Globaloney

GLOBALONEY

Unraveling the Myths
of Globalization

MICHAEL VESETH

ROWMAN & LITTLEFIELD PUBLISHERS, INC.
Lanham • Boulder • New York • Toronto • Oxford

ROWMAN & LITTLEFIELD PUBLISHERS, INC.

Published in the United States of America
by Rowman & Littlefield Publishers, Inc.
A wholly owned subsidary of
The Rowman & Littlefield Publishing Group, Inc.
4501 Forbes Boulevard, Suite 200, Lanham, MD 20706
www.rowmanlittlefield.com

P.O. Box 317, Oxford OX2 9RU, UK

British Library Cataloguing in Publication Information Available

Library of Congress Cataloging-in-Publication Data

Veseth, Michael.
Globaloney : unraveling the myths of globalization / Michael Veseth.
    p.   cm.— (Globalization)
  Includes bibliographical references and index.
  ISBN 0-7425-3658-0 (cloth : alk. paper)
  1. Globalization.   I. Title.   II. Series: Globalization (Lanham, Md.)
JZ1318.V47   2005
303.48'2—dc22   2004018542

Printed in the United States of America

♾ ™ The paper used in this publication meets the minimum requirements of American National Standard for Information Sciences—Permanence of Paper for Printed Library Materials, ANSI/NISO Z39.48-1992.

CONTENTS

ACKNOWLEDGMENTS

I have run up more than the usual number of intellectual debts in the process of writing this book. I'd like to acknowledge my creditors in partial repayment of their generosity without in any way implicating them for the mistakes that remain.

First let me thank my colleagues at the University of Puget Sound for their unstinting support and frequent assistance: David Balaam, Nick Kontogeorgopoulos, Matt Warning, Richard Anderson-Connolly, Jan van der Veen, Ross Singleton, Arpad Kadarkay, Jeff Matthews, and Doug Goodman. Thanks as well to the University for the John Lantz Fellowship that gave me needed time to pull it all together.

I owe a special debt of gratitude to Scott Bailey, who read the entire manuscript and provided uncommonly clear direction on revisions. Many people helped me with the case studies that form the core of *Globaloney*. Thanks to Paul Tourville, Justin Hughes, Ken Willman, Pam and Michel Rocchi, Jeffrey Matthews, Valerio Franchi, Roberto Ferranti, Gabriele Forni, Neal Ibbotson, Jane Hunter, Steve Smith, Don Bird, David Barnsley, and Jeff McMullin. Jarrod Weiner and Erik Jones helped me refine my ideas about the rhetoric of globalization. Kristi Veseth kept me well-informed about what globalization looks like in practice.

Finally, thanks to Sue Veseth for helping me recognize globaloney in the first place and for putting up with my compulsive interest in finding out where things come from and why.

INTRODUCTION

The devil is in the details. Mark Twain learned this lesson as a boy working at a Missouri newspaper, setting printer's type by hand. If you want to get a sentence right, you've got to get all the right letters lined up in just the right order. Every detail must be exactly right; getting close isn't good enough. A single mistake can corrupt the meaning of an entire story.[1]

But the devil isn't *always* in the details. Sometimes the devil lurks in the big picture, the grand design. You can get all of the bits and pieces lined up perfectly, but it doesn't make any difference because the design itself is flawed. I don't know if Mark Twain coined a phrase to this effect, but he certainly knew it from personal experience. He lost his vast publishing fortune investing in an unsuccessful attempt to manufacture an automated typesetting machine. All of the expensive little details of this complicated and temperamental machine were right, but somehow the darn thing never worked.

What is true about complicated machines can sometimes also be true about complex social and economic systems. In fact, Mark Twain wrote a book about this problem, *A Connecticut Yankee in King Arthur's Court*. It is the story of a modern fellow named Hank who gets knocked unconscious and unexpectedly wakes up in sixth-century Camelot, not nineteenth-century Hartford. With his advanced knowledge of science, technology, and commerce, Hank is soon running King Arthur's realm along more efficient lines. He becomes Sir Boss.

Mark Twain tended to make up his stories as he went along, so as we read his books we can see how his attitudes and outlook changed. The beginning of *Connecticut Yankee* is all about how well the technical and commercial details of nineteenth-century America worked and how much better and more efficient they are than the products, practices, traditions, and institutions they replaced. It reflects Twain's inherent optimism. Sir Boss gets all the details right, and the prospect for progress is bright.

By the end of the book, however, the scene is not so sunny. All the little details of modern life, when transplanted to King Arthur's time, have arranged themselves in patterns of conflict and misery. In the end, *Connecticut Yankee* is less a celebration of modern industrial life than an indictment of its harsh and bitter consequences.[2] In the course of writing *Connecticut Yankee*, Mark Twain came to believe that the devil in industrial capitalism was not its details, but the way those details came together, in the patterns they formed. The details were correct, but the grand design was flawed. This distinction is a useful insight that can be applied to many situations, especially our current concern, globalization.

Globalization is real, and we must take it seriously, but it is not easy to understand because of its complexity. Globalization is not one single thing; it is a collection of things, some tightly intertwined, some loosely connected if at all. James H. Mittelman calls globalization a *syndrome*, or a group of related signs and symptoms that produce a recognizable pattern.[3] Impossible to define with precision, but you know it when you see it: that's globalization. It might not be too strong to say that globalization is in the eyes of the beholder. If you stare at its details long enough, some pattern may eventually appear, like one of those Magic Eye 3-D images that were so popular a few years ago.

You need to understand the details of globalization if you are going to make any sense of it, but the *devil* isn't in the details, it is in the pattern, the big picture, in how we organize and make patterns out of those details. Because globalization is too complicated to understand directly, through the details, we tend to think about it using metaphors, parables, and other rhetorical and heuristic methods that create for us a comfortable sense of the big picture, the grand design.

But that's where the devil comes in. It is easy to manipulate the details to create false patterns and to distort the big picture. Clare Boothe Luce coined a term to describe an argument that intentionally misunderstands globalization or misrepresents it in order to make a questionable point. She called it *globaloney*. I've borrowed her term for the title of this book.

Globaloney is a critique of the rhetoric of globalization: the vivid images, clever metaphors, and persuasive narratives that manipulate and distort our understanding of the globalization syndrome. In writing this book I'm not trying to defend globalization against the forces that oppose it. Rather, I'm trying to defend my understanding of globalization as a messy, complicated process against rhetoric that tries to simplify it in order to sell a particular viewpoint or political agenda. I want to look closely at the "stories" that people tell about globalization and compare them to the factual details. And I want to tell a few globalization stories of my own to show how various are the patterns that the details can create. In short, I want to muddy and complexify globalization so that my readers will think more critically about globalization arguments—and recognize globaloney when they see it.

From *Selling Globalization* to *Globaloney*

Globaloney broadens and extends an argument that I began in 1998 in *Selling Globalization: The Myth of the Global Economy*.[4] This book started out as an application of chaos theory to international finance and ended up as a critical examination of the methods and motives of the neoliberal pro-globalization movement.

Selling Globalization was initially a book about financial bubbles, speculative attacks, and chaos theory. It argued that the fundamental instability of global financial markets makes it impossible for globalization to be as complete, as powerful, and as encompassing as some people seem to think. Globalization is built on a foundation of global finance, but this foundation is inherently unstable. The more global the finance structure becomes, the less stable it is. It cannot possibly support the elaborate global structures that some people hope for and other people fear.

It was a sound argument, but I had a hard time getting people to take it seriously at first because, in the boom years of the late 1990s, it just didn't fit the way that most people had been conditioned to see the grand design of globalization. How could I get people to take the idea of *fragile* globalization seriously when they were conditioned to see it as an unstoppable universal force?

I decided to try to undermine the conventional wisdom about globalization's grand design through close analysis of its details. I put together four brief case studies of "global" corporations and then looked closely to see if the details of their businesses were consistent with the most common metaphors and images of economic globalization. In

3

other words, I asked, do the facts fit the stories that we tell about the facts?

One of the companies I selected—Nike—fit the standard globalization/multinational corporation story very well. But Nike turned out to be the noteworthy exception, not the representative case. The other three firms I studied—Boeing, Microsoft, and the Frank Russell Company, a global investment advisor widely known for its Russell 3000 index—all were very different indeed, and the details of the differences revealed a lot. For most global firms, I concluded, the fact that they are global is a secondary attribute. The most important factors are specific to their particular businesses or industries.

These case studies attracted a lot of interest not because they were so good but mainly because they were so rare—hardly anyone looks to see if the facts of globalization fit the popular stories and images. The stories that are told about globalization are seldom questioned, much less tested, because the rhetoric of globalization is so convincing, the simple images used to reinforce the rhetoric are so compelling, and the interests of the "sellers" are so strong. *Selling Globalization* showed that some of the pro-globalization rhetoric was used to sell the idea of globalization in order to advance a particular set of economic, political, and intellectual interests.

My goal this time is not to persuade you that global financial markets are an unstable foundation for global capitalism—hopefully my previous book and the continuing series of international financial crises have already done that. Now I want to persuade readers that they might be misunderstanding the very nature of globalization because they have accepted a distorted "big picture" that is fundamentally different from the facts. And I want them to consider that this might be a very serious problem. The way we understand problems affects the choices we make, the votes we cast, and the causes and interests that we support by accident or design. I picked *Globaloney* as a title for this book because, although it isn't a very elegant term, it sure gets the point across.

When I first started working on this project I created a "Globaloney Test" webpage. It showed a slice of mortadella, the big, plump, savory Italian meat, alongside an image of the earth as seen from outer space. The first caption read, "This is Mortadella, a complex and subtle pork product made in the Bologna, Italy. Don't confuse it with Baloney, its one-dimensional, highly processed, mass-market substitute." Under the globe I wrote, "This is Globalization, a complex and subtle web of economic, political, and social change. Don't confuse it with Globaloney, its one-dimensional, highly processed, mass-market substitute." I hope that readers of this book will pass the globaloney test.

How *Globaloney* Is Organized

It is best to begin at the beginning, and this book begins with the first recorded use of the term *globaloney* in a heated 1943 political debate between the vice president of the United States, Henry Wallace, and an ambitious new member of Congress, Clare Boothe Luce. Luce coined the term to describe Wallace's vision of the postwar world. But the debate wasn't really about globalization, or even global policy; it was about the domestic policies of the Roosevelt administration on one hand and the political ambitions of a very junior member of the House of Representatives on the other. The techniques and even some of the images that Wallace and Luce used in the 1940s bear a close resemblance to arguments you heard in the 1990s. The moral of chapter 1, "The Globaloney Syndrome," is that globaloney is not really new and that sometimes it is not even about globalization. It is about interests and the arguments that best advance them. There is always an interest at the center of a globaloney argument that seeks to advance itself by creating a persuasive image of the grand design.

What is globalization? I argue that a lot of what we mistake for facts about globalization is really the result of the clever application of standard rhetorical forms. Adam Smith, the father of economics, was also a master of rhetoric (he even lectured on it). Smith wasn't the father of globaloney, but he was perhaps its most successful early practitioner. In a real sense, I think Adam Smith taught today's globalonists their trade. So, as the title of chapter 2 suggests, you can "Blame It All on Adam Smith."

I am particularly interested in arguments that globalization is the end of local culture and that it is essentially the Americanization of the world, with all the bad effects you might imagine. This means I need to confront arguments like Benjamin Barber's *Jihad vs. McWorld* and Walter LaFeber's *Michael Jordan and the New Global Capitalism*.[5]

Sports metaphors and images are powerful rhetorical tools. I don't think Adam Smith talked about the need for a "level playing field" or the ability of transnational corporations to "slam dunk" negotiations with emerging market countries, but he would probably take advantage of such devices if he were writing today. I examine one of the most persuasive examples of sports globaloney in chapter 3, "Michael Jordan and NBA Global Fever." Just like professional basketball, globalization is a U.S.-centered, media-driven, capitalist enterprise that destroys local culture and exploits everyone but those at the very top. This narrative makes a good story, but it is so one-sided that it would make a very boring game. I feel the need to organize a more effective opposition, if only to add some excitement to the game.

And it isn't hard to do, because if you accept the premise that globalization is the National Basketball Association, then you will see many stories, not one. You will find the story of Air Jordan, of course, but you will also find Yao Ming and Emanuel Ginobili, among others. The full story of globalization and basketball is a complicated pattern that weaves together global market forces, local culture, national pride, and individual opportunity. It is almost as much about foreign influences on a U.S. game as it is about American domination abroad. Globalization as we usually think of it is part of the story, but the real story is different, more complicated, and more interesting. The real story of Air Jordan and the Global Game is the kind of globalization story I am interested in.

But is basketball *really* the global game and therefore a valid metaphor for understanding globalization? The *truly* global spectator sports, some would argue, are Formula One auto racing and soccer, or football as most of the world calls the game. The global soccer industry is the subject of chapter 4, "The Beautiful Game and the American Exception." The American exception? I said soccer was a global spectator sport, but that's not really true. In the United States soccer is widely played but not widely watched. That's the American exception that helps us appreciate the limits of the argument that sports equals globalization equals Americanization.

If you examine the global soccer industry you will find some patterns that repeat those of the Air Jordan story of globalization, but you'll also see much that is very different. I hope that this will raise a number of disturbing questions about the ways we misunderstand globalization through sports. I think you will see that the Air Jordan story, for example, is deeply rooted in an American view of America. Ironically, all the classic globalization stories are rooted in very specific local perspectives, and often reveal more about local attitudes than global patterns.

Food—fast food—is the basis for perhaps the most popular image of globalization—McWorld—and is the subject of chapter 5. Globalization is so closely associated with American hamburgers that the entire complex process of economic and social change is often characterized simply as McDonaldization, a process that destroys local cultures and traditions, replacing them with the fat-filled empty calories of American capitalism. Thomas Friedman, in his book about globalization, *The Lexus and the Olive Tree*,[6] cannot seem to resist having "Golden Arches" moments that define globalization wherever he goes.

Although it is tempting to see the spread of fast food as the essence of globalization, it is also wrong to do so. Even the McDonald's story is more complicated than is commonly appreciated; it is *both* a story of global business *and* the story of the vitality of local culture, as we will learn as we search for the truth about the McAloo Tikki Burger. More than anything, however, McDonald's story is the story of the process of rationalization, which Max Weber identified years ago. Rationalization is related to globalization, I suppose, but they aren't the same thing.

But *are* hamburgers the essence of globalization? One problem with the McDonaldization story is that it uses an exceptional case—the world's most successful single restaurant chain—to argue a general case (almost a universal case). What happens when we look beyond hamburgers? Chapters 6 and 7 try to find out.

The people who oppose global McDonaldization often champion the merits of *terroir*, although they usually don't call it that.[7] *Terroir* is a French term for the special qualities associated with particular places. *Terroir* is about how wines are affected by local soils, techniques, traditions, and microclimates. If generic "chablis" from California doesn't taste the same to you as the eponymous dry white wine from Chablis in the Burgundy region of central France, then you might be someone who appreciates *terroir*.

The logical place to look at globalization versus *terroir* is the wine industry, a seriously interesting example of global markets at work and not, as some of my friends have suggested, just an excuse to drink a lot of wine in the name of research. The classic patterns of global trade and investment are present in the global wine industry. Gallo, Mondavi, Beringer, and other U.S. firms have established systematic global networks of vine and wine. Meanwhile, the French are expected to be vigorously resisting these trends, even as they enthusiastically embrace them. There are clear links between core and periphery (or Old World and New World, as wine people like to say), which fit an expected pattern, too. It's all there. The story of wine is the story of globalization as McDonaldization. Except that it's not.

Although it is easy to make the wine industry fit the preconceived notion of the globalization debate, in fact what is happening in the wine business has little to do with globalization and everything to do with particular patterns and practices that have existed in the wine business for hundreds of years. When you go looking for certain patterns of globalization, you sometimes see them both when they are present and when they aren't. Analysis of the wine industry shows that "globalization" is just one of the special arrangements that characterize this business. I hope this will make you wonder how many other "globalization" stories aren't really about globalization, either.

What does globalization look like to the people who don't live in McWorld, who are too poor to buy a Big Mac, who live in the countries that cannot even attract a McDonald's in the first place? How does it change their lives down at the grassroots level? Does it give them hope and opportunity, or does it crush them and their cultural heritage?

The conventional wisdom, which I call "Grassroots Globaloney," is that globalization is like the Borg Collective in the *Star Trek: The Next Generation* series and movies: Resistance is futile; you will be assimilated (and homogenized and dehumanized). Because I am suspicious of simple, deterministic conclusions, I suspect that resistance is possible and that even the poorest people in the world have at least some ability to shape globalization to suit their needs. I explore these ideas in chapter 7 through case studies of global trade in used clothing (the rag trade) and the Slow Food movement, a global network that uses the methods of McWorld to offer an alternative to it.

Taken together, these case studies make an argument for a more complex definition of globalization and suggest the types of local, regional, national, international, and global patterns that we need to visualize if we are going to try to understand globalization in a meaningful way. I say that we need to *try* to understand globalization, with emphasis on the *try*, because I'm not really sure that we can understand any complex system of which we are so much a part.

Globaloney concludes with an exercise in creative destruction, where I try to uncover some deeper truths about globaloney and globalization. Chapter 8, "Globalization and the French Exception," presents my own theory of why the French hate globalization so. Like all great global narratives, my theory contains a lot of globaloney (but it is high-quality globaloney, I assure you). I then subject my own theory to critical analysis, an exercise that raises doubts about the premise—the notion that the French really do hate globalization—as much as the theory and sets the stage for my attempt to draw a conclusion about why globalization is so difficult to understand clearly. Maybe it's impossible to really understand globalization, given all the devils and all the details that are at work, but we don't have to try so hard to *misunderstand* it. And that's not globaloney.

THE GLOBALONEY SYNDROME

Globaloney, she said. Globaloney! Clare Boothe Luce, playwright, editor, and now politician, was making her maiden speech in the U.S. House of Representatives on February 9, 1943, when she coined this new word.

"Mr. Wallace's article in the *American* magazine is on a very high plane, indeed," said the new Republican congressman from Connecticut. "In it he does a great deal of global thinking. But much of what Mr. Wallace calls his global thinking is, no matter how you slice it, still globaloney."[1]

Mr. Wallace (Vice President Henry A. Wallace) was indeed guilty of global thinking, as we shall soon see, but globaloney? Then as now, calling someone's argument globaloney is not a compliment. To call something baloney is to condemn it as pretentious or silly; globaloney is a silly or pretentious argument about globalization. Globaloney is a hot new buzzword, according to *Newsweek* magazine,[2] an idea whose time has come, but in fact globaloney has changed very little since its introduction on the floor of the House of Representatives.

If we want to understand what globaloney is, where it comes from and how it can be used, there is no better introduction than Mrs. Luce's quarrel with Mr. Wallace. So let me tell you the story of globaloney's birth as a colloquial expression as a way to identify some of the rhetorical techniques and political issues that are often associated with it.

Henry A. Wallace: Globaloney Vision

Henry A. Wallace was, according to John Kenneth Galbraith, the second most important person in Franklin Delano Roosevelt's Depression-era New Deal administrations—second to Roosevelt himself. As secretary of agriculture and then vice president, Wallace was on the political front lines and in the front pages, generating ideas, crafting policy, and selling his vision of peace and prosperity. It was a vision largely in line with Galbraith's own view: a Keynesian vision of government as an investor of last resort, actively fighting domestic poverty and economic stagnation, which probably explains Galbraith's high regard. By 1943 Wallace's views had evolved into the global vision that Clare Boothe Luce decried.

Although the front pages of 1943 were dominated by news of the war in Europe and the Pacific, it was difficult not to think ahead—to think about what the postwar world would look like and what problems it would face. Would the end of war bring the return of the economic problems of the 1930s? So much was this question on the public mind that, in 1944, the Pabst Brewing Company sponsored an essay contest on the subject of postwar full employment that drew nearly thirty-six thousand entries. Herbert Stein and Leon Keyserling, two future chairs of the President's Council of Economic Advisors, won the top prizes.

Henry Wallace laid out his ideas about postwar policy in a series of essays and speeches between 1941 and 1943, which were collected and published under the title *The Century of the Common Man*.[3] To modern eyes, the book reads like a war-weary response to *The Economic Consequences of the Peace* (1919), the book that John Maynard Keynes wrote condemning the injustices of the Treaty of Versailles. "The seeds of the present world upheaval were sown in the faulty economic decisions that followed the war a generation ago," Wallace wrote.[4] "In very truth, this nation sowed the wind by its policies of isolation, high tariffs, unwise foreign loans, and high-pressure sales abroad. It could not avoid reaping the whirlwind."[5] Wallace's essays still read well today, so much do the problems of his day resemble the ones we face and so much does his thinking anticipate later authors. For our purposes, however, it is best to focus on the eleventh chapter, "Business Measures," which reprints the *American* magazine article that so displeased Clare Boothe Luce.

How to prevent a postwar depression was the subject of Wallace's essay. "Business men," he said, "realize that the shock of this war's end will probably be at least seven times as great as that which was felt in the beginning of 1920."[6] Just as war had required planning, he wrote, peace will require planning, too. "Peace unplanned could be a disaster worse than war."[7] To prevent disaster, Wallace argued, the United States and the world needed to be ready with what we might call today a Global New Deal. The Global New Deal would have several key elements: first, strong multilateral economic agencies to stabilize commodity prices and to channel private and public investment funds for reconstruction and growth; second, free trade policies, so that investors will not fear that foreign markets will be closed to their products. A stable and growing global economy, Wallace argued, would be a ready market for U.S. goods. Rising foreign demand could at least partly replace war production as a source of income for U.S. businesses and workers in the early postwar years.

If in the likely case that a smooth transition from global war production to global peace production could not be managed and a postwar recession occurred, the United States and other countries would need just the sort of domestic New Deal programs that Roosevelt and Wallace organized in the 1930s. Farmers would need farm programs, he said, and businessmen and laborers would need programs, too, to help them pick up the slack in a world where pessimism would no doubt discourage private investment initiatives. Although he thought that wartime technological advances would create opportunities in many industries, Wallace seemed to be especially enthusiastic about the potential for home construction. "In nearly every country of the world one of the most feasible projects will be construction of low-cost houses on a scale never before contemplated," he said. "Few people realize the multitude of construction devices and gadgets of all kinds which are available to make houses livable at lower cost."[8] Government could help here, as well as with deposit insurance for banks, social security insurance, and so forth.

The Wallace plan, broadly stated, was to remember the lessons of the 1920s and 1930s: to avoid the postwar errors of World War I (isolationism and protectionism) and to embrace the advantages of New Deal government programs and Keynesian economic policies. Okay so far, but where's the globaloney?

Wallace needed a device to help him sell his plan for postwar recovery to the public and to his fellow politicians—and to camouflage the holes in his argument. He needed a popular image that would capture the imagination and carry his proposals along better than they could carry themselves. He found it, he thought, in globalization, which he called global vision and Mrs. Luce invented the term globaloney to describe.

We have entered the age of air power, Wallace argued, which is a borderless age, an age of globalization. "Airplanes and air power have eliminated the old significance of national boundaries. . . . The seas will no longer separate the continents in the way they once did. Information and goods will flow with ever-increasing freedom."[9] Freed of the constraints of time and space, he wrote, Americans will become internationalists (globalists, we might say today), with global interests in global markets.

Business leaders would boldly take flight, taking advantage of global airline routes that condense time and space. Their initiative would unlock the world's wasted resources and put them efficiently into use. Just as the railroad opened up the American west, the airplane would open up the world to commercial opportunity. "What the United States has done," he wrote, and what Russia was doing to exploit resources in Siberia, "[gives] a clue to what is possible in such regions as China, Alaska, and Latin America."[10]

To make all this possible, Wallace proposed a freedom-of-the-air plan that would open airports to commercial traffic from all nations. U.S. airports would open themselves to foreign carriers in exchange for similar privileges abroad—all subject to governance by an "international air authority," of course. Freedom-of-the-air, he said, would be to air travel and transport, the engine of twentieth-century globalization, what freedom-of-the-seas had been to nineteenth-century globalization.

The plan that Henry Wallace presented in 1943 for postwar full employment was not especially radical, but he knew it would generate some political opposition. Broadly, he called for something like the World Bank to stimulate reconstruction and promote growth, something like the General Agreement on Tariffs and Trade (GATT) to promote free trade, and for the sort of domestic economic programs that were actually adopted once conflict ended. He probably knew that isolationists would oppose the international side of the package and conservatives would oppose the domestic programs because they would promote big government, high taxes, and regulation of the marketplace.

By playing the globalization card in the form of freedom-of-the-air, I think Wallace was trying to create a distinct business constituency for his plan that would cut across the existing political fault lines (and especially, perhaps, undermine Republican opposition). Globalization, he proposed, would create global opportunities for American businesses and workers and unleash a global engine of economic growth.

More than prosperity, globalization would bring peace, too, by merging our separate national interests and by cultivating cosmopolitan attitudes. "Boys and girls of the rising generation are already air-minded to a degree which is not possible for most of their elders who grew up earth-bound," he argued. "Education courses in the future might well include airplane trips to one or more foreign countries. It is infinitely more important to make the people of the United Nations space-minded for peace than it was for Germany to make its people space-minded for war."[11]

The essay closes this way.

> Airplanes and airpower have eliminated the old significance of national borders. . . . [I]nternational air travel will cause the American businessman to think in international terms as never before. The narrow selfishness of the past will more and more seem foolish and harmful. The seas will no longer separate the continents the way they once did. Information and goods will flow with ever-increasing freedom. . . . Modern technology, the wings of air, and the waves of air mean that the common man will demand and get a better education and a higher standard of living. In serving the common man, the business leader will have opportunities for initiatives such as he has never dreamed of before.[12]

Like contemporary discussions of globalization, Wallace linked globalization, technology, and communications with education and rising living standards. Like Adam Smith, he linked the self-interest of business men with social welfare.

Henry Wallace's freedom-of-the-air argument is a classic globalization story, one that includes elements that we see repeated again and again in this book. It paints a picture of a borderless world, where time and space have been condensed. Indeed, in a previous essay titled "World Organization," Wallace explained just how small the world had become: "Today, measured by travel time, the whole world is actually smaller than our little country was. . . . [W]hen George Washington was inaugurated, it took *seven* days to go by horse-drawn vehicle from Mount Vernon to New York. Now Army bombers are flown from the United States to China and India in less than *three* days."[13]

The small world is also a borderless world, Wallace argued, because national boundaries are irrelevant in the air. This borderless world is a world of prosperity and a world of peace—for those who seize upon the opportunities that it presents. If the United States failed to seize the opportunity presented by freedom-of-the-air (and the other policies that Wallace advocated, which depended in part on the opening of global markets to U.S. goods), then evildoers would take advantage and shape a world of war.

Technology has made the world small and borderless—always a questionable premise, but a vivid image nonetheless. This image is used in place of detailed argument or evidence to justify broad generalizations and universal conclusions that, in turn, justify policies and legitimize interests that may have little to do with globalization at all. This is a classic globalization story, all right, and a classic globaloney story too. But not for the reasons that Clare Boothe Luce proclaimed on the floor of the House.

Clare Boothe Luce: The Globaloney Threat

Clare Boothe Luce successfully campaigned for her seat in Congress based upon her internationalist credentials. As a journalist, she had traveled the world, visiting foreign leaders and U.S. troops abroad, developing personal and direct knowledge of foreign affairs. Once elected on the 1942 Republican ticket, however, she found deeply entrenched isolationist and protectionist interests blocking the path to power and influence within Congress. She needed to appeal to these dark forces to achieve status within Congress, but how? She found the answer in Henry Wallace's globaloney.

Judging by her later actions, which I will discuss below, I am not sure that Clare Boothe Luce really strongly opposed the broad outlines of Henry Wallace's international or global agenda. Her personal experiences had probably already persuaded her that foreign affairs and domestic interests were tightly interwoven and that isolationism was both unwise and fundamentally impossible. But Wallace's freedom-of-the-air plan gave her the opportunity she needed to establish a reputation and curry favor with the powerful isolationist leaders. Thus, quite unexpectedly, Luce's much anticipated maiden speech did not address any of the great issues of the day, but rather focused intensely on a few paragraphs from Henry Wallace's just-published *American* magazine piece. It provided a text that Luce could spin into globaloney that would serve her own political agenda perfectly.

Clare Boothe Luce's strategy was to take the powerful image of the airplane that Henry Wallace used to advance his globalist agenda and convert it into a weapon to use against him. I know, she said, that "the airplane has been the most dynamic instrument of this war and that the airplane will surely be the most dynamic instrument of the peace. The question of America's place in the present and post-war civilian air world is for this reason the most important question which confronts us today. If we fail to answer it intelligently, although the United Nations will win the war, America can lose the peace."[14]

Much as Wallace did in his *American* magazine article, Luce began her speech touting the airplane as the high-tech creator of a shrinking and borderless world, with the United States at its center. The airplane made it possible to reach "any important city" in Europe, Asia, Africa, or South America in forty-eight hours or less, she said. The view of the future was the view from the air—a borderless world as far as the eye can see. It was critically important, therefore, that the United States should continue to dominate this world in peace as it did in war because "the masters of the air will be the masters of the planet, for as aviation dominates all military effort today, so will it dominate and influence all peacetime effort tomorrow."[15]

Here Luce borrowed a rhetorical trick from Adam Smith, who sometimes overcame logical difficulties by simply leaving them out. Smith made arguments along the lines of "what is true for every individual cannot be false for a great nation," which sounds grand but says little unless supported by reasoning or evidence. What is true about war (that air power dominates) cannot be false about peace, Luce argued. It was both clever rhetoric and canny political strategy: the battlefield is the best place to preach protectionism.

"We already know the danger in war of an enemy airplane to a nation's home front," she reminded the congressmen and reporters in attendance. "It is elementary, or should be, that human nature being what it is, and some nations forever greedy and contentious, to grant this free transit, this free look-see to all nations of the world might be very unwise from our point of view."[16] She was especially worried about Stalin and the potential postwar communist threat—a concern that Wallace shared. But where Wallace imagined a borderless airspace that would permit U.S. values and interests to spread smoothly over the globe, Luce saw only enemies and threats.

Freedom-of-the-air, to Luce, meant dropping your defenses and exposing vital interests to unscrupulous enemies. No military leader would ever do that in war; no civilian leader should consider it in peacetime. "[W]e shall have most efficiently laid the groundwork for America's certain defeat in World War No. 3. Then indeed the air over our heads will be full of the sound of wings—the wings of the chickens come home to roost, but to roost uncertainly in these steel girders above us, as the bombs of the enemy send them squawking in terror, and us squealing with shame, out of this great hall."[17]

What about the economic benefits? After all, Henry Wallace initially justified his freedom-of-the-air idea with its economic potential. A postwar economic slump was likely, Wallace had argued, unless global markets for U.S. goods could be developed quickly to fill the holes left by declining war and defense needs. Luce addressed the economic aspect, but twisted it to serve her purposes. She shifted the battleground from Wallace's global markets to the domestic air industry, then invoked again the peace-as-war imagery. Doing this, Luce could argue that globalization of the airspace would be ruinous to U.S. industry as well as destructive to national security.

She grabbed onto Wallace's seemingly offhand remark that freedom-of-the-air would be as beneficial to postwar world commerce as freedom-of-the-seas had been in the nineteenth century. "What did Freedom of the Sea mean to the world of the past?" Luce asked. "As Freedom of the Seas prevented neither World War No. 1 nor No. 2, there is no reason to suppose that Freedom of the Air would prevent World War No. 3."[18] Going further, she argued that freedom-of-the-seas was actually damaging to U.S. economic interests, by defining those interests narrowly as the U.S. shipping industry, ignoring the benefits to the farmers and factories whose products were carried by sea. "America's merchant marine had languished, and all but died, in an effort to compete, under freedom of the seas and internationalization of ports, with all the cheap labor, low-operating cost, government subsidy countries of the world." And what was true on the seas, Luce suggested, cannot be false in the air: "Shall freedom of the air, like freedom of the seas, in the year '49 or '59 have made it impossible not only for America's merchant airway systems to compete against the low-cost countries of the world, but for America to protect her sky lines?"[19]

The cheap labor threat is a common element of globaloney arguments today, made most famous perhaps by U.S. presidential candidate Ross Perot, who predicted in 1992 that the North American Free Trade Agreement (NAFTA) would cause a "giant sucking sound" of high-wage U.S. jobs going to low-wage Mexico. By arguing, in essence, that what was true for nineteenth-century shipping cannot be false for twentieth-century air travel and transport and by declaring cheap unskilled foreign workers a threat to high-tech U.S. industries, Clare Boothe Luce engaged in globaloney as high art.

Global airspace was so important that it needed to be protected, and U.S. security and economic interests protected as well, she argued. But in doing this, we are not being selfish or truly protectionist, she continued. "We have a higher purpose. I believe that we should maintain our position of international civil air supremacy for the greatest and best of all reasons: Our responsibility to the whole world and to ourselves, to assume democratic political leadership."[20] There is no evidence in the *Congressional Record* that any of the members present appreciated the irony of this argument. We need to keep skies closed (isolation) and dominate foreign competitors (protectionism) in order to free the world (democracy).

"Mr. Wallace's article in the *American* magazine is on a very high plane, indeed," Luce said, a play on words that is not apparent when the quotation is read outside of its proper context. "In it he does a great deal of global thinking. But much of what Mr. Wallace calls his global thinking is, no matter how you slice it, still 'globaloney.'"[21] "We, gentlemen, were not elected by our constituents, on either side of this aisle, to preside over the liquidation of America's best interests, either at home or abroad," she concluded. "The sky's the limit of those interests. The time is now." [22]

Both Henry Wallace and Clare Boothe Luce can be accused of globaloney in this famous exchange. Each used global metaphors and images to disguise or shore up an otherwise unsustainable argument and to advance or protect their interests. It is hard to say who is the worse offender. Wallace's argument uses globaloney to make the largest jump: from unregulated airports to peace and prosperity. But Luce's globaloney is more powerful and profound. Whose globaloney was best? Clare Boothe Luce gets the nod here, based upon immediate effects.

Wallace's freedom-of-the-skies proposal did not prove to be a very effective tool in selling his internationalist agenda; it faded from the scene. Luce, however, got the attention and recognition she sought from the powerful leaders of the isolationist wing of her party and was appointed to the Military Affairs Committee—a real plum for a first-term congressman. Ironically, however, Luce voted in favor of many of the foreign policy programs that Wallace's Democrats proposed during her two congressional terms, a fact that makes the tone of her "globaloney" speech sound more like calculated opportunism than heartfelt conviction.

Clare Boothe Luce might have been the first person to utter the term *globaloney* in print, but she was not the first person to use globaloney to further her interests. And she sure was not the last.

The Globaloney Syndrome

The episode of Clare Boothe Luce versus Henry Wallace would be little more than an interesting historical footnote if globaloney had stopped there and then. Instead, however, this was simply a very public moment in an ongoing process that I call the globaloney syndrome.[23] A *syndrome*, as the term is typically used in medical discussion, refers to a combination of indicators—symptoms, signs, and so forth—that are associated with a particular disease. A syndrome is not a disease itself, although it is easy to confuse the two, but the signs used to diagnose the presence of a disease. Tourette's syndrome, for example, is an inherited neurological disorder, which is characterized by its outward symptoms, involuntary body movements and vocalizations. A person with severe Tourette's syndrome may experience uncontrollable physical or vocal outbursts. While these behaviors might be personal problems for the patient, friends, and family, they are not the disease itself, just the symptoms.

The globaloney syndrome is a set of political, social, and economic arguments that draw upon certain vivid images, persuasive narratives, and memorable anecdotes or examples that are claimed to represent the causes or effects of globalization. These images, narratives, anecdotes, and examples are used to create or reinforce bogus syllogisms and half-baked arguments that intentionally misrepresent aspects of globalization in order to further particular intellectual, political, or economic interests. As I wrote in an earlier book titled *Selling Globalization*, these arguments use what's hot—globalization—to sell what's not—a particular political agenda, economic interest, academic program, or combination of all three.[24]

The core of the globaloney syndrome, as I have defined it, are the interests that the globalization arguments serve, much as the core of Tourette's syndrome is the neurological disorder. The key to understanding the globaloney syndrome, therefore, is to recognize it by its symptoms and then to ask, what interests do these global arguments serve? The globaloney syndrome is best treated, I think, by first identifying the symptoms and then by probing for the interests behind them.

I've already identified the symptoms of globaloney in both Henry Wallace's global vision and Clare Boothe Luce's response to it. Both were guilty of kidnapping vivid images of globalization—airplanes, air travel, and a borderless world—and using them to advance their own political agendas. They covered weak logic and missing evidence with these images and then moved by leaps and bounds to otherwise impossible conclusions. Henry Wallace, wanting to advance an internationalist agenda, needed to camouflage the likelihood of a postwar recession and sought to forestall the reemergence of protectionism. He used the image of the airplane and prospect of global opportunities for American business to link them all together.

Unfortunately for Wallace, Clare Boothe Luce jumped on his images and turned them to her own purposes, to advance her own political career. She saw no friendly skies—they were filled with enemies and threats, which suited well the interest of House Republican elites and, therefore, Luce's interests too. It's nothing personal—just business— she might have said to Wallace in private, since their international interests seem aligned in some areas. But as far as I am concerned, it is really just globaloney.

Globaloney Past and Present

Sometimes history is a distant mirror that reflects the present. Perhaps this is true about globalization and globaloney.

By some measures the world at the turn of the twentieth century was as globalized as the world today, a hundred years later. The historian Harold James examined the reactions to early twentieth-century globalization in *The End of Globalization: Lessons from the Great Depression*, one of the best books about globalization that I have read.[25] Anti-globalization reactions came to a head in the 1930s, James argues, taking three forms. First, there was a reaction against the financial crises associated with global finance. Money became more national, not global, and more highly regulated. Second, there was a reaction against foreign goods and international trade as beggar-thy-neighbor protectionist policies were enacted everywhere. Finally, James argues, there was a reaction against immigrants, the human face of globalization. By the end of the 1930s, fear of foreign money, foreign goods, and foreign people was very strong. Globaloney emerged both to exaggerate and reinforce these fears and to attempt to reverse them. Wallace and Luce were just two voices among many in this swirling debate.

I tracked globalization's rise and fall and rise again in a book that I edited for a *New York Times* series: *The* New York Times *Twentieth Century in Review: The Rise of the Global Economy.*[26] I tried to tell the story of twentieth-century globalization by piecing together nearly five hundred articles, book reviews, editorials, and op-ed pieces, cartoons, and photographs from one hundred years of the *New York Times*. The term *globalization* was probably first used in the *Times* by Clyde H. Farnsworth in a 1981 article about the Tokyo Round of the GATT, but the word didn't catch on until the 1990s. One of striking things I learned from working on this book was that the emerging global economy was not much discussed in the press while it was developing. Globalization only got attention when problems occurred and antiglobalization reactions erupted.

In the early 1990s, for example, "globalization" appeared in the *Times* about once a week or less on average. By the end of the decade, however, it was being used once a day or more. The turning point in the trend line came with the Asian financial crisis of 1997, which really put globalization on the map by making its inherent problems completely obvious. Globalization in the press tends to be defined only indirectly, by its failures and the reactions against them.

It almost makes you wonder if globalization itself actually exists, except as metaphor or a rhetorical device. This possibility has been explored by Australian politics professor Jo-Anne Pemberton in her book *Global Metaphors: Modernity and the Quest for One World.*[27] In *Global Metaphors* Pemberton compares the globalization discourse today with that of the 1920s and 1930s, when the last round of globalization fell apart. She finds little that is really new in the contemporary debate; the rhetorical patterns that I call globaloney have deep roots that extend back to that previous era that caused so much anxiety and ended so very badly. Why?

One reason, Pemberton argues, is basic supply and demand. There is a particularly strong market for this sort of rhetoric during periods of disruptive economic and social change. "The rhetoric of new orders is a way of responding to perceptions of crisis and an attendant sense of social insecurity," she writes. "However, predictions of dramatic social transformation coupled with attempts to generate excitement about possible tomorrows are also strategies of persuasion with the aim of rearranging intellectual and political priorities."[28]

Anxious people want to know how the story will end—the demand side of globaloney—and there are people who respond to this opportunity by supplying stories shaped to serve particular interests. As anxiety about globalization grows, as it does during periods of turmoil like the Asian financial crisis, globalization rhetoric is magnified until globalization narratives become the subject of their own discourse. Pemberton goes as far as defining globalization itself as rhetoric. "The term globalization denotes a set of inducing arguments and seductive images rather than a stark and incontestable fact of life. . . . Globalization, understood in an expansive fashion, is in many ways a rhetorical effect, as was international rationalization before it."[29]

Henry Wallace and Clare Boothe Luce built their globaloney arguments around the image of a borderless world as seen from the air. Such images are part of a continuing pattern in globalization discourse, according to Pemberton. "Narratives of globalization seduce through emotional and aesthetic appeals and the play of metaphors," she writes. "Quite striking is the use of organic and technological imagery."[30]

Globalization is real; it is not just rhetoric. But so strong are the demand and supply for globalization rhetoric that the substance of globalization can easily be lost in the chatter about it. The rhetoric of globalization replaces globalization itself. Jo-Anne Pemberton's work suggests that globalization attracts certain particular types of arguments and images. If this is true, then we should hear these arguments and see these images in the globalization stories of the 1990s as much as in those of the 1930s and 1940s.

And we do. Herewith, as prelude to the more detailed analysis to come, are three classic globaloney scenarios from the 1990s that illustrate Pemberton's points, provide examples of the reactions that Harold James finds in globalization history, and echo in various ways the images produced by Wallace and Luce in 1943. They are contemporary reflections of that earlier time. You might think of them as "the good, the bad, and the ugly" of globaloney for reasons that will shortly be clear.

Thomas Friedman: The Lexus and the Globaloney

The Lexus and the Olive Tree, by *New York Times* columnist Thomas L. Friedman, was probably the most widely read globalization book of the 1990s—and its appearance coincided with the increasing use of the G-word in the *Times* and elsewhere.[31] When read closely, it is a thoughtful and intelligent analysis of the tensions and trade-offs inherent in economic globalization. The Lexus, which represents the high-tech, high-speed, money-driven forces of economic globalization, needs to be balanced against the Olive Tree, which represents traditional social and cultural norms and practices. People want to have both a future and a past, to frame the two qualities a bit differently, and the burden of globalization is to find a way to make it so.

When my students read *The Lexus and the Olive Tree*, we listen carefully to both sides of Friedman's argument, both that of the optimist, who hopes that globalization can make the world more prosperous and peaceful without doing too much damage to nature and culture, and that of the pessimist, who is afraid that it won't and will instead incite a violent backlash. It is true that, in the end, Thomas Friedman really is a global optimist (although not an unthinking hyper-globalist). But he is certainly aware of the risks and dangers.

When I discuss Friedman's book with intelligent civilians (nonacademic friends), however, I find that they have overlooked his nuanced olive tree concerns and retained only his optimistic bottom line. Why don't people remember both sides of Thomas Friedman's globalization argument? Maybe they are uninterested in the logic of an argument and concerned only with the bottom line. There is probably some truth in this view, but I think a more powerful explanation is that Friedman's best rhetoric—his most memorable images and metaphors—is used to support the optimistic scenarios, not the pessimistic ones. It is not difficult to create antiglobalization images and metaphors (see the discussion of William Greider's rhetoric below), but Friedman decided not to use them. So perhaps my civilian friends are right and I am wrong. Although a word count might find that the book is fairly balanced between optimist and pessimist views of globalization, an audit of memorable phrases and vivid images would be decidedly one-sided. What follows, therefore, is not a summary of what Thomas Friedman actually wrote in *The Lexus and the Olive Tree*, but an inventory of what most readers actually retain, constructed from five vivid images.

The Electronic Herd

Globalization for Thomas Friedman is driven by money and technology, and he combines them in the image of the Electronic Herd. The Electronic Herd represents global investors, who charge into emerging market economies like the bulls in the old Merrill Lynch commercials and that, if spooked, charge out again, trampling anything in their path. Bulls, in the lexicon of Wall Street, are optimists who rush in to seize opportunities, unlike the cautious Bears. A herd of bulls, therefore, is an image of opportunity, not destruction (or not just destruction). In the age of financial globalization, Friedman suggests, a country needs to attract the attention of the Electronic Herd that will bring capital and technology with them.

The Golden Straitjacket

What determines which nations attract the Electronic Herd and achieve prosperity and which do not? The state, Friedman suggests, is the main factor, because unwise state policies can discourage foreign investors. In order to grow rich (become Golden), the state has to keep its hands off business by donning the Golden Straitjacket. To wear the Golden Straitjacket means to swear off protectionist trade policies and state interference in the economy. The tighter a nation wears the Golden Straitjacket, the more attractive it will be to the Electronic Herd, and the greater the prosperity it will be able to achieve.

DOS Capital: Software and Hardware

What attracts the Electronic Herd is not just a smaller state, Friedman writes, but a *better* state. He draws upon somewhat outdated computer terminology to create the image of the better state through DOS Capital. DOS stands for "disk operating system," the set of software instructions that controlled a computer's hardware in the days before various versions of Windows dominated the personal computer scene. Friedman's DOS is the rules and practices that guide government policy. Old versions of DOS lack rule of law, financial transparency, and efficient capital markets—"software" that the Electronic Herd needs to have to make its business hardware function efficiently. Countries that want to wear the Golden Straitjacket and get the gold need not only to stop the state from doing counterproductive things, they also need the state to upgrade their software, to make their markets more appealing to foreign investors.

DOS Capital is of course a play on words besides being a metaphor. The phrase is meant to remind us of *Das Kapital*, Karl Marx's famous book on capitalism. The metaphor is not especially memorable, but it is extremely effective in establishing the idea that globalization is a progressive movement. We all know that computer software systems are *supposed* to get better and better as they are revised and renumbered (even as we suspect that this does not always happen in practice). Windows 98 was an improvement on Windows 95, for example, because it was supposed to be more reliable and less prone to crashing. Computer updates these days typically feature better and more effective security features. By comparing a nation's laws, rules, and practices to a computer software system, Friedman introduces a progressive tendency. Such systems get better, more reliable, and more secure as they are upgraded to accommodate global capitalism. And this metaphor quietly assigns blame for problems. Anyone who fails to upgrade has no one else to blame for the crash when it comes; if this is true about a computer system, it cannot be false about a global economy.

The Golden Arches Theory

The Golden Arches Theory of Conflict Prevention holds that countries that have put on the Golden Straitjacket tightly enough and upgraded their software far enough to attract transnational investment (in the particular form of McDonald's—the Golden Arches) are unlikely to make war with one another. The Golden Arches Theory reflects the common argument that globalization promotes peaceful relations among nations because it makes war too expensive. War panics the Electronic Herd. Any gains from war must be weighed against the lost benefits of foreign trade and, especially, international investment.

In general terms, the theory that globalization makes war too costly is a familiar one that reaches back at least as far as David Ricardo and was popularized by 1933 Nobel Peace Prize recipient Norman Angell in *The Great Illusion*. More recently this idea has been developed and revised by Michael Mandelbaum in *The Ideas That Conquered the World*.[32] Friedman's contribution here is to link it to the Electronic Herd and especially to create the memorable image of the Golden Arches itself.

In its original form, the theory was that no two countries with Mc-

Donald's stores had ever gone to war because, as Friedman put it, the people would rather buy hamburgers than take up arms. When explained in more detail, this is really a theory of democracy rather than hamburgers. For the theory to work, a nation needs a large enough middle class to form a McDonald's-friendly fast-food market and a system of government where the interests of that middle class can influence policy.

After North Atlantic Treaty Organization (NATO) forces invaded Yugoslavia in 1999 and violated the Golden Arches Theory, Friedman modified the idea slightly, but stuck to the bottom-line conclusion.

> Today's version of globalization—with its intensifying economic integration, digital integration, its ever-widening connectivity of individuals and nations, its spreading of capitalist values and networks to the remotest corners of the world and its growing dependence on the Golden Straitjacket and the Electronic Herd—makes for a much stronger web of constraints on the foreign policy of those nations which are plugged into the system.

"It both increases the incentives for not making war and it increases the costs of going to war in more ways than in any previous era of modern history."[33]

Globalution

In a famous scene in *The Lexus and the Olive Tree,* Indonesian revolutionaries praise McDonald's, saying that every time they eat a hamburger under the Golden Arches they feel they are striking a blow against government corruption. These men were engaged in a process Friedman calls Globalution—a combination of globalization and revolution that Karl Marx never imagined. Globalution is how globalization creates democracy.

Globalization not only promotes peace between nations, Thomas Friedman argues, it also promotes democracy within nations through Globalution, revolution driven from abroad by the Electronic Herd. Dictatorships and oppressive regimes are bad news for transnational businesses, the argument goes, so the Electronic Herd puts lots of pressure on these governments to reform and punishes them by stampeding out if they do not. Transnational corporations and Electronic Herd investors, who are only concerned with their own profits, thus take actions to undermine dictators and corrupt government, benefiting the oppressed masses and promoting democracy, as if guided by an invisible hand to do so.

A Composite Image of Globalization

If you string together these images and metaphors, leaving out the counterexamples, qualifications, and conditionalities that are layered through Friedman's work, you get an outrageous claim that qualifies for the globaloney hall of fame: globalization equals peace, prosperity, and democracy. Global investors (Electronic Herd) create prosperity (Golden Straitjacket), forcing governments to adopt democracy-friendly reform (DOS Capital) or be overthrown (Globalution). War is too costly in the world that results because the economic systems are too interconnected (Golden Arches Theory). And besides, people would rather stand in line to eat hamburgers than go to war anyhow.

Connecting the dots in this highly selective way gives you a picture that has a lot in common with the one that Henry Wallace sketched in *American* magazine. Both are globaloney, of course. Both Wallace and Friedman promoted internationalist agendas and used vivid images and powerful metaphors to cover holes and support arguments that could not otherwise support themselves. It is not clear, for example, that the Electronic Herd is the harbinger of prosperity. Bulls created bubbles and financial crises in both the 1920s and 1990s. Nations that insert themselves into straitjackets, electronic or manual, find it impossible to protect themselves and their citizens from such catastrophes (hence the necessity of Wallace's Depression-era New Deal programs). And so on—it is easy to see that each of Friedman's laws of globalization are really special cases, albeit memorable ones.[34]

Friedman's argument, as written, is more nuanced, as I have suggested above, but still sketchy in many places. Without the images and metaphors it would command little attention. But with those features included, Friedman's columns and books shaped the globalization debate and created its vocabulary. Thomas Friedman's Golden Arches image of globalization is "the good" in this brief rhetorical trilogy since his images reinforce positive aspects of globalization, just as Henry Wallace did.

Giant Sucking Sounds: Fear, Loathing, and Globaloney

You can think of *The Lexus and the Olive Tree* as a grander version of Henry Wallace's *American* magazine article. But, as I said a few pages ago, where Wallace imagined a people-driven globalization, where free-dom-of-the-air would let people move seamlessly across the face of the earth, doing business, making contacts, understanding each other a bit better, Thomas Friedman has to rely upon a faceless Electronic Herd. This difference reflects an important change between Wallace's day and ours.

Henry Wallace was probably able to remember the time before World War I when international travel was essentially open and international migration not too severely regulated. A people-driven globalization was not out of the question in Wallace's time as it was in the 1990s, when Thomas Friedman wrote. Pity poor Friedman, forced to manufacture peace and prosperity out of global money alone! He had little choice, however, because finance is the most global of all the structures that connect the nations and peoples of the world. People are hardly global at all by comparison, in terms of their unregulated global mobility.

Clare Boothe Luce knew, however, that nothing frightens people as much as other people and that fear of enemies—foreign people and for-eign competition—can be even stronger than love of money. That's one reason her protectionist globaloney was so effective and is so popular today. Although there are many contenders for the honor, my choices for the three most successful practitioners of the global rhetoric of fear and loathing of the 1990s are Jean-Marie Le Pen, H. Ross Perot, and José Bové.

Jean-Marie Le Pen

Jean-Marie Le Pen is the leader of the National Front, a French political party often characterized as ultra-right-wing or nationalist. Despite his party's status on the political periphery, however, Le Pen advanced all the way to the final round of France's 2002 presidential election, where he faced and was defeated by the incumbent, Jacques Chirac. Le Pen's great gift is his ability to create vivid images of enemies who sneak in through open doors and windows, taking jobs and opportunities. Rising crime and unemployment rates are the result. Although his writings and speeches strike many notes, a common theme is a version of the giant sucking sound, as Arab immigrants are drawn from Northern Africa to France. "Massive immigration has only just begun," he has said, according to a BBC News profile. "It is the biggest problem facing France, Europe and probably the world. We risk being submerged."[35]

Recent data indicate that migration into France has been relatively stable over the past twenty-five years. About 7.4 percent of France's population is foreign-born. Net inward migration is estimated at about 0.64 migrants per 1,000 of population, much less than the equivalent figures for Germany (3.99 new migrants per 1,000 population), the United Kingdom (1.06), the United States (3.5), or Denmark (2.01), for example. In statistical terms, France's "migrant problem" is no different than those of other developed countries.[36]

Despite these facts, I am sure that Le Pen's supporters saw supporting evidence everywhere they looked in France. Each time they saw a darker complexion or foreign-looking outfit, they knew that Le Pen was right. Each time they heard someone speak a foreign language, they understood Le Pen's fears. They saw and heard these things more and more, and became more convinced that Le Pen's fears were valid, for three reasons. First, of course, because their eyes and ears were sensitized to these stimuli and so focused upon them, much as someone who is thinking of buying a Volkswagen car suddenly sees them everywhere on the street where they went unnoticed before. Second, France draws tourists and students from around the world, so one might expect to see and hear more foreign dress and language based upon this alone. But third, and most important, most of the people that Le Pen's supporters saw and heard and feared were not migrants at all. They were native-born French of foreign heritage. This group is much larger than the group of actual migrants and gets larger every year as the general population grows.

Le Pen played upon the economic and social fears of French voters very successfully. Globalization, for Le Pen, means dropping all protective barriers and being flooded by foreigners who take your money and perhaps even your life. He exploited these fears just as Clare Boothe Luce did.

H. Ross Perot

Texas billionaire H. Ross Perot coined the term *Giant Sucking Sound* when he ran for the U.S. presidency in 1992. Although Perot's ballot opponents were Bill Clinton and George Bush, he really ran against globalization. And lost. Both Bush and Clinton supported economic globalization in general and its regional variant, NAFTA, in particular. (Clinton, who supported NAFTA with somewhat mixed emotions during the election headed the most pro-globalization administration thus far in U.S. history.) Perot could not have defeated Bush or Clinton on personal merits, in terms of his political experience, knowledge of the issues, or telegenic appeal. He stood a better chance opposing globalization, so he ran against it instead.

Whereas Le Pen's image of globalization was of foreigners sneaking in, Perot's was of jobs running away, or being pulled away, actually, drawn by low wages abroad. The specific attraction was low wages in Mexico, but wages in most countries are lower than the United States. The first sound you will hear once NAFTA is signed, Perot told his television audience, will be a giant sucking sound—the sound of U.S. jobs being sucked abroad.

Perot expanded on the themes raised by his presidential campaign in a 1993 book titled *Save Your Job, Save Our Country: Why NAFTA Must Be Stopped—NOW!*[37] NAFTA/globalization, he argued, threatens individual jobs and national economic sovereignty. NAFTA would make U.S. borders more permeable, allowing illegal migrants and illegal drugs to flow in from Mexico more easily. It would open up U.S. businesses to foreign investment, foreign influence, and foreign control. U.S. wages would be driven down and U.S. national security jeopardized as vital defense industry production moved offshore. It will be only a matter of time before the United States becomes a nation of hamburger flippers (another McDonald's reference!).

None of the fears that Ross Perot raised proved valid in NAFTA's first ten years—not one. This is not a surprise since, for example, the threat that Mexican investors would take over many key U.S. industries just doesn't make any sense given the vast differences between the two economies. Studies of NAFTA tend to focus upon its *lack of* significant effects on the U.S. economy rather than its dramatic power. Most economists agree that the jobs of low-skilled U.S. workers were threatened by technological change rather than by global trade or investment. Studies show that foreign wage rates are not a high priority in foreign direct investment decisions (if they were, the United States would not be the largest single recipient of foreign direct investment in the world). Low foreign wages are generally offset by low foreign productivity. To the extent that transnational corporations consider wages, they look for *bargain* wages—wages that are low relative to the skills and productivity of the workers who receive them—not low wages per se.

The fear of low-wage competitors is a classic globaloney argument that Clare Boothe Luce used too. Why was Perot's sucking sound globaloney so effective? Clearly not because it is based upon facts. Rather,

Perot spoke out to an audience engulfed in change and fearful of it and provided them with a simple reason for their dilemma and a clear enemy to resist. Simple images of the future are comforting in times of stress and change because they tell fearful people what is wrong, and that it is not their fault. They provide the appearance of understanding and the illusion of logic. The details of the argument connecting cause, effect, and action are mostly missing, but this serves to strengthen the appeal rather than weaken it.

José Bové

Many people observe that José Bové looks a lot like Astérix the Gaul, a French cartoon character. In his comic strip, Astérix and his friend Obélix fight to preserve France from foreign invaders. His motto is, "Ils sont fous ces Romains!" These Romans are crazy. Bové fights globalization by behaving crazily himself.

José Bové is probably best known for his attack on a McDonald's restaurant in Millau, France, which demolished the structure, sent Bové to jail, and made him a hero. Such is life in France. Bové said that McDonald's "provoked" him by opening a fast-food restaurant in the village. He could not help himself after that.

Bové is now waging war against globalization on a broad battlefield, campaigning against industrial farms, genetically modified foods, free trade, and so on.[38] His task is made easier by the fact that he is able to define his own enemy. He does not fight globalization so much as an image of globalization—the image of McDonald's hamburgers. He creates an enemy, giving it only the characteristics that make it a suitable target for attack. The rest he ignores; it isn't there. It is a good strategy, and he has been very successful.

Are you concerned that McDonald's name has been showing up frequently in this chapter? McDonald's is a very common ingredient in globaloney recipes because it is a common sight around the world. Once a suggestion is planted about McDonald's (such as McDonald's equals industrial), every time you see McDonald's you think of industrial food. Then it is a simple step to argue that McDonald's equals globalization, therefore industrial food equals globalization. That's the lexicographic algebra that José Bové employs, and the conclusion slides down easily. We are humans, not machines; we need human food, not industrial food. Down with McDonald's. Down with globalization.

The problem is that McDonald's, like many of the images of globalization, can represent a great many things. That's why Thomas Friedman could use McDonald's so effectively in *The Lexus and the Olive Tree*. It is just as easy to take some desirable characteristic of McDonald's (a safe place with clean restrooms) and employ Bové's algebra to arrive at a conclusion that presents globalization in a favorable light.

José Bové has used globaloney to become an international celebrity, capable of bringing out the press to any demonstration. So great is his personal fame that photographers rushed to take his picture at the Seattle World Trade Organization (WTO) meetings, defiantly munching a Roquefort sandwich outside a local McDonald's store. The store provoked him, I suppose, and it soon stood vandalized. Ils sont fous, ces Romains.

William Greider: The Manic Globaloney Machine

If, as the Nike advertisements used to say, image is everything, then William Greider is the master of everything. Greider is national editor of *Rolling Stone* magazine and has written books with such titles as *Secrets of the Temple: How the Federal Reserve Runs the Country*, *The Trouble with Money*, and *Who Will Tell the People? The Betrayal of American Democracy*. Since globalization is, according to Thomas Friedman, "everything and its opposite," it makes sense that Greider would write a book about it, opposing it, and he did, *One World, Ready or Not: The Manic Logic of Global Capitalism*,[39] an example of the sort of globalization narrative that Jo-Anne Pemberton discusses in *Global Metaphors*. I want to point out five techniques that Greider uses in *One World* that make it a classic of globaloney.

The Coming Crisis

You may not realize it, but the world is on the verge of dramatic change, Greider tells his readers. "The logic of commerce and capital has overpowered the inertia of politics and launched an epoch of great social transformations," he says boldly, creating a powerful yet incomprehensible image.[40] The crisis is earth-shattering, in the figurative sense, although the book's cover displays the image of a literal world globe that has been shattered and patched back together again using masking tape. This is a serious crisis. Be afraid. Be very afraid.

Global Metaphors

The best way to understand what is happening, Greider writes, is to think of global capitalism as a machine—a huge, destructive machine that destroys everything that it touches. And who is driving the machine? Who is in command? No one. Pemberton noted that the metaphors used in globalization are often organic or technological. Organic images can suggest natural order or uncontrolled chaos. Technological images are used to describe progress, rational order, or, as here, destruction. One of Thomas Friedman's principal metaphors—the Electronic Herd—is both organic and technological. Greider presents an image of nature destroyed by the machine.

Clear Agenda

William Greider makes no bones about his agenda in *One World*. You cannot write a book with chapter titles like "The Ghost of Marx" and "These Dark Satanic Mills" and not have readers suspect that you are advancing a radical agenda. Greider proposes, as many others have done with less effect, that Marx's analysis of capitalism is truer today than it was in the nineteenth century and that the Workers of the World have more reason to arise now than they did in 1848. Greider calls for creation of a global labor movement to offset the interests of capitalists and the manic logic of capitalism, which he sees as destroying itself and taking the rest of the world with it.

The Power of Exceptional Cases

There are many facts and figures in *One World*, describing global production capacity, for example, or the distribution of national income. Greider is smart enough, however, to know that statistics never persuade or convince by themselves, but they can be useful when connected to a powerful story. This is perhaps why journalists like Friedman and Greider are so influential in framing the globalization debate—they are trained storytellers, after all.

One common technique in globaloney is to tell the story of an exceptional case and then argue as if it were really the general case. The reader, stuck with only one piece of evidence, usually goes along. We see this technique at work repeatedly in the chapters that follow.

To a certain extent, of course, it is impossible to avoid talking about special cases, because they are the only ones that really exist. "[T]he notion of '*global*' in '*global*isation' invites us to take the world as our unit of analysis," Jarrod Weiner has observed, "and clearly it is impossible to observe everything. One must necessarily and unavoidably select what one believes to be the most important; the only difference is whether someone does, or does not, make those criteria of selection explicit."[41]

In *One World*, for example, Greider tells the tragic story of the 1993 Bangkok toy factory fire—a truly horrific event. It was, he says, "the worst industrial fire in the history of capitalism."[42] In terms of loss of life, it was even worse than the Triangle Shirtwaist Company fire of 1911. Both cases are notable, of course, because they are exceptional—they are not representative of any general trend. They are so far beyond the norm that they demand attention and action. Logically, exceptional cases like these require specific and immediate responses. Greider, however, uses the exceptional case to justify a generalized response. He calls for global social standards for production and trade. Clearly Greider has his reasons for citing these specific cases, and I think they are probably good reasons. But the reasons aren't clearly stated, and the reader is left to imagine that all factories everywhere are like these exceptional cases.

Fighting Fire with Fire

Finally, one important characteristic of globaloney that we find in *One World* is the strategy of creating a virtuous globaloney in order to oppose an evil globaloney. What do capitalists believe, you might ask? Greider creates a globaloney version of capitalist ideology in order to poke holes in it. Capitalists think that the market can do everything, organize every aspect of human society. They have no religion; they only worship the market. They see no value except the market value. You know, that sort of thing. If capitalists do believe this, they should be ashamed of themselves. Maybe people like this *do* exist. If they didn't, of course, someone would have to invent them to promote an anticapitalist and antiglobalization agenda.

But William Greider didn't entirely have to invent exaggerated pro-globalization rhetoric in order to poke holes in it. *One World, Ready or Not* was inspired in part by a best-selling book that appeared in the United States in 1943—the same year as the Henry Wallace–Clare

Boothe Luce globaloney exchange that began this chapter. It was called *One World* and its author was Wendell L. Wilkie.[43]

One World reported Wilkie's experiences as he circled the globe, meeting with Allied leaders at the request of President Roosevelt. It's a small world, he discovered, as his converted bomber, the *Gulliver*, ran up 31,000 air miles in 46 days (but only 160 flight hours, as Wilkie made sure to point out, to stress how small the world had grown). "There are no distant points in the world any longer," he said. "Our thinking in the future must be world-wide."[44]

In *One World*, Wilkie pieced together a globalization scenario that must have scared the daylights out of the isolationist and protectionist members of his own political party. The airplane makes this a small world, he said. One world, not many. One world, indivisible. The interests and concerns of other peoples cannot help but be our interests too. If we believe in freedom we cannot tolerate imperialism abroad or at home. If we believe in equality, we cannot tolerate inequality or discrimination abroad or at home. If we do tolerate imperialism, inequality, and discrimination, we will become the very enemy we now oppose. And we must work hand in hand with other countries to achieve our lofty goals. *One World* is a call for truly radical change—change that few of his readers were prepared to embrace. But Wilkie embedded change in a vivid image that comforted his anxious reader—an image of airplanes creating an international brotherhood devoted to American values.

That round-the-world flight transformed Wendell Wilkie. It provided him with a radical agenda for domestic reform and international engagement. Or rather, since I am a bit cynical about this, perhaps the flight provided only the images and metaphors that he needed to market his ambitious agenda to a fearful country. And created the opportunity of a lifetime for Clare Boothe Luce to brand this sort of thinking "globaloney."

Globaloney? So What?

As you can see, I am very critical of people who use distorted images of globalization to advance personal or intellectual agendas of their own. It isn't that I am in love with globalization; I don't worship it as some people seem to do. I'm not a "market-hugger" the way some people are "tree-huggers." It's just that I've become a skeptic. I am suspicious of any argument that uses an image of globalization to arrive at a bogus or self-serving conclusion.

I made a special effort to identify pro-globalization interests in an earlier book, *Selling Globalization: The Myth of the Global Economy.* I thought that the hyper-globalizers, who exaggerate the benefits and inevitability of globalization, were dangerous. I wanted to poke holes in their arguments before they pushed the case for global markets and investments too far. In this book I'm changing targets, to a certain extent, trying to take particular aim at the antiglobalizers and those who attack globalization as an indirect way of attacking something else—America, capitalism, or both.

Why switch targets now? One reason is that I think that the speculative excesses of the 1990s and the brutal consequences of the financial crises they spawned have taken some of the steam out of the hyper-globalization engine. I am not so worried that people will accept the consequences of bogus pro-globalization logic as I once was.[45] It is the antiglobalization rhetoric that worries me now.

Where do these antiglobalization arguments lead us? I know that idealists hope that they lead to a world of greater security, justice, and equality, but I fear that they could lead to a world of greater conflict, repression, and poverty, particularly if they are based upon globaloney, not facts. We saw in the 1930s how fearful people can react to the apparent loss of control to external forces, peoples, and cultures and how they can be manipulated by clever rhetoric into socially destructive acts. After reading Harold James's book, I can't help but see some of the same acrid reactions in the news today. I don't want to go down that road again.

Is it inevitable that we must choose between distorted images, between the hopeful globaloney of Henry Wallace and Thomas Friedman and the fearful globaloney of Clare Boothe Luce and Jean-Marie Le Pen? Or is history a pendulum that swings between these extremes, as Daniel Yergin suggests in *The Commanding Heights?*[46]

I don't think that we have to accept that globaloney of one sort or another need always dominate public debate, tilting the agenda in favor of one set of interests or another. I am optimistic that we can learn to tell the difference between globalization and globaloney and make up our own minds about important issues, not simply fall headfirst into clever rhetorical traps.

*   *   *

Globaloney the word was born in 1943, but globaloney arguments are much older. In chapter 2 I try to pin the blame for globaloney on Adam Smith, who was not just the Father of Economics, but also the founder of globaloney rhetoric. I'll show how Smith's techniques are used in globaloney arguments today.

BLAME IT ALL ON ADAM SMITH

At least we know who's to blame. When the time comes to assign guilt for the fact that almost everyone misunderstands globalization, I don't think the jury will have to deliberate very long. If most people confuse globalization with globaloney, if they perceive the complex patterns of global markets as simple images of hamburger stands and soda pop cans, if they are so mesmerized by globalization rhetoric that they fail to see what's right before their eyes—well, you don't need to be Sherlock Holmes to deduce the reason why.

You can blame it all on Adam Smith.

Now if this were one of those popular antiglobalization books, like *One World, Ready or Not: The Manic Logic of Global Capitalism*[1] by *Rolling Stone* writer William Greider, I'd be blaming Adam Smith for going too far in his praise of free markets and the next couple paragraphs would read something like this:

> Globalization is a vast turbo-powered machine that circles the globe destroying all that it touches. Who is in control of this unstoppable manic machine? No one. No one can control it. The best we can do is

to offer up human sacrifices to try to satisfy the demands of the nameless, faceless market gods.

Who created this twenty-first-century Frankenstein? You can blame it all on Adam Smith. Adam Smith created the myth of the Invisible Hand, which falsely justifies the ruthless pursuit of individual greed and personal power on the grounds that it is somehow in the public interest for market forces to make children work in sweatshops. There is no Invisible Hand, just the fact of greed, exploitation, and the ultimate destruction of civilization as we know it.[2]

On the other hand, if this were one of those popular pro-globalization books, like *The Borderless World: Power and Strategy in the Interlinked Economy*[3] by business consultant Kenichi Ohmae, I'd be damning Adam Smith for not going far enough in his praise of market forces and the next paragraphs would read something like this:

Globalization is the new world of unlimited opportunity and unimaginable prosperity. Globalization essentially frees humankind from all of the barriers that have for centuries kept people from achieving their true potential. We are all connected by the vast global web where time and space are irrelevant and authoritarian rule is impossible.

Why has it taken us so long to realize the unlimited potential that global markets offer? Adam Smith is to blame because he failed to appreciate the full potential of the Invisible Hand of Self-Interest. He wrote how the Butcher and the Baker, seeking no end other than their own profit, unintentionally benefit society as well, as if guided by the famous transparent appendage. Smith's examples are quaint and charming, and his conclusion is no doubt correct, but he missed the point. What the Invisible Hand really does is to push inevitably for one vast stateless, border-free world where friction-free capitalism can weave a seamless web of peace and prosperity.

But this chapter isn't going down either of these roads. Adam Smith is to blame because he taught both the antiglobalizers like Greider and the hyper-globalizers like Ohmae how to sell bogus arguments and to make extravagant claims on the basis of the flimsiest evidence (or even in spite of evidence). Forgive me, Adam Smith. I am a trained economist, and you are the father of my discipline. But you taught the world how to manufacture globaloney.

Pins. It's All about Pins.

Adam Smith is the godfather of globaloney, although hardly anyone thinks of him that way, despite the work of Friedrich List and many others. He is more famous as the father of modern economics. His book *The Wealth of Nations*, published in 1776, is one of the most influential books of all time.

Adam Smith wrote about a lot of things in *The Wealth of Nations*, but globalization wasn't one of them. The world of 1776 was still trying to figure out how *international* relations worked; they weren't ready for the idea of *global* affairs. Adam Smith's contribution wasn't so much that he created globaloney itself as that he popularized a way of thinking and writing that lends itself to globaloney. I guess you'd say he perfected the rhetorical technology that powers the modern globaloney factory. Here's how it happened.

For the most part, *The Wealth of Nations* was a work of synthesis, not something Adam Smith whipped up from scratch. Smith drew together ideas that had been in the air for decades and pieced them into a coherent system of economic thought. This systematic organization of economic ideas was a great achievement, and it made him famous.

Surprisingly, *The Wealth of Nations* contained only one truly original concept: the division of labor, the idea that you can break down a big task into specialized functions that can be more efficiently performed. Henry Ford's assembly-line system is a famous example of the division of labor at work. The division of labor is an important idea, and we should remember Adam Smith because of it, but of course it is not what we actually remember him for. For most people, Adam Smith stands for "laissez-faire"—free markets and free trade. But the division of labor is where it all begins and where globaloney technology was first put to use.

I suppose that Rule #1 in the globaloney guide is Be Bold! Don't dillydally. Make your claim loud and clear. Page one, chapter one, book one of *The Wealth of Nations* therefore starts out with a bang.

> The greatest improvement in the productive powers of labour, and the greatest part of the skill, dexterity, and judgement with which it is any where directed, or applied, seem to have been the effects of the division of labour.[4]

Adam Smith begins *The Wealth of Nations* with an incredibly broad generalization about the division of labor. Labor productivity owes more to the division of labor than to anything else, where anything else includes most of the factors that we usually associate with increasing productivity—innovation, learning-by-doing, technology, capital investment, etc. You cannot fault Smith for understating his main point! And remember that this is the very first sentence in the book.

How can Smith possibly convince the reader that the division of labor, which hasn't even been defined yet, is the main factor in the production of prosperity? The claim is so broad and the notion so abstract that it would probably be impossible to support it using figures and statistics. But Smith isn't bothered by this because he isn't trying to *prove* that the division of labor is the key to productivity growth, he only needs to *persuade* the reader that it is—and this is a much easier task. So instead of statistical analysis he tells us a story.

> To take an example, therefore, from a very trifling manufacture; but one in which the division of labour has been very often taken notice of, the trade of the pin-maker; a workman not educated to this business (which the division of labour has rendered a distinct trade), nor acquainted with the use of the machinery employed in it (to the invention of which the same division of labour has probably given occasion), could scarce, perhaps, with his utmost industry make one pin in a day, and certainly could not make twenty. But in the way in which this business is now carried on, not only the whole work is a peculiar trade, but it is divided into a number of branches, of which the greater part are likewise trades.[5]

This is the beginning of the famous "pin factory" story, which is, along with the "Invisible Hand," the most memorable part of *The Wealth of Nations*. The pin example is a clever choice. Pins must have been among the most common manufactured items in Smith's day. If he were writing today, Smith might pick pencils (as Milton Friedman did for his 1980 television series, *Free to Choose*), but pins worked fine in 1776. Common, ordinary, cheap. Smith is right, however; I cannot imagine making pins (or pencils) myself. If pins are so hard to make, why are they so cheap? Glad you asked, Smith says. The answer is the division of labor.

> One man draws out the wire, another straights it, a third cuts it, a fourth points it, a fifth grinds it at the top for receiving the head; to make the head requires two or three distinct operations; to put it on, is a peculiar business, to whiten the pins is another; it is even a trade by itself to put them into the paper; and the important business of making a pin is, in this manner divided into about eighteen distinct operations, which, in some manufactories, are all performed by distinct hands, though in others the same man will sometimes perform two or three of them.[6]

The use of detail in this paragraph is very effective, don't you think? In my mind's eye I can see each of the steps he enumerates, and I am

42

instantly convinced that the division of labor can be extended to at least eighteen steps or stages of production. How does Smith know so much about ordinary pins? Glad you asked, Smith replies. I once visited a pin factory myself.

> I have seen a small manufactory of this kind where ten men only were employed and where some of them consequently performed two or three distinct operations. But though they were very poor, and therefore but indifferently accommodated with the necessary machinery, they could, when they exerted themselves, make among them about twelve pounds of pins in a day.[7]

Seeing is believing, it is said. The fact that Smith reports on a personal observation is very persuasive, more persuasive than if he reported industrial statistics of some sort. It is *so* persuasive, in fact, that it is the only actual example that he provides. It is all he needs, however, because it is such a great example. The global relevance of the division of labor, in terms of Smith's argument, rests upon ten men and a pail full of pins. How many pins is that, anyway? Glad you asked, says he. I counted them.

> There are in a pound upwards of four thousand pins of middling size. Those ten persons, therefore, could make among them upwards of forty-eight thousand pins in a day. Each person, therefore, making a tenth part of forty-eight thousand pins, might be considered as making four thousand eight hundred pins in a day. But if they had all wrought separately and independently, and without any of them having been educated to this peculiar business, they certainly could not each of them have made twenty, perhaps not one pin in a day; that is, certainly, not the two hundred and fortieth, perhaps not the four thousand eight hundredth part of what they are at present capable of performing, in consequence of a proper division and combination of their different operations.[8]

Since Adam Smith cannot possibly *prove* his broad assertion that the division of labor is responsible for all improvements in labor productivity, he doesn't even try. Instead he tells the story of his own observations with just enough detail to establish his own credibility. If Smith is credible, that makes Smith's argument credible. By choosing an example that you can readily imagine, he makes his story almost as trustworthy as if you had actually been to the pin factory. The picture is vivid, so the example is persuasive.

It is a good thing that the story is so appealing, because the conclusion is astounding, and all the more astounding for being true. Working alone, ten men might make between 10 and 200 pins in a day altogether. But working together (and taking advantage of the division of labor), they produce 48,000 pins. The division of labor is responsible for a 240-fold increase in the productivity of labor. No wonder pins can be so cheap despite being so difficult for a person to make. The division of labor is indeed a miracle—in regard to pins, in any case, and ignoring any other forces that might be at work.

If you found the pin factory example convincing, then you have swallowed Smith's bait and he will now reel you in, because he means to draw a universal conclusion from this one particular example. Does the pin story apply just to pins? Glad you asked.

> In every other art and manufacture, the effects of the division of labour are similar to what they are in this very trifling one; though in many of them, the labour can neither be so much subdivided, nor reduced to so great a simplicity of operation. The division of labour, however, so far as it can be introduced, occasions, in every art, a proportionable increase in the productive powers of labour.[9]

This is a powerful paragraph because it smoothly extends the argument from pins to everything else. The division of labor has the same sort of effect as you saw at the pin factory in *every* other situation. No support of this claim is offered; it is just simple logic. Smith is saying, more or less, that what is true about pins cannot be false about the great majority of human productions. Pins are a "trifling" example; if the division of labor so powerfully increases the productivity of simple pins, it must be even more powerful when applied to matters of substance.

In short, Smith leads us quickly from a single memorable and convincing example to a general conclusion. The division of labor makes (or can make) all things as cheap and common and abundant as pins. The division of labor is the key to unlocking vast quantities of goods and services generally just as it enables the production of uncountable numbers of pins. Say, who profits from this mass production? Glad you asked.

> It is this great multiplication of the productions of all the different arts, in consequence of the division of labour, which occasions, in a well-governed society, that universal opulence which extends itself to the lowest ranks of the people.[10]

Pins are so cheap that even the poor can afford to buy some and taste a bit of "opulence." And what is true of pins is generally true. So the division of labor benefits everyone in society, bottom to top.

Now if the division of labor is so beneficial, it should be maximized, expanded, exploited. What determines how much division of labor can take place? Glad you asked. It's the market. The division of labor is limited by the extent of the market.

> As it is the power of exchanging that gives occasion to the division of labour, so the extent of this division must always be limited by the extent of that power, or, in other words, by the extent of the market.[11]

Broader markets, finer division of labor, greater opulence; simple as that. Regulating markets, restricting their growth, or restraining international trade necessarily limits market extent, limiting the division of labor, hurting everyone, even the poor. If you wanted to maximize labor productivity, it is obvious that you would favor global markets—free international trade connecting free national markets—and the laissez-faire policies that are necessary to avoid limiting them.

So there you have it. Globalization (global markets and laissez-faire policies) increases opulence, providing benefits that reach even to the lowest ranks of society. Proof? Well, the whole argument is really built on just one single fact: ten men working *together* can make a lot more pins than if they work *by themselves*. It is really not much of an argument, evaluated objectively, but it is great rhetoric. Once you have that pin factory centered in your mind's eye, the conclusion of global laissez-faire is just a few steps away.

The Newtonian System

The tight little chain of principle, example, assertion, and logical conclusion that starts on the first page of *The Wealth of Nations* is one of Adam Smith's best rhetorical achievements. It sure was effective at converting readers to Smith's point of view. And it didn't happen by accident. Smith knew economics, but it might be true that he knew rhetoric even better.

Adam Smith studied rhetoric in addition to jurisprudence and moral philosophy, and he even gave lectures on this topic in both Glasgow and Edinburgh. Although he never wrote a book on rhetoric, we do have good notes taken at his lectures, which reveal quite a lot about Smith's thinking in this field.[12] He was part of a movement called the New Rhetoric, which sought to rationalize argument. The Old Rhetoric was flowery and indirect; it relied upon allegory and metaphor more than cold facts and logic. The New Rhetoric was intended to be plain, rational, and almost scientific by comparison.

Three elements of the New Rhetoric, as explicated in Smith's lectures, interest us here. Smith argued for plain language, for the effective use of historical example, and for tight organization of an argument. Plain language, he said, makes arguments clear and persuasive. He cited Jonathan Swift in this regard. The use of historical examples, Smith argued, gives weight to an argument and provides it with a solid foundation. According to the notes, "It sets before us the more interesting and important events of human life, points out the causes by which these events were brought about and by this means points out to us by what matter and method we may produce similar good effects or avoid Similar bad ones."[13] He cited Thucydides as a master of this method.

Finally, Smith championed a systematic approach to argumentation. The Old Rhetoric, which he associated with Aristotle, among others, was a leisurely pursuit. It examined all the various possible lines of reasoning one by one, drawing insights and making comments here and there as appropriate, until all possibilities had been exhausted. Smith contrasts this with what he called the Newtonian system, which is to identify a principle right at the start of an argument (say, on page one) and then to construct a chain of observations that are all connected by that principle. Smith did not invent the Newtonian system—his biographer Ian Simpson Ross indicates that it went back at least as far as Plato—but he vigorously championed its use.

Adam Smith had strong views about effective rhetoric, but he didn't always practice what he preached. He didn't always follow all of the principles of the New Rhetoric in *The Wealth of Nations*, for example, and even his lectures on rhetoric didn't strictly follow his rules of rhetoric, according to Vivienne Brown.[14] In particular, Smith could not resist violating the first rule, stick to straight talk. His writing is often complicated and indirect, and it can try the patience of modern readers (one reason why Smith is more read about than read today, I suppose). Smith didn't bend the rule about history, however. The whole of Book III of *The Wealth of Nations*, for example, is a survey of the "Progress of Opulence" from the ancient through the modern worlds. More generally, however, Adam Smith used examples and details very effectively both to give weight to arguments and to capture the imaginations of his readers.

Where Smith really excelled, however, is in his use of the "Newtonian" form of argument, and this is why he is to blame for so much of the globaloney that is written. The idea of the Newtonian argument is to take a principle and use it to connect several observations in ways that entice and convince the reader. Smith took the principle of the division of labor and, in just a few paragraphs, made it a powerful image. Once this image was created, he encouraged the reader to see it everywhere in forms big and small and to see its influence at all levels. Smith exploited fully the psychological impact of the Newtonian system. "It gives us a pleasure to see the phenomena which we reckoned the most unaccountable all deduced from some principle (commonly a well-known)," according to notes from one of Smith's rhetoric lectures, "and all united in one chain."[15] Readers of *The Wealth of Nations* are thus not only willing to accept universal conclusions based upon sketchy arguments and minimal evidence, they are in fact pleased to do so. Smith delights his readers by solving easily and at once these otherwise puzzling and troublesome problems of the real world.

So powerful is the Newtonian technique in *The Wealth of Nations* that Adam Smith can even disclose the limitations of his argument without undermining its effectiveness. He writes, for example, that the division of labor cannot be as complete in some products as it is for pins, but that really doesn't undermine his point that it has *some* effect in all products. He notes that the case of the pins is really a trifling matter (it is—man does not live by pins alone), but that doesn't really undermine the gee-whiz impact of the example (ten men, 48,000 pins). Opulence extends even to the lower classes, he writes, when a society is well-governed, but poorly governed societies were probably the norm in 1776 and are in much of the world today. But, again, the main point or the image of that main point is so clear and strong and compelling that its impact is undiminished, indeed it is unaffected, by these notes and conditions.

In other words, Smith can have it both ways. He can paint a simple universal picture based upon the principle of the division of labor and at the same time be able to claim a more complex, nuanced argument. Nice work, Adam Smith.

Political Economy versus Cosmopolitical Economy

I am not the first person to accuse Adam Smith of globaloney. The nineteenth-century German political economist Friedrich List did it before me in *The National System of Political Economy*, first published in 1841, his mercantilist response to Smith's *Wealth of Nations*.[16]

List is little known in the United States today, but his influence on European and Japanese economic policy has been profound. I think of List as a sort of German twin brother of the Frenchman Alexis de Tocqueville because both based major works on what they observed in the United States. De Tocqueville famously conned the French government into sending him to the United States in 1831 for the purpose of studying American prisons. He studied American society instead and wrote *Democracy in America*, still perhaps the best statement of American domestic political culture.

Friedrich List came to the United States just a few years before de Tocqueville, but under somewhat different circumstances. List was a professor and liberal member of the Representative Assembly of Würtemberg who was driven by the idea of free trade. He agitated and schemed and finally, in 1825, mounted a major legislative action to create a Commercial Union (a sort of European Union) among the German states of the time. His forceful advocacy of free trade so offended the entrenched protectionist interests that he was expelled from the assembly, convicted of agitation, and sentenced to ten months' hard labor in prison. List escaped this punishment by fleeing German territory, going first to Paris and then, armed with letters of introduction supplied by a sympathetic Lafayette, to the United States, where he found work as a journalist.

Like de Tocqueville, List was deeply influenced by the relative peace and prosperity that he found in the United States. Unlike de Tocqueville, who was most impressed by the quality of America's "civil society," List was intrigued by the power of the federal government and the effectiveness of American economic policies that dated from Alexander Hamilton's era. A strong and forceful state, List decided, was needed to promote industry and build a nation. Free trade, however beneficial in theory, he argued, meant dominance by Great Britain in practice, since Britain already had such a head start and so many advantages. No one could catch up with Britain if exposed to unprotected competition.

List went public with his views in a series of newspaper articles on U.S. tariff negotiations with Great Britain, which were collected and published in 1827 as *Outlines of a New System of Political Economy*. Protectionist interests were drawn to List's elegant prose and effective argumentation, much as similar interests would later be drawn to Clare Boothe Luce's protectionist rhetoric. They saw to it that his articles were widely circulated. So well known did List and his views become that he was sent on a trade mission in 1830 by President Andrew Jackson, who appointed him as U.S. consul to Hamburg. List was still considered an outlaw in German eyes, however, and Hamburg refused to accept him.[17] Although List himself was unacceptable, his new American ideas were eventually embraced; Germany under Bismarck adopted many of the trade policies List's American newspaper articles advocated.

The foundation of List's case is a critique of Adam Smith. List contrasted his own theory of *political* economy with Smith's doctrine, which he called the theory of *cosmopolitical* economy. The difference between political economy and cosmopolitical economy, according to List, is the fact that the nation-state is a fundamental element of the economic system. Smith, he argued, assumes that there are no nation-states or that they are in a state of "perpetual peace." With states and nations assumed away, List said, one can approach economic problems from the pure perspective of the individual. Sans states and the power and conflict associated with them, the principle of laissez-faire and the policy of free trade are indeed valid in theory.

"A true principle, therefore, underlies the system of the popular school," List wrote, referring to the economic liberal school of thought, "but a principle which must be recognized and applied by science if its design to enlighten practice is to be fulfilled, an idea which practice cannot ignore without getting astray; only the school has omitted to take into consideration the nature of nationalities and their special interests and conditions, and to bring these into accord with the idea of universal union and an everlasting peace."[18] In assuming away nations and the state, and thus essentially assuming a borderless world of individuals, List said, Smith put the cart before the horse. Nations and nationality are facts of life and we cannot pretend that they do not exist, because they do.

"The popular school has assumed as being actually in existence a state of things which has yet to come into existence," List continued. "It assumes the existence of a universal union and a state of perpetual peace, and deduces therefrom the great benefits of free trade. In this manner it confounds effects with causes."[19] List firmly believed that political union was a necessary precondition for economic union or free trade and, given his personal history in Germany, it is easy to see why. Nations at war or facing the possibility of conflict put security ahead of potential economic benefits and reject free trade and economic union.

What are the consequences of free trade in a world of nations, national interests, and state power? Not perpetual peace, List argued, but rather domination.

That, however, under the existing conditions of the world, the result of general free trade would not be a universal republic, but, on the contrary, a universal subjection of the less advanced nations to the supremacy of the predominant manufacturing, commercial, and naval power, is a conclusion for which the reasons are very strong and, according to our views, irrefragable.[20]

What should the state do? Free trade and laissez-faire invite disaster. The best course, both for the nation and for the society of nations, List argued, is American-style protectionism.

The system of protection, inasmuch as it forms the only means of placing those nations which are far behind in civilisation on equal terms with the one predominating nation . . . appears to be the most efficient means of furthering the final union of nations, and hence also of promoting true freedom of trade. And national economy appears from this point of view to be that science which, correctly appreciating the existing interests and the individual circumstances of nations, teaches how every separate nation can be raised to that stage of industrial development in which union with other nations equally well developed, and consequently freedom of trade, can become possible and useful to it.[21]

List was right that nations and politics matter, of course, and he made the most of his opportunity to undermine Adam Smith's vision of a borderless world. He was also correct that Smith's rhetoric in this case did not so much assume away an important problem as simply ignore it. In other words, I think List accused Smith of globaloney and made it stick. But then List managed to sneak in some globaloney of his own.

It is not true, as List says above, that a system of protection really does or necessarily can place nations on an *equal* footing except in the narrow sense that import prices are driven up to equal or exceed those charged by domestic businesses. The underlying differences between the countries may remain vast, creating a chasm that is in fact impossible to span, but List ignores these differences. Having just pointed out that Smith neglects the existence of nations, List is confident that the reader will not notice that he has neglected culture, geography, and history. No matter, List said, because there is no *real* difference. Even taking individual circumstance into account, he said, "science" teaches us that every separate nation can be raised by protection to a level approximately equal to the highest and therefore trade on equal footing with them.

List's greatest globaloney achievement only becomes apparent when we step back and consider where he has taken us. Globalization—in the form of peaceful free trade among equal nations—is impossible without protectionism, which is its opposite. The way to tear down walls, therefore, is to build them higher. The way to promote equality is to reinforce difference. The way to achieve peace is to make war. It is an argument right out of 1984. Or, more precisely, out of 1943.

List's critique of Adam Smith, you see, reminds me of Clare Boothe Luce's sarcastic criticism of Henry Wallace's 1943 "global vision," which was featured in chapter 1. Having freedom-of-the air, Luce might have said, is all very well in Mr. Wallace's *cosmopolitical* theory, but we live in a world of *political* reality, where open borders put all our security at risk. Much of the rest of the argument would be the same, with one exception. The America of Friedrich List was afraid that Great Britain would dominate them with its technical superiority. The America of Clare Boothe Luce, which had achieved technological superiority, feared dominance by low-wage competition abroad. Such double-edged fears are common elements of the globaloney syndrome.

Manufacturing Globaloney

One of the most powerful Old Rhetoric images of globalization was created by William Greider in his best-selling book *One World, Ready or Not: The Manic Logic of Global Capitalism*.[22] On page one of chapter one he describes globalization as a "wondrous new machine, strong and supple, a machine that reaps as it destroys." He goes on:

> It is huge and mobile, something like the machines of modern agriculture, but vastly more complicated and powerful. Think of this awesome machine running over open terrain and ignoring familiar boundaries. It plows across fields and fencerows with a fierce momentum that is exhilarating to behold and also frightening. As it goes, the machine throws off enormous mows of wealth and bounty while it leaves behind great furrows of wreckage.[23]

This sure is a powerful image, easy to visualize and full of emotion. It is so powerful that the reader initially fails to consider that there is no particular reason to think of globalization as a machine or its domain as a farm field. You could just as easily use an organic metaphor (globalization is a cancer) or a geologic metaphor (globalization is an earthquake) or a meteorological one (it's a hurricane). Choose the metaphor you like and it determines a particular way of understanding globalization.

If your metaphor is strong enough, you can even warn the reader that the image distorts without fear of undermining your argument. Caveats give such arguments the appearance of objectivity and thus actually reinforce the point. Thus Greider, for example, points out that

> The metaphor is imperfect, but it offers a simplified way to visualize what is dauntingly complex and abstract and impossibly diffuse—the drama of a free-running economic system that is reordering the world.[24]

People who talk or write about globalization use both Old Rhetoric (metaphors) and Adam Smith's New Rhetoric, where the key is to establish an organizing principle and then to push it as far as it will go. I think that Smith's "Newtonian" method of connecting a chain of observations is especially effective in making arguments about globalization. Globalization is such a large, ambiguous idea that it necessarily contains lots of examples of just about everything, so it is no challenge to link it up to whatever principle you like.

To choose a trifling example, suppose that I say that globalization is based upon the principle of the network, especially computer networks that share information. This is not a big stretch, it seems to me, since globalization is all about markets and markets are networks that link together buyers and sellers and other interested parties. Everyone knows that market networks are pretty dependent on computers these days, and there are computers almost everywhere, many of them networked. So if I provide one or two memorable examples, like Adam Smith did with his pin factory, then pretty soon you will be *looking for* computer networks wherever you go. And, because you are looking for them, you will see them. And every one of them will reinforce the idea that globalization is based on the principle of the network.

Once the globalization network principle is established, there are two ways we can go. One approach would be to examine how networks actually work and what real principles networks embody to see if there are insights to be gained from this analysis. This might be a fruitful path to take, but it would involve research, not persuasion.[25] It is the road not taken. Let's see where rhetoric alone can take us.

Once I've got you thinking about globalization in terms of networks, then I think I can manipulate the concept of the network to encourage you to interpret globalization in some particular way. Networks, like markets, can be very decentralized, with no strict decision-making hierarchy. Networks connect everyone in the system to everyone else, so you might say that networks are democratic, pushing power out to the grass roots. Since globalization is based upon the principle of the network, it follows that globalization is democratic, too.

Globalization is democracy: isn't this a crazy conclusion? Yes, I think so. But it is not much crazier than Adam Smith's chain linking the pin factory to global free trade via the principle of the division of labor. There is nothing particularly democratic about either markets or networks—at least not in the sense that Thomas Jefferson would use the word. Not according to Thomas Frank, either, who wrote a whole book to refute it.[26] But the Newtonian method of the New Rhetoric is powerful, so powerful that even Thomas Friedman, whose book *The Lexus and the Olive Tree* is one of the better globalization reads, cannot resist concluding that finance, information, and technology—three critical elements of globalization—have been democratized.

Of course, the happy conclusion that globalization is democratic isn't the only way that the network principle can be applied here. Networks can be dangerous—they can crash and spread damaging viruses. So network globalization is a threat. Networks also have the effect of excluding those who are not part of the system (the digital divide). So network globalization is unequal and creates haves and have-nots. The network principle, it seems, can be used to make all sorts of arguments about globalization, and each can be made as logical and appealing as Adam Smith's pin factory story.

Searching for the Soul of Capitalism

As I was revising this chapter for a discussion at the Johns Hopkins Center in Bologna, Italy, I started reading William Greider's latest book, *The Soul of Capitalism: Opening Paths to a Moral Economy*.[27] Perhaps it was just because I had been studying Smith's rhetoric so closely, but I could not help but see Smith's New Rhetoric strategy at work: principle, example, connect the dots, generalization.

William Greider is a longtime critic of capitalism, and it must be said that capitalism has a lot to criticize. Where Smith intentionally painted an artificially optimistic vision of global market expansion, Greider makes it his business to do just the opposite. Although Greider says in the opening chapters of *The Soul of Capitalism* that he just wants to reform capitalism a bit—to iron out the harsh creases, more or less—in fact his agenda is a lot more radical. But how do you make the case against capitalism at a time when it is seen by many as a great success? Oh, Greider says, you think capitalism is working because it generates economic growth and material abundance? Then you are obviously missing the point—capitalism steals your soul. Let me tell you a personal story.

The story Greider tells is of his grandfather Franklin S. McClure, who farmed the land in western Pennsylvania a hundred years ago. Greider treasures the memories of the summers he spent at the farm the way most of us, I suppose, embrace such recollections. Grandpa was a stubborn man, Greider says, and he resisted change pretty much across the board: no phone, no electricity, no indoor plumbing—he even continued to farm with horses long after everyone else turned to tractors and farm machines.

Why did Greider's grandpa give up all the comforts of life that global capitalism can provide? Here's where the globaloney part begins. "Though I never heard this said," Greider writes, "my hunch is that what my grandparents resisted was the encroaching loss of self-reliance, the steadily vanishing complexity of their own self-contained lives, the capacity to do many things well and provide well enough for themselves. Put in those terms, it seems a huge and frightening loss. They were unwilling to accept the trade-offs."[28]

Do capitalism and its comforts create a giant sucking sound of alienation that takes away our souls? It is a big jump from what grandpa *didn't* say to such an all-encompassing condemnation, but the right rhetoric makes it easy. You just say that it does, using grandpa's unspoken words as your only evidence. "The same alienating exchange is occurring in our own time," Greider says on the next page, "and not just for those workers displaced by new technologies."[29]

Now Greider has a good point about capitalism's ability to alienate. Adam Smith even said that working in a pin factory could be pretty discouraging, and the pin factory was as close as Smith ever got to the modern industry. What I want to point out is how closely Greider has followed the outline of the "Newtonian" type of argument that Smith advocated in his lectures on rhetoric and used so cleverly in the first chapter of *The Wealth of Nations*. Paralleling the pin factory example, Greider starts with a bold assertion, then follows with a single memorable example, complete with details about outhouses and farm livestock, which forms the basis for a universal conclusion. The fact that one example is pretty slim evidence doesn't matter; the fact that the key parts of that example are imagined rather than observed doesn't matter either. And, in fact, Greider even acknowledges that visiting that farm wasn't much fun after the first couple of days. He and his brother couldn't wait to leave.

None of this matters, because the rhetoric has done its job. The image of the soulful farm and noble farmer has been created and capitalism blamed for the alienation we feel today. Cause and effect, simple as that. Feeling alienated? Soulless global capitalism's to blame! Just connect the dots.

Although I disagree with a lot of what William Greider says and the way that he says it, I do give him credit for two things. First, he is a wonderful writer who can create powerful images and who wields both Old Rhetoric metaphors and New Rhetoric organization with equal skill. So strong are the images found on the pages of *The Soul of Capitalism*, for example, that the publishers, Simon & Schuster, were forced to pull out all stops to provide appropriate cover art: the Stars and Stripes is merged with the image of an old-fashioned apple pie. Two of the three most powerful symbols of American values are deployed to represent a book that argues that those values need fundamental reform.[30] And, of course, a piece of the pie is missing: its soul has been cut out.

I also credit Greider with being completely honest about what he is doing. Obviously he is not providing a fair and balanced picture of capitalism, and he doesn't say he is. That's very hard to do in any case and impossible if you also want to advocate an agenda for radical change. In the penultimate chapter, however, Greider explains his real purpose.

Societies don't use facts to define themselves, Greider argues, or to help them justify their actions. Social elites use myths, narratives, and stories to create what Antonio Gramsci would have called intellectual hegemony. It hardly matters whether the story is true or false. What matters is that people accept the story and use it to justify a set of actions and to further a set of interests.

Adam Smith's pin factory example provides such a narrative. Although on the surface it is nothing more than a tiny insignificant case study in preindustrial productivity, the story as told by Adam Smith has vast implications and justifies a world of free-trade, open-market, and pro-industry policies. Society should encourage pin factories and other factories and bear the costs associated with factories, factory work, and open markets, because the ends justify the means. And the ends, you will recall, are increased material abundance from the bottom to the top.

These narratives are important, Greider, believes; they shape the world. Images are everything. "America needs to develop a new narrative for itself," he writes. "The old story is no longer working to the mutual benefit and general satisfaction of the society and, in fact, does great damage to many lives and to our prospects for the future."[31] Greider's aim, to put it more bluntly than it deserves, is to replace one globaloney with another. To replace one narrative—the pin factory's story of *more*—with another narrative—a story of *moral*. And that's what he tries to do in *The Soul of Capitalism*.

How to Fight a Fire

You need to fight fire with fire, Greider believes. The only way to beat a story about capitalism or globalization is with a better story. Although he may be right, I still disagree. I think (or perhaps I only hope) that you can defeat distorting stories with facts—and that is what this book tries to do in the next several chapters. The problem with trying to shape or reform society by fighting stories with stories is that victory goes to the best storyteller, and that may not be you.

This is the danger that Paul Krugman points out in the introduction to his book *The Great Unraveling*.[32] Krugman argues that many of the supporters of President George W. Bush, who say that they support traditional American values and social principles, intend, in fact, to produce radical social change—and not the kind of change that William Greider has in mind. They justify their policies with stories, not facts. Indeed, the stories they tell about many policies, such as the tax cuts and Social Security reform proposals, are almost wholly divorced from the facts of the situation, a point that Krugman makes again and again in his *New York Times* columns. Krugman never tires of pointing out the fallacies these stories contain. Krugman seems to think that the best way to fight fire is with facts.

My study of globaloney from Adam Smith to George W. Bush has made me suspicious of arguments about globalization that are based upon images, metaphors, and memorable exceptional cases. I don't want to be drawn into a storytelling contest, however, because I am not as confident as Greider that I would win. There is too much at stake to risk that.

I'll side with Krugman on this one, then, and resort to facts. I won't be able to *prove* that the stories we examine in the next several chapters are globaloney, but I hope that I can *persuade* that they might be and that you might therefore need to reexamine what you think you know about globalization.

*   *   *

What connects Adam Smith, the Father of Economics, with Michael Jordan, the famous basketball player? It is difficult to find a direct connection, since Smith died in 1790, about a hundred years before James Naismith invented basketball and about two hundred years before Michael Jordan won his first NBA title. But a link does exist: globalization. The image of Michael Jordan defines globalization today much as the image of Smith's pin factory defined globalization in 1776. Let's see if image is everything, or if it's just more globaloney.

MICHAEL JORDAN AND NBA
GLOBAL FEVER

The 1999 Seattle World Trade Organization (WTO) meetings were intended to give globalization an upbeat, prosperous, happy human face. The ministerial meetings of the WTO were supposed to launch a new round of global trade negotiations—the positive political face of globalization. Seattle, the home of Boeing, Microsoft, Starbucks, and Amazon.com —the economic face of globalization—was supposed to symbolize the new agenda, a focus upon upscale, high-tech products and intellectual property rights.

Even the face of Washington governor Gary Locke, the first U.S. governor of Chinese American heritage, was supposed to symbolize China's anticipated entry into the WTO in particular and the world community in general (as if anyone needed to be reminded about China and its potential power). In the planners' minds, Seattle, green and prosperous, must have presented a perfect picture of globalization.

But that's not how things turned out. And that's not the image of globalization that the Seattle meetings produced. In many ways, the most important achievement of the Seattle WTO meetings was that they gave a human face to the antiglobalization movement. Or *faces* (plural), to be more accurate, because antiglobalization has three faces: modern, premodern, and postmodern. All three were on display in Seattle.[1]

The Three Faces of Antiglobalization

The first image that was revealed in Seattle was the modern face of anti-globalization—the anxious faces of union workers fearful that their good-pay, good-benefits jobs would be taken by Mexican or Chinese workers who were willing to do them for a few dollars a day. I call these union members and the activists who marched with them the *modern* face of globalization: unions are relics of the modern era, when nation-states forged national markets that could be organized, regulated, and protected. Unions exist on the principle that the fundamental work-place conflict is labor versus management and that unions are a coun-tervailing power, sanctioned and encouraged by democratic national governments. This principle is threatened fundamentally by globaliza-tion, which is seen to weaken the state's ability to control domestic markets and mediate the balance of power. The whole idea of labor ver-sus management in Muncie, Indiana, loses relevance in a global econ-omy, where the *real* competition is seen as Muncie versus Malaysia.

The union faces feared the global economy and looked to elected leaders to protect them from foreign competition. The Seattle WTO meetings were about everything that they feared. The union protesters weren't interested in changing the world system; they wanted to influ-ence the domestic political debate so that their concerns would get more attention in the 2000 presidential election. No one paid much at-tention to the union faces, however, despite their large numbers. There was nothing unexpected or newsworthy about them.

Street violence in Seattle *was* unexpected and newsworthy and most of the violent and destructive acts that featured in news reports of the WTO meetings were the work of a relatively small group of black-clothed, masked anarchists. They were the premodern face of antiglob-alization.

The goal of the Anarchist Action Collective (headquarters in Eu-gene, Oregon, birthplace of the global giant Nike) was not to try to seize power from "discredited" modern institutions such as unions and national governments. "The oceans are dying and humanness is being strangled. Species are made extinct every hour while the artificial and the commercialized flourishes. The blight of techno-capital is spread-ing, leaving the individual ever more isolated and disempowered," their manifesto proclaims. "The only sensible solution is to make a break with the whole dying mess. It's time to face up to it. It's time to erase what is really destroying everything. It's time to create a new world after the ashes of the ruined one."[2]

I call the anarchists the premodern face of antiglobalization for the obvious reason that they seek to destroy both globalization and the modern institutions that have created it—the WTO, national governments, unions, corporations, the works. It's all rotten, all corrupt. They yearned for the sort of world that I imagine existed in the Middle Ages—and they were willing to tear down everything that stood in their way. Or at least they were willing to trash any Starbucks or McDonald's that provoked them.

Caught between the vast legions of modern unionists and the small group of premodern anarchists were the antiglobalization protesters that interest me the most, the postmodern face of antiglobalization. They didn't want to reinvigorate the nation-state, like the unionists, or tear it down, like the anarchists. Their goal was at once much more modest and vastly more radical.

The postmodern protesters were united in what they opposed—the pro-globalization globaloney that fills the air at events like WTO meetings.[3] But unlike the anarchists and union groups, they didn't have an alternative; they had no shared vision of a modern or premodern past worth returning to. Their goal was simple and dramatic—to be antithesis to the WTO thesis. Whatever synthesis would arise from this dialectic would be an improvement over the present mess.

The postmodern response to globalization was to create a repulsive but persuasive narrative of globalization that would discredit the WTO talks and the modern system of global capitalism that the WTO symbolizes. They sought to do through action what William Greider has tried to do through words: to establish a counterhegemonic rhetoric that undermines the legitimacy of the established interests. So long as people accept the dominant pro-globalization narrative, the argument goes, there is little chance for reform or revolt. To change people's actions you must first change their minds, by telling a story about globalization that explains how wrong it is.

But image is everything today, so an antiglobalization narrative has to be more than a manifesto and a slogan. It needs a symbol, a human face to remind the world of their antiglobalization story, a face to represent globalization as Americanization, destroying local culture; globalization as capitalism, exploiting the weak; globalization as an unequal bargain, privileging the rich and exploiting the poor. And, most particularly, the human face of postmodern antiglobalization would need to be a vivid image that could be portrayed effectively through the global media.

Although globalization is often portrayed as a faceless, inhuman process, the face of postmodern *anti*globalization is real. Ironically, it is the face of an African American man from North Carolina, the grandson of a sharecropper. He is not, as one might suppose, given the requirements of a memorable counterhegemonic narrative, a poor textile worker, exploited sweatshop employee, or undocumented-immigrant nonunion Wal-Mart store cleaner. Quite the opposite: he is rich and famous. The postmodern face of antiglobalization lives, and his name is Michael Jordan.

Michael Jordan and the New Global Capitalism

Michael Jordan would seem to be an unlikely candidate for the job of poster child for the antiglobalization movement. He is, most readers will already know, arguably the best professional basketball player of his generation. Starting from humble (but not impoverished) beginnings, he became a college All-Star basketball player at the University of North Carolina and a member of two Olympic gold medal teams (1984 and 1992). Jordan led the Chicago Bulls of the National Basketball Association (NBA) to six league titles (1991–1993 and 1996–1998) and was named the league's most valuable player five times. Jordan's image off the court was extremely popular, and he earned huge sums for product endorsements. As if to prove that he was only human after all, Jordan briefly retired from basketball in the mid-1990s to pursue an unsuccessful career in professional baseball only to return to the NBA and championship success. Jordan retired for good in 2003 with the highest scoring average (30.1 points per game) in league history.

How could such an authentic sports hero be transformed into an antiglobalization villain? The answer to this question is, of course, globaloney. Globaloney is not about the facts of globalization, it is about metaphors, images, and slanted arguments. Globaloney is about using Adam Smith's Newtonian rhetoric to establish a principle and then use carefully chosen observations to connect the dots in the reader's mind from assumption to conclusion and beyond.

This is what the distinguished diplomatic historian Walter LaFeber has done in his book *Michael Jordan and the New Global Capitalism*, first published in 1999, the year of the Seattle WTO meetings.[4] LaFeber quite literally wrote the book that forms the narrative, or part of it, that the postmodern antiglobalizers required. Here's how the story unfolds.

Following the example of Adam Smith, LaFeber establishes his critical principle on page one of chapter one: Globalization is Americanization and its human face is Michael Jordan. "At the end of the twentieth century, Americans, their economy, and their culture seemed to dominate many parts of the globe," he writes. "A basketball player who lived in Chicago, Michael Jordan, was arguably the most recognized and revered of those Americans to billions of people worldwide."[5]

In China, we learn, some schoolchildren were asked to name the two greatest figures in the twentieth century. Their choices: Zhou Enlai, the Communist revolutionary, and Michael Jordan.[6] Michael Jordan? How did they know about him? Earlier, on the second page of the preface, LaFeber explained that a young college student, Max Perelman, was traveling in a remote region of China and met a group of Tibetans who, learning that he was American, asked him how Michael Jordan was doing. Michael Jordan is so famous, apparently, that his name is known and his face recognized in even the most remote corners of the world.

LaFeber has come to bury Jordan/Americanization/globalization, however, not to praise it, so he quickly darkens the image. Jordan may be the best that ever played the game, as they say on ESPN, but what does he represent? To some, LaFeber reveals, "Jordan personified not only the imaginative, individual skills that Americans dream of displaying in a society that adores graceful and successful individualism, but the all-out competitive spirit and discipline that Americans like to think drove their nation to the peak of world power." But Jordan's American skills, LaFeber notes, "quickly translated into money and power in the world of the late twentieth century."[7] And that's the real point of the narrative.

The story of Michael Jordan is not the saga of an African American basketball player, as readers might have expected; it is a narrative of globalization, Americanization, capitalism, and—above all—the story of power. LaFeber tells how Michael Jordan became the willing and well-paid tool of the "new global capitalism." What is new about this capitalism—and what makes it a useful foil to the postmodern antiglobalizers—is that it is, well, postmodern itself. *Modern* capitalism is about mass production of products for mass markets—it is the Karl Marx/Henry Ford version of capitalism. *Postmodern* capitalism is about producing images or impressions and selling them to a global market. Post-modern capitalism is, to use George Ritzer's term, "the globalization of nothing."[8]

Clearly Jordan cannot be postmodern global capitalism by himself. He, after all, is *something*—the world's best basketball player. Joining Jordan on the new global capitalism team are four more capitalists, Jerry Krause, head of the Chicago Bulls basketball team; Rupert Murdoch and Ted Turner, representing global news and sports media (the "edutainment telesector" in Benjamin R. Barber's terminology); and Philip Knight, the head of Nike.

"The ability of basketball, U.S. advertising techniques, and American-dominated media to penetrate other cultures amazed observers," LaFeber notes.[9] Nike, and its vast advertising budget, promoted Jordan to sell its overpriced "Air Jordan" line of shoes. Krause and Murdoch and Turner used each other to promote Jordan, the Bulls, the NBA, and the global media empires that they forged in the process. Along the way they gained vast wealth and the power to enter and transform new markets and, essentially, Americanize them through basketball telecasts, high-priced shoes, and celebrity advertising.

Postmodern customers wanted to "be like Mike," which was the theme of an advertising campaign. They sought to transfer some of the image of Michael Jordan to themselves, to associate his cool success with their own lives, through the purchase of otherwise unexceptional consumer products. A Nike advertising campaign of the time summed it up beautifully: "Image Is Everything." In a section called "The Swoosh-ifying of the World," LaFeber engages in some classic "borderless world" imagery, the postmodern version of images that date back to Henry Wallace and Clare Boothe Luce. "Wearing his Nikes, Jordan's image flew around the world and across geographical boundaries that seemed increasingly to be—especially for the media that carried that image—almost meaningless lines on maps."[10] I point this out to remind the reader that, as good as this story is, we are dealing with globaloney here, not globalization.

Some of what LaFeber says about Jordan and postmodern global capitalism is the sort of hyperbole that sportswriters seem unable to resist. And some of what he says is absolutely on target. Nike really is a postmodern global corporation, for example. When I studied Nike for my 1998 book *Selling Globalization*, I was surprised that it had only 14,000 employees (in 1995)—not very many for a corporation with $5 billion in annual sales. Those employees produced very few of the products that Nike sold, however. Most Nike-branded goods were produced abroad by contract manufacturers. Nike's own employees mainly worked to create and maintain Nike's image—and to protect its valuable trademarks. That's what made Nike a postmodern corporation then, and it is still true today.

According to its 2003 Annual Report, Nike's sales roughly doubled between 1995 and fiscal 2003, and its employee ranks grew to about 23,300 (most of the increase was through corporate acquisitions, including Cole Haan shoes and Bauer Hockey). Nike still produced very few of its products itself, as before, and had little in the way of direct sales. Thirteen company-owned Niketown stores polished the brand image while seventy-five Nike outlets sold off surplus stock, but for the most part Nike let other companies handle the retail end of the business. Nike is no General Electric when it comes to manufacturing (it carefully characterizes itself as the world's largest seller, not producer, of athletic shoes and apparel) and no threat to Wal-Mart as a retailer, either.

Nike's particular specialty remains its image, which it manufactures both directly through advertising and indirectly through endorsements and sponsorships with athletes and celebrities like Michael Jordan. As Nike's annual report suggests,

> We utilize trademarks on nearly all of our products and believe that having distinctive markets that are readily identifiable is an important factor in creating a market for our goods, in identifying the Company. . . . We consider our Nike® and Swoosh Design® trademarks to be among our most valuable assets and we have registered these trademarks in over 100 countries.[11]

Image really is everything with Nike, and that's what makes it a perfect example of a postmodern business.

But is Nike a *representative* example of globalization? Is the truth about Nike the truth about globalization? No. That's what I concluded when I surveyed global corporations for *Selling Globalization* and that's what I conclude again today. What makes Nike noteworthy is that it is different from almost all of the other firms that you might put on a "global capitalism" list. Nike is the exception, not the rule. Then why is it so easy to persuade people that it is the general case? I suppose it is the power of the Newtonian rhetoric system, which I discuss in chapter 2. Once you have read that Nike is the quintessential global firm, they you will begin to notice Nike wherever you see it and, because it is Nike, you will see it everywhere. And each observation—in print, on television, on your teenager's shoes—reinforces the initial principle. You have connected the dots (or the swooshes, I guess), and this act satisfies you more than asking pointed questions ever could.

Nike is an exceptional case. Michael Jordan is an exceptional case. The six-time champion Bulls were an exceptional case. The story that Walter LaFeber tells is interesting and noteworthy not because it is ubiquitous and universal, but because it is exceptional and particular. It is a "man bites dog" story in a world where that doesn't happen very often. If it were wise to generalize on the basis of exceptional cases like these then, I suppose, we would be wise to build arks after every exceptionally rainy day.

The story is persuasive, however, because, like the best globaloney, it draws upon compelling images and employs effective rhetorical principles.[12] Once you have accepted the principle that Michael Jordan is the face of globalization, then all daily encounters and references to Jordan, the Bulls, the NBA, Nike and its swoosh, and televised sports serve to reinforce the story. Consciously or not, your mind connects the dots (and, as Adam Smith said, gets satisfaction from the exercise). But where do the dots lead? What is the point of the Michael Jordan story?

Imperialism, that's what Michael Jordan stands for. Economic imperialism and cultural imperialism. And that's what makes him a powerful tool of postmodern antiglobalism. The link between Michael Jordan and economic imperialism is easy to trace. Jordan gets millions to endorse Nike shoes, which are ultimately produced by workers in China and other low-wage countries (by Nike contractors, not Nike itself) and then sold for large sums to gullible consumers around the world, who are entranced, literally, by Jordan and Nike and the image that the NBA and ESPN have helped create. Sweatshops are built and consumers duped for the gain of a tiny global elite. Sounds like imperialism to me!

What makes this new postmodern global imperialism different from the older versions? Classical imperialism, with its exploitation and dependency, was based upon the control of power—military power. Modern economic imperialism, the kind that Lenin wrote about, was based upon control of capital and technology. The new global imperialism, however, provides profits to whoever can create, control, and promote powerful global images. That's what makes this a postmodern phenomenon. Anyone can make the shoes, more or less, and sell them. But the shoes and hats and T-shirts and the rest are just cheap reproducible commodities without the link to an image that validates the buyer's action. Image, in this line of reasoning, really is everything. Everything. The key to creating and controlling these images is technology (and the capital to implement it). What makes the new global capitalism possible are the communications technologies of the 1990s.

The emphasis on technology is one factor that makes me suspect that there is globaloney here. As noted earlier, globaloney tends to appear when disruptive change occurs. The globaloney stories provide simple explanations to anxious or frightened people, telling them what is happening and how it will turn out. These simple narratives frequently draw upon natural or, as in this case, technological images and metaphors—like Michael Jordan's image being beamed across a borderless globe.

But it gets worse. Not only does Michael Jordan and the image-as-commodity chain that he represents exploit the world's population, it also transforms them into (shudder!) Americans. "The Jordan-Knight-Murdoch-Turner phenomenon" is an example, according to LaFeber, of how the new capitalism goes about "creating the markets that quite willingly absorbed American popular culture once the media represented that culture."[13] American culture, of course, is fatally flawed. It is a market culture, based upon market values, not human values, controlled by images, defined by commodities. It is a culture that exploits without guilt. Indeed, exploitation gives it satisfaction. Michael Jordan always seems satisfied, doesn't he?

If this is what Michael Jordan stands for, then isn't he the perfect symbol of globalization for the postmodern antiglobalists? Doesn't he represent an intolerable condition? Doesn't this image undermine fundamentally any attempt by corporations or governments to portray globalization as a benign or beneficial phenomenon? And the ultimate beauty is that, once the dots are connected, every commercial dunk or swoosh, real or virtual, reinforces the notion of globalization as postmodern imperialism and undermines the obvious intent and personal or corporate interest of whoever is footing the bill. Postmodern globalization doesn't just contain the seeds of its own destruction, it actively sows them.

Walter LaFeber's book constructs the image of Michael Jordan as postmodern imperialism/globalization. His book, like this one, is a work of synthesis. He did not invent this image of Michael Jordan and postmodern capitalism, he just assembled the pieces that were already there and, by making his story interesting and accessible, helped spread the word. He states the principle and helps the reader connect the dots, but the principle was already there and the dots were already pretty well lined up.

LaFeber himself expresses some doubts about the ultimate conclusion he draws. Perhaps people will come to their senses, he speculates. Perhaps it is possible to resist these apparently irresistible forces. In the final chapter, which makes too much, in my view, of the coincidence of Michael Jordan's temporary retirement from basketball and the September 11, 2001, attacks on the World Trade Center, he suggests that perhaps we will come to our senses when we see how the rest of the world has reacted to globalization/Americanization. LaFeber seems to hope that Michael Jordan will stand tall in real life as on the basketball court and renounce the system he helped create. But he hasn't. Walter La-Feber is obviously a fan—he must sincerely love basketball and admire Michael Jordan's skills. No wonder he is so discouraged. It is always the true believers who are most bitterly disappointed.

Obviously I don't think that globalization is a simple equation: Jordan plus Nike plus ESPN equals sweatshops plus overconsumption plus inequality equals Americanization. Actually, I do think that this is *part* of what globalization is, and I believe these effects must be included within a nuanced understanding of globalization. But the Michael Jordan story goes too far.

Or perhaps it does not go *far enough!* For the most part, I think, the basketball and globalization narratives are separate stories that just intersect in several places—and the intersections are interesting and get our attention precisely because they are unexpected. But let us suppose that the story of basketball really *is* the story of globalization. Then, as I have just said, Nike and Michael Jordan are part of the story, but there are at least three other stories that must be told, too. The whole story of basketball as globalization must include Michael Jordan, but also Doc Naismith, Yao Ming, and Steve Kerr—real people who represent the complicated different elements of real globalization.

Doc Naismith and the Old Global YMCA

The best book about globalization and basketball is probably *Big Game, Small World: A Basketball Adventure* by *Sports Illustrated* writer Alexander Wolff.[14] Michael Jordan never makes a direct appearance in this book, alas, because he became unhappy with Wolff's reporting some years ago and refuses to speak to him. Absent Michael Jordan, Wolff is forced to deal with *the rest* of global basketball. He begins, logically enough, at the beginning: in Almonte, Ontario, birthplace (in 1861) of the man who invented basketball, James Naismith. Ironically, if basketball promotes Americanization, then Americanization has Canadian roots.

James "Doc" Naismith seems to have been an exceptionally serious man, perhaps even an austere one. He was certainly well educated. He studied philosophy at McGill University in Montreal (1887), took a divinity degree from Presbyterian College, also in Montreal (1890), and eventually earned a medical degree from the University of Colorado in 1898. He is best known, however, for the work he did in Springfield, Massachusetts, in 1890 and 1891 while studying physical education at an institution called the YMCA Training School (which later became Springfield College). That's where he invented basketball, nailing a peach basket to a gym wall and tossing a leather ball into it. But I am getting ahead of myself. Naismith may have invented basketball, but the YMCA globalized it.

YMCA stands for Young Men's Christian Association. It is a movement that was founded by George Williams in London, England, in 1841. Its original mission, framed in response to the Industrial Revolution urban environment that Karl Marx and Charles Dickens famously described, was to get young men off the streets and into a healthy environment where Christian ideals could be fostered. I think that today we would call it a "faith-based social welfare initiative," but not one based narrowly on the doctrine of a particular Christian sect. Bible studies were promoted as a healthy alternative to drinking and fighting, but the YMCA's mission expanded to address broadly the needs of young people's "spirits, minds, and bodies." It was from the start an open, expansion-minded evangelical organization. The YMCA movement (and it can legitimately be called a movement) expanded to the United States by the 1860s, where it grew deep roots that included the Springfield Training School. The YMCA needed trained leaders for its urban programs in the United States and to serve as missionaries abroad, and Springfield was where they were trained.

Now we can return to the peach basket. With university degrees in philosophy, divinity, and (eventually) medicine, and with an outstanding record as a high school and college athlete, James Naismith pretty much epitomized the YMCA's ideal of healthy spirit, mind, and body. But that did not make his work at the Springfield YMCA easy. He was assigned a particularly rowdy group of eighteen young men, and he apparently struggled, as others had done before him, to find a healthy outlet for their energies during the winter months, between the outdoor sports seasons. The idea for basketball, an active indoor team game that stressed skill over brute force, seems to have come to Naismith all at once. He arrived at the school one morning with the original thirteen rules and ordered the janitor to hang a couple of baskets (half-bushel peach baskets, as luck would have it) from the balcony of the gym. And the first game was played.

The game caught on, both within the United States and around the world. Basketball's first globalization was no accident, but neither was it a capitalist plot. Basketball became one of many tools that the Christian evangelicals who attended the YMCA Training School in Springfield learned how to use. "As Training School graduates fanned out on missions around the world, and Naismith shared his game with anyone who showed an interest, basketball spread rapidly and widely," Alexander Wolff writes. "So widely that before his death in 1939, the inventor had collected translations of the rules in almost 50 languages and dialects."[15] Thousands of missionaries and war relief workers fanned out from the United States in the late 1800s and early 1900s, and many of them took basketball with them.[16] By the time Michael Jordan won his NBA titles with the Chicago Bulls, basketball was already celebrating its hundredth birthday as a global sport.

It is interesting to speculate why YMCA missionaries found basketball such a useful tool in their work. The fact that it was a completely new game without a lot of cultural or political baggage attached to it might help account for its ready acceptance. It wasn't a French game or a German game, or even an American game; it was a YMCA game. Teaching the game was a good way to establish and build relationships that could be deepened later. Certainly the values that Naismith intended the game to embody—teamwork and skill over brute force—are universal enough, not the domain of any particular country or religion. (Ironically, these are *not* the values currently associated with America by its critics.) It is also a fact that people who learn to play together well can often find ways of doing other things together.[17]

Perhaps the flexibility of the game itself was a factor in basketball's spread. Basketball can be played indoors or outside, weather permitting, half court or full court, on a wood court, concrete, or packed earth, day or night. The baskets can be set at the standard 10-foot level for adults (that was the height of the balcony in the Springfield gym) or lowered for children. The game can be played by both men and women, five-a-side or four or three or two or one-on-one. Odd numbers of players can challenge each other to match shots in a version called "HORSE" on U.S. playgrounds. One person can even play alone, and this is often done, a kind of hoops solitaire played for the satisfaction of achieving an individual challenge: can you hit ten free throws (or jump shots) in a row? Wheelchair basketball is an authentic and highly competitive sport.

In any case, basketball really did catch on and seems to have outgrown its connection with YMCA missionaries or the United States very quickly. It became just another popular sport for people to play and watch. It was, I guess, localized or—to use a phrase I find awkward—glocalized.[18] The extent to which basketball outgrew its missionary roots in countries like China is simply stunning to someone conditioned to think about sport as part of the new global capitalism. Basketball was and remained a popular pastime in China during the Cultural Revolution, for example, because it had lost all of its non-Chinese associations. "Basketball flourished during that benighted period of Chinese history, when Red Guards roamed the land, stamping out with sometimes whimsical ruthlessness anything suspected of being intellectual or foreign," writes Alexander Wolff. "The game might have been implicated as the latter, but at the time of the founding of the army in 1927, basketball was already the most popular pastime among the troops."[19]

If it seems strange that foreigners would take an American game as their own, consider this. People in China and New Zealand and other countries learned basketball in exactly the same way as people in the United States did: *they learned it from YMCA missionaries.* Basketball was introduced into the United States in exactly the same way, at almost exactly the same time, and for exactly the same reasons as it was introduced in China. It's not an American game or even a Canadian game. It *was* a YMCA game. And now, of course, it is anybody's game.

The fact that missionaries created global basketball a hundred years ago in a purposeful attempt at cultural imperialism deflates somewhat the achievements of the "new global capitalism." Walter LaFeber's book leaves the impression that Jordan, Nike, and the media created global "NBA Fever" out of whole cloth.[20] They somehow took people who really knew nothing about basketball and cared even less and transformed them through media manipulation into Nike junkies. Once you realize that basketball has for decades been an important sport in Bhutan and the Philippines, for example, it is not so surprising that you might meet a Chicago Bulls fan there. If you and I are interested to know about the exploits of the greatest basketball player in the world, why shouldn't basketball fans somewhere on the other side of the world share our interest? And, with the Internet and other technological innovations, there is no reason that they should not be as well informed as you.

So people who think that Michael Jordan is globalization will have "globalization moments" constantly, because they will run into basketball and people who know about Michael Jordan everywhere. They will connect these dots back to their presumed source: Jordan/Nike/NBA and media-driven globalization. But is it because of Nike? Maybe. But I think it is really because of the YMCA.

In writing *Big Game, Small World*, Alexander Wolff traveled around the world, to Italy, Croatia, Bhutan, China, Israel, Lithuania, the Philippines, and beyond—to many of the places where basketball thrives today. At one point he says that he was looking for pieces of America in these foreign lands, but he doesn't follow up on this idea. He sees basketball everywhere, but because he takes the time to consider the local context, he doesn't seem to find much of America in the games that are played. He does sometimes find Americans—American athletes who play for foreign teams in foreign leagues. But the ones who stick seem to adapt to local culture, customs, and priorities. The ones who don't disappear.

So perhaps basketball is not Americanizing the rest of the world in quite the way that globalization critics imagine. But maybe, just maybe, the rest of the world is globalizing America. This is my segue to the third element of globalization and basketball: the globalization of the NBA.

Yao Ming and the New Global NBA

If you want to talk about basketball and globalization—and if you are an American, like Walter LaFeber or Alexander Wolff, looking for American influences—then the story you would tell would be how basketball and its commercial or Christian values expanded out from the United States through the vectors just discussed. Michael Jordan or Doc Naismith is a featured character, depending upon which version of the story you tell, along with Nike or the YMCA.

But suppose that you are not an American or perhaps that you are an American who fell asleep twenty-five years ago and, upon awakening, are told that the NBA has now become a global phenomenon. What would you think? After spending only an hour watching ESPN or reading the sports page of *USA Today*, you would almost certainly agree with the conclusion, but not for the reasons discussed so far. You would quickly conclude that the NBA has been globalized not because it has transformed the sports world outside the United States (remember, basketball has been a global sport for a hundred years). No, what would strike you is how much the rest of the world has come to influence professional basketball in the United States.

The National Basketball Association is the world's premier professional basketball league, attracting skilled athletes from around the world. It is not so much America's league as the world's league. Seventy international players from thirty-three countries and territories were on NBA team rosters on January 2, 2004, for example. Every team had at least one international player, as far as I could tell, and it was theoretically possible for the Dallas Mavericks to play the San Antonio Spurs using only international players: Dirk Nowitzki (Germany), Tariq Abdul-Wahad (France), Eduardo Najera (Mexico), Steve Nash (Canada), and Jon Stefanson (Iceland) for Dallas and Tim Duncan (U.S. Virgin Islands), Manu Ginobili (Argentina), Tony Parker (France), Rasho Nesterovic (Slovenia), and Hedo Turkoglu (Turkey) for San Antonio. San Antonio could even make one substitution, Alex Garcia (Brazil), without losing its all-international status.

An all-international NBA? Unthinkable. But in many respects it is already here. Glancing at the morning box scores, I found a game between the San Antonio Spurs and Denver Nuggets where five of the ten starting players were internationals: Tim Duncan, Rasho Nesterovic, Tony Parker, and Hedo Turkoglu for the Spurs and Nenê for the Nuggets (like Pelé, Brazilian Nenê uses a single name).[21] There is no indication that local support for an NBA team is diminished by the addition of international players to team rosters. The Michael Jordan exception aside, professional basketball fans tend to be more loyal to teams than to individual players. Players come and go very frequently in professional sports—today's local hero is tomorrow's opponent. To a certain extent a new face is a new face, whether he comes from Boston or Bulgaria. Whether he contributes to the continuing story of the local franchise is what counts.[22]

Many of the best players in the league are "internationals," including two-time MVP Tim Duncan, 2001–2002 Rookie of the Year Pau Gasol (Spain), and 2003 All-Stars Zydrunas Ilgauskas (Lithuania), Steve Nash, Dirk Nowitzki, Peja Stojakovic (Serbia and Montenegro), and Yao Ming (China).[23] The 2003 NBA finals series between the New Jersey

Nets and the San Antonio Spurs featured four international players: the Nets' Dikembe Mutombo (Congo) and Duncan, Ginobili, and Parker for the Spurs.

It is tempting to interpret the internationalization (if not globalization) of NBA rosters as evidence of the Michael Jordan effect—the Americanization of the world through Jordan-based, Nike-driven U.S. media power—but the evidence doesn't support such a view. The NBA is unexceptional with respect to its international elements compared with other U.S. spectator sports or with foreign sports leagues. Only the National Football League (NFL) and NASCAR auto racing of the major U.S. spectator sports lack a significant international influence among players. Latin American players have long been prominent in Major League Baseball (MLB), the American "national pastime," for example, being joined in recent years by players from other regions where baseball is popular including Asia (Japan and Korea). The internationalization of the National Hockey League (NHL) has progressed to the point where an All-Star game was played with stars of North America versus the World. (The NBA has enough international talent to play such a game—perhaps it will.) The CART and Indy Racing League auto racing competitions are currently dominated by international drivers. Paul Tracy (Canada), Bruno Junqueira (Brazil), Michel Jourdain, Jr. (Mexico), Sebastien Bourdais (France), and Patrick Carpentier (Canada) were the top five drivers on the CART circuit in 2003, for example. Scott Dixon (New Zealand), Gil de Ferran (Brazil), Helio Castroneves (Brazil), Tony Kanaan (Brazil), and Sam Hornish, Jr. (United States) were the top five Indy Racing League drivers in 2003. As noted before, American football and NASCAR auto racing are the exceptions to the rule that the major U.S. spectator sports are highly "globalized."

The globalization of professional basketball in the United States reflects the globalization of professional sports more generally. A survey of the players on top professional basketball teams in the first-rank national leagues in Europe, for example, shows just how ubiquitous international players are generally. Although there is only one foreign player (Buljubasic Mirko from Bosnia-Herzegovina) on the roster of Triglav Osiguranje Rijeka, the top team in the Croatian A1 league at the time this was written, most teams combine many nationalities. Partizan Beograd, the team at the top of the Yugoslavia league, started two Americans and three Yugoslavs. Maccabi Elite Tel-Aviv of the Israel Premier league starts two Americans, a Lithuanian, a Croat, and Tal Burstein, an Israeli. Le Mans Sarthe, top of the French ProA league, has players from

France, the United States, Croatia, Canada, the Ivory Coast, and Mali. The top players for Spain's Tau Ceramica Vitoria come from Lithuania, Argentina, Hungary, and England. So the NBA's international rosters don't make it special. The fact that so many international players are now in the league reflects how much American basketball has adopted foreign practices.

Bologna, where I taught a few years ago at the Johns Hopkins Center, is crazy about basketball. It supports two high-level professional teams, Virtus and Fortitudo. Virtus, the richer and more successful team, is currently evenly divided between Italian players and internationals (half from the United States and half from Greece). The roster of Fortitudo, the working man's club, includes four Italian players, two each from Argentina and Slovenia, and one each from Belgium, Yugoslavia, Finland, and Portugal. Judging by the numbers, globalization shaped the team rosters of Virtus and Fortitudo of Bologna in roughly the same way as it did the Spurs and Mavericks of Texas. (There's even one direct connection: Manu Ginobili of Argentina, who currently plays for San Antonio, wore a Virtus Bologna uniform when he was named most valuable player of the 2001 Euroleague finals—Bologna defeated Tau Ceramica three games to two.)

The globalization of basketball is matched by several other "global" sports, the most obvious being soccer. Team rosters in the highest-level leagues around the world reflect a complex pattern of international migration that is discussed in greater detail in chapter 4. Going into the 2003–2004 season, Manchester United's soccer squad included players from France, Ireland, the United States (!), Spain, Brazil, Uruguay, Norway, Holland, South Africa, and Cameroon. Paris St Germain of the French league listed players from Spain, Morocco, Argentina, Brazil, Tunisia, Portugal, Cameroon, and Nigeria among others. Bayern Munich's roster included players from Argentina, Croatia, Ghana, France, England, Bosnia, Brazil, Serbia, and Paraguay. Juventus of Turin in Italy's Serie A league listed players from France, Croatia, Ghana, Holland, and Uruguay. Internazionale of Milan, as befits its name, was more international than most, with players from Colombia, Paraguay, Denmark, Uruguay, Argentina, France, Turkey, Senegal, Greece, Holland, the Czech Republic, Sierra Leone, and Nigeria in addition to its Italian stars.

While the conventional wisdom seems to be that NBA basketball is an important part of and appropriate symbol for Americanization and the new global capitalism, it is perhaps more precisely true that the

NBA has been globalized *by* the rest of the world and that, in the process, American professional sports have become much more like spectator sports in the rest of the world. If we wanted to put a face on the new global capitalism this represents, we might not pick Michael Jordan. We might choose instead Manu Ginobili or Yao Ming.

The YMCA came to Argentina in 1902, during the peak period of Christian missionary globalization, opening its first center in Buenos Aires. There was from the start a very strong emphasis on physical education and training—the international YMCA website uses words like "pioneering" and "outstanding organization" to describe the early physical education programs.[24] I'll bet that the first gym had basketball hoops, although I cannot find any records to confirm it. A second YMCA was opened in 1929 in nearby Rosario, followed by a third in Bahía Blanca, a port city 400 miles south of the capital. This is where Jorge Ginobili ("Yoyu" for short) learned to play basketball. He played for the local team and was at one point its president. His son, Emanuel ("Manu" for short), learned to play the game in the local community center. Although he was born into a country known for its devotion to soccer, Manu Ginobili grew up in a basketball town and in a basketball family (he even had a Michael Jordan poster on his bedroom wall).[25] The family home is only 100 yards from the gym.

Manu Ginobili started his basketball career playing for his father's team, Club Bahiense del Norte in the Argentine professional league. Significantly, Pepe Sanchez, the first Argentine to play in the NBA, also began at Bahiense del Norte. Following a pattern familiar to fans of Argentine soccer, Manu soon left for the greener pastures of European leagues, retracing the footsteps of his older brothers, Leandro and Sebastián, who played basketball in Spain and Italy. Manu played first with Calabria and then with Virtus Bologna, where he achieved great success, winning the Euroleague cup and twice receiving the Italian league MVP award. He moved to San Antonio in 2002 at the age of twenty-five.

Although Michael Jordan is the postmodern face of antiglobalism, Manu Ginobili would be a better candidate to represent the actual face of global basketball (but not a perfect one because he, like Jordan, is an exceptional case). Ginobili's history shows how complex the real world is and how the three stories of basketball as globalization that I've told so far can come together. Ginobili is, first of all, part of the story that Walter LaFeber has told. He grew up with Michael Jordan's image looming above him. On the court today he is covered with Nike swooshes.

No doubt his image is used to sell Nike products in Argentina and elsewhere. No doubt the people who respond to the images become a little more consumerist in the process. Certainly the global media profit from the linkages he helps create, especially through Argentine subscriptions to the Sky satellite sports channel.

But Ginobili is also part of the Doc Naismith story. Basketball isn't the number one sport in Argentina—it isn't even number two or three. Soccer dominates the sports scene. Thanks to the publicity generated by Sanchez, Ginobili, and others, some think that basketball might eventually catch up with rugby and field hockey in popularity. That basketball exists at all in Argentina is due to the enthusiasm and skill of those early YMCA pioneers. They created islands of basketball in a sea of soccer. The globalization of the YMCA a hundred years ago is at least as important as Jordan and Nike to the way that the global game developed—and probably more important.

Finally, Ginobili also illustrates the third story of the globalization of basketball—the nearly complete internationalization of the professional game in the United States. If you believe that basketball is an important force in Americanizing the world, then consider what America must mean if its principal homegrown game features names like Manu Ginobili and Yao Ming.

Yao Ming stands 7 feet, 6 inches (2.29 meters) and weighs 310 pounds (140.6 kilograms). He plays center for the Houston Rockets. Yao was the number one draft choice in 2002, but he was not the first Chinese international player in the NBA. That honor goes to Wang Zhizhi, who was drafted by Dallas in 1999 and left the league in November 2003, cut by the lowly Los Angeles Clippers. The story of how Yao came to the NBA—and why Wang had to leave it—adds another layer to the saga of the globalization of the NBA.

Which is more surprising, that a Chinese man is so tall or that a Chinese man plays the "American" game of basketball—and plays it very well? Neither should surprise you very much, I think. Yao gets his vertical stature honestly. His mother, Fang Fengdhi, is 6 feet, 2 inches in height, and his father Yao Zhiyuan stands 6 feet, 10 inches.[26] That Yao plays basketball is ultimately due to those pioneering YMCA missionaries, of course, who brought basketball to China a hundred years ago.

But there are more immediate causes, too. Yao's father and mother both played basketball—he for the Shanghai team and she for the Chinese national squad. Yao, like his parents, may have been born to play basketball, to use a sportswriter's cliché, but the fact is that all three were carefully selected at an early age and then trained to excel on the court. China was and is a Communist country, and sports are a serious matter. International competitions have traditionally been a way that Communist countries have sought to form and strengthen national identity. Yao was first recruited as a 5-foot, 7-inch third grader. "He didn't much like basketball," according to his first coach, Li Zhangming, "He was tall, but slow and uncoordinated."[27] Yao continued his basketball studies, despite his initial ambivalence, out of a sense of duty more than personal joy in playing the game.

The fact that Yao plays for Houston today is a matter of political economy as much as basketball. On the U.S. side, as you might imagine, the economy aspect is key and the politics takes place with an eye toward building the global market. With Yao in the starting lineup, broadcasts of Houston games are popular in China. The NBA hopes to build China into its largest market—larger than the U.S. market![28] Of course, everyone who thinks about selling products in China has such dreams. I don't know if this one is any more realistic, but it has captured the imagination of the folks at the NBA headquarters in New York and stimulated the creation of a special website for Chinese fans at china.nba.com/ (one of nine international portals to the NBA site).

Politics played a bigger role on the Chinese side of the bargaining. Yao's transfer straight from the Chinese national team to the Rockets was carefully negotiated by Chinese sports authorities. Yao benefits from the deal, of course. He is famous, he has money, and he is able to develop his basketball skills at the highest possible level. But he must be careful to obey the Chinese authorities and contribute to the national team, both in terms of time and talent and in monetary terms. He must be careful to toe the line if he wants to avoid the fate of Wang Zhizhi.

Seven-foot, 1-inch Wang Zhizhi came into the NBA in 1999 in a complex deal between the Houston Rockets and the state-run Chinese Basketball Association. Wang played for the Bayi Rockets, a team organized by the People's Liberation Army (Wang held the rank of regimental commander in the PLA).[29] Wang entered the NBA on terms not so different from Yao's, but his career was cut short when he decided to stay in the United States during the summer of 2002, to develop his individual skills in the NBA's summer league, rather than returning to China and the Chinese national team's training camp. He put his own interests above those of the state. The Chinese authorities made their displeasure known, and a little more than a year later Wang's U.S. career was essentially finished.

First Wang was traded by Dallas to the Los Angeles Clippers, in part because the Dallas management did not wish to sour its good relations with the Chinese. Then China banned telecasts of Clippers games to avoid showing the traitor Wang. The Communist state made Wang an economic liability for any NBA team. He was released by the Clippers in November 2003. You often hear it said that the decision to cut a player is not personal, it is "just business." In Wang's case, however, it was "just politics."

To sum up, this third image of basketball globalization incorporates elements of the first two and adds several new twists. The classic Michael Jordan story of basketball's commercialization and links to name-brand products (Nike) and high-tech media (Sky Sports) is here. We can see clearly, however, that the Michael Jordan effect rests on the foundation built by Doc Naismith's YMCA missionaries, who planted the seeds of the global game a hundred years ago. Those seeds have grown and evolved to reflect the particular natures of their local environments, conditioned by the culture of soccer in Argentina and by the priorities of the Communist state in China, for example.[30]

Finally, the outward push of the Nike/NBA marketing strategies has been matched in recent years by an inward pull of international players to the NBA, transforming in some ways the nature of the game on the court far more than Michael Jordan jerseys could ever alter indigenous culture abroad. The globalization of the NBA itself is a complex process, however, that opens the game and the business of basketball to foreign influences even as it also opens up foreign markets. Basketball globalization is not just the push of American capitalism abroad, it is also the assimilation of foreign influences in the United States.

Steve Kerr and the Global Game of Winner-Take-All

Steve Kerr played on six NBA championship teams during his career, which began in 1988 and ended with his retirement in 2003 (he is now a sportscaster). Kerr earned four of the fancy rings that champion team members receive playing with Michael Jordan's Chicago Bulls and two more with the San Antonio Spurs (the last one, in 2003, on the same team as Tim Duncan and Manu Ginobili). As near as I can tell, he appears nowhere in Walter LaFeber's story of Michael Jordan and the new global capitalism because LaFeber is interested in star power and Steve

Kerr was not an NBA star. His career averages are these: 6.0 points, 1.8 assists, and 1.2 rebounds in 17.8 minutes per game. Kerr was a role player, known for his ability to hit long-range three-point shots at critical moments (a "clutch player," it is said).

Steve Kerr made a lot of money as a professional basketball player, but that goes without saying. According to the collective bargaining agreement between the NBA and its players, each team must spend a minimum of $32.8 million on player salaries. The minimum wage for a first-year player is $367,000. A player with ten or more years experience must receive at least $1 million per year (all figures are for the 2003–2004 season). So the lowest-paid NBA player makes more per season than the highest-paid college professor, for example.

I suspect that Steve Kerr made more than the minimum wage during his career, but even the minimum is nothing to complain about. Unless we compare it to what the highest-paid NBA players received. On every one of Kerr's teams there were athletes who were just a little bit taller (he is 6 feet, 1 inch), just a little bit faster, who played just a little better defense, or had slightly better moves. At this highest level of play, after all, the difference between the best player on a team and the average player is absolutely small, but relatively crucial to the player's and the team's success. How much more did those *slightly* better players receive? Well, you know the answer. They earned vastly more money. For 2002–2003, for example, the top five NBA player salaries were paid to Kevin Garnett ($27.9 million), Shaquille O'Neal ($26.5 million), Dikembe Mutombo ($17.0 million), Rasheed Wallace ($16.9 million), and Allan Houston ($15.9 million). Yao Ming earned $4.1 million in 2003–2004 and Manu Ginobili was paid $1.5 million.[31] The highest-paid veteran star player, Garnett, therefore made seventy-six times as much as the lowest paid rookie—$27.9 million compared with $367,000.

But the real gap between rich and richer in the NBA is even greater. Star players earn millions over and above their playing salaries through endorsement contracts of one kind or another. Lesser players earn little or nothing from these sources. LeBron James, the high school student who was the first pick in the 2003 NBA player draft, for example, receives just $4.0 million in salary from his team, the Cleveland Cavaliers. This is much less than the highest-paid Cleveland player, the Lithuanian center Zydrunas Ilgauskas ($13.5 million), but much more than Jason Kapono, a shooting guard from UCLA who receives the rookie minimum of $367,000. James, however, is a player of Jordan-type potential. Before he played his first professional game he had already signed a seven-year endorsement contract with Nike worth $90 million, according to a *Sports Illustrated* article.[32] He also agreed to a deal with Upper Deck sports trading cards. The value of the contract was not announced but the signing bonus was: $1 million. I am sure he will sign more deals for more money as his career develops. Perhaps, like Michael Jordan, LeBron James will eventually find his playing salary to be of more symbolic than tangible value. Near the end of his career Jordan earned so much from outside sources that he could afford to donate his token Washington Wizard salary of $1 million to the victims of the September 11, 2001, terrorist attacks.

The economic gap between Michael Jordan and Steve Kerr, or between LeBron James and Jason Kapono, does not reflect a corresponding difference in their absolute basketball skills. Rather it is a result of the globalization of the professional basketball industry. Basketball fan Thomas Friedman made this connection in *The Lexus and the Olive Tree*, written during the glory days of the Chicago Bulls, using Michael Jordan and Steve Kerr to make the point.[33] For Friedman, Jordan represents the winners from globalization and Kerr the ones who get left behind. "I use the example of the NBA," he writes, "not because I sympathize with players who make only $272,250 [the NBA minimum at that time], but because it is an easy device to use to explain the widening income gaps that are helping to feed a backlash against globalization around the world."[34] Friedman is right that globalization can increase income differentials in certain cases, but inequality is not the only problem and perhaps not even the most important one. Robert H. Frank and Philip J. Cook explained this final connection between basketball and globalization in their 1995 book *The Winner-Take-All Society*.[35]

In many situations, a worker's pay is based upon *absolute* productivity. A house painter's income largely depends upon how many houses get painted. Paint more houses, get more money. There are some situations, Frank and Cook wrote, where *absolute* differences in quantity are less important than *relative* differences in quality in determining a worker's compensation. The reward that a fine arts painter receives, for example, depends in part upon how many pictures she paints, but it depends even more upon how that painter's work compares with that of other fine artists. The twentieth-best painter in the world probably can command a great deal more for her paintings than the thousandth-best painter. The gap between the value of a painting by the number one painter versus that of one by the twentieth best is probably vast. By contrast, the thousandth-best painter may get the equivalent of the minimum rookie salary for her work.

Why is the gap so huge? The answer that Frank and Cook give, to summarize very briefly, is that although the absolute differences in artistic ability among top painters (or singers or actors or basketball players) are very small, the price that buyers are willing to pay is determined by relative performance, not absolute accomplishment. Who would want to hear the thirty-seventh-best soprano in the country, for example, if you can hear the best—or one of the ten best—and especially if your self-worth or social status is enhanced by your taste for the best? Sometimes people are willing to pay outlandish sums for concert tickets (or basketball shoes) because what they are really buying is priceless—their own self-esteem. No price is too high if you want to be seen to have the very best.

Any market where it is possible to list a top ten (ten best movies, best actors, best point guards, best Bordeaux wines, best luxury sports utility vehicles, best liberal arts colleges, best gourmet restaurants, best law schools, best country clubs, etc.) is likely to be a winner-take-all market. Sometimes these factors compound themselves, as with parents who want their child to get into the best prep school, to increase the chances of getting into the best college, to improve the odds of getting into the best law school, so that their son or daughter can go to work for the best law firm, live in the best neighborhood, and drive the best car. For the prep schools, colleges, car companies, and so forth there is a strong economic incentive to be placed in the top group, so as to receive economic rewards disproportionate to absolute quality differentials.

The magnitude of the winner-take-all effect depends upon the size of the market. The bigger the market, the more purchasing power will be focused upon the top choices and the greater the gap between the best and the rest. The biggest effects, of course, occur in markets that are truly global in size. Technological change—the Internet, satellite and cable television, and so forth—makes it possible for the local or regional markets for some types of products to be linked up to the global market. By connecting the market dots, technology magnifies the existing winner-take-all effects.

This is how globalization has worked in professional basketball. I am sure that Michael Jordan and Nike and ESPN are all marketing geniuses and that their skill and manipulation are one reason for the high profits they have received. But I find the winner-take-all scenario based upon Frank and Cook's analysis even more persuasive. Here's how I would connect the dots. The YMCA established local basketball outposts around the world, but they remained largely isolated from one another until recent years. Each national league rewarded relative performance: the spoils, status, endorsements, preferential treatment, trips to foreign competitions, and so forth, went to the victors and to the very best players. (This was even true in otherwise egalitarian Communist China!)

Technological changes in the 1990s made it possible for these various leagues, teams, and fans to merge into a global arena, a disruptive event. The rewards for the best players and teams increased dramatically both in absolute and relative terms. Even if Michael Jordan and Nike had not tried very hard (and I am persuaded that they *did* try hard), I think they would have benefited from the emergence of a global winner-take-all basketball market. Why *wouldn't* an Argentine teenager like Manu Ginobili put Michael Jordan's poster on his bedroom wall in the 1990s? Why would he or she choose to identify with the second-best player on the Bulls or the best player on a lesser team? Why *not* choose the best, the number one? Teenagers today in Bahía Blanca, Argentina, probably have posters of Ginobili or LeBron James on *their* bedroom walls.

The globalization of these winner-take-all markets has two important effects. The first and obvious one is that relative inequality rises: rewards are concentrated at the top. The average absolute level of reward may rise (remember that NBA minimum wage), but the gains to those at the very top increase much, much more. Thomas Friedman is probably right to be concerned that this vast gap could generate a backlash against the rich or perhaps even against the system that made them rich.

Frank and Cook, however, are worried about a different reaction. Faced with Michael Jordan's tremendous financial success, they fear that young people will choose to "Be Like Mike" and devote their energies to competition in the winner-take-all markets. Instead of getting a good education, which will tend to increase their incomes proportionate to their increase in productivity, they will dump their books and hit the courts, trying for the big payoff that comes to the number one performer. But the thing about winner-take-all markets is that such efforts only pay off for the few. For the majority, it is a sucker's game.

The winners of basketball globalization—a winner-take-all market if there ever was one—gain enormously in terms of money and prestige. The near-winners get much less. I don't feel sorry for these losers, however, because at least they are playing in the top global league, and that is worth a great deal (the $367,000 rookie minimum) compared to rewards in lesser leagues.

The losers? In one sense they are the players like Steve Kerr, with slightly inferior talents, who earn grossly inferior salaries. But by now you know that the real losers of basketball globalization are not the Steve Kerrs of the world, they are the nameless dreamers who never make it to a professional league. Inspired by the riches of the best, they gamble that they can make it to the top, unaware of how tough the competition really is and how little separates the big names from the no names. These individuals lose their individual gambles (the odds were always against them), but their societies lose even more through the wasted resources absorbed in winner-take all competition—basketball and otherwise.

Basketball as a Metaphor for Globalization

Globalization is a technologically driven, capitalist-based process of Americanization of the world, which exploits the poor for the benefit of those few who control the power to create irresistible images. This is a useful image of globalization, for the postmodern antiglobalizers, because it thoroughly discredits the claims of hyper-globalists: that globalization is culturally benign and generally beneficial to the majority of people.

It is also a very incomplete image of globalization, and arguments based upon it can rightfully be labeled globaloney. If we look at how and why basketball has become a global phenomenon, we find elements of the Michael Jordan narrative, but we also discover patterns that run in the opposite direction, as international players (following NBA practice, I have carefully avoided calling them "foreign players") crowd onto U.S. team rosters. It may be convenient to believe that what happened to basketball can easily be generalized to other cases of globalization, but it seems highly problematic to do so. Global basketball seems to me to be very much a particular creation, not a general phenomenon, based to a considerable degree upon the efforts of YMCA missionaries a hundred years ago.

Without those pioneering YMCA workers, basketball might be a sport played mainly in the United States, like baseball, or it might not be played at all. And Michael Jordan would have been just another washed-up former minor league baseball hopeful who couldn't hit a big-league curve ball. Unknown, forgotten "baseball Michael" Jordan might have been a truer face of globalization than the famous man in the Nike ads.

When you tell the whole story of globalization and basketball, it is not necessarily a pretty story and it does not necessarily make you love globalization. But you have to tell the whole story if you want to understand even this little piece of globalization. Otherwise it is just global-oney.

*   *   *

Only an American would even suggest that it is possible to understand globalization through basketball. That's because only an American would think that basketball is the global sport. The *real* global spectator sports are Formula One auto racing and soccer. What does globalization look like if we use soccer as organizing metaphor? Turn the page to find out.

THE BEAUTIFUL GAME AND
THE AMERICAN EXCEPTION

David Beckham is the best-known player in the world's most popular spectator sport, soccer (or football as most of the world calls it), aka "the beautiful game."[1] Every day, in season and out, his image is pushed and pulled into homes, schools, and businesses around the world through all known forms of modern communications media. If global professional sports has a human face, it's probably Beckham's.

Do you know who Beckham is? The basic facts are these: David Beckham's career with the Manchester United soccer team began at age twelve (as a "trainee" or member of the club's youth squad). He played his first Premier League game in 1995 at the age of twenty and played midfielder in 394 games for Manchester United after that debut, winning six league titles. He is captain of England's national team. He was transferred to Real Madrid, another elite soccer club, for a fee of £25 million in 2003.[2] He wears jersey number 23 at Real Madrid in honor, he says, of Michael Jordan. His face is one of the most recognized images on earth.

David Beckham wears the symbols of global capitalism comfortably; they are embroidered on his chest. At Manchester United his playing jersey featured the logos of Nike and Vodafone (the team sponsor—professional soccer players are human billboards to a degree not allowed in America's major professional sports leagues). At Real Madrid he is a walking advertisement for Adidas and Siemens, the German industrial giant. The transfer from Manchester United resolved an awkward commercial conflict: Manchester was signed with Nike, but Beckham himself was Adidas property—the beneficiary of a £100 million lifetime endorsement contract. The Beckham/Manchester mixed message (Nike shirt, but Adidas soul and contract) is now reconciled: Adidas through and through.

Nothing about the move from Manchester to Madrid was simple. "The diverse nature of Beckham's personal endorsements means that any negotiations would have been complex and time-consuming," Gavin Hamilton reported in *World Soccer*. "The player's acceptance of Madrid's demand for 50 percent of his image rights—in return for an annual salary of around £4.5 million—suggests he was desperate to join them."[3] It is rumored that Real Madrid was able to recoup the full cost of Beckham's transfer fee in the first year through global sales of the new number 23 Beckham replica jersey. Sales were especially strong in Asia, when Real Madrid toured prior to the start of the 2003–2004 European season.

David Beckham is a global media superstar, whose face appears on magazine covers and newspaper pages every week. And not just on the sports page, either. His wife, Victoria, is better known as Posh Spice of the Spice Girls singing group. His, her, and their every action, emotion, and personal appearance is captured, analyzed, and promoted by the global tabloid press to an extent that Michael Jordan could not even imagine. A Google search of Internet news sources on January 12, 2004, found nearly two thousand Beckham news stories that had been posted during the previous few days.

Bank It Like Beckham

David Beckham is so famous—and so bankable from a commercial standpoint—that the mere use of his last name was enough to guarantee an audience for *Bend It Like Beckham*, a 2002 film directed by Gurinder Chadha, which was the highest grossing British-financed, British-distributed film in history.[4] The film tells a soccer story, but it is really about globalization, of course, and so worth a brief digression.

David Beckham's signature play on the soccer pitch is the free kick—a focused moment of high drama in a game that otherwise features a flow of continuous motion. He is known for his ability to strike the ball so that it rises and bends around the opposing side's defensive wall, then arcs downward quickly, zooming into the net just beyond the goaltender's frustrated grasp. In the film, a teenaged girl named Jess Bhamra dreams of playing soccer and bending her shots like David Beckham, but she faces two obstacles: she is a girl, and therefore subject to gender prejudice in sexist English sports, and her parents are immigrants from India who are opposed to the prospect of assimilation. She is expected to behave like a proper Indian girl and obedient daughter, which makes bare-legged sports out of the question. An interesting subplot concerns her father, a cricket player back in India, who quit the game after experiencing humiliating prejudice in England.

The critical question that this film asks is not whether Jess can really bend it like David Beckham (she can), but rather whether she and her teammates, coach, and family can become "globalized," which is to say whether they can transcend or overcome the obstacles that prevent them from becoming equal competitors. It is tempting to say that the question is whether they can be assimilated and "Americanized," so to speak, for a reason that will become clear shortly.

Jess is invited to join the girls' youth squad of the local soccer club. With the other girls she experiences English sexism and bonds with her coach, who is no stranger to English prejudice—he is Irish. The film ends happily, which is to say it ends with globalization triumphant. Jess's Indian family accepts her as a competitive female soccer player (her father even takes up cricket once again). Jess wins a big game by bending it like Beckham (in my favorite scene, she imagines that the defensive wall is made up of all her adult female relatives, dressed in colorful saris—an extra incentive to kick past them). Jess and teammate Jules gain the ultimate prize: they receive scholarships to play soccer in America, at the University of Santa Clara.

I call *Bend It Like Beckham* a globalization film because it is about how the forces of international or global competition empower individuals and allow them to overcome prejudice and cultural constraints. They transcend race, gender, and nationality. They become globalized. And they do it in Adidas logo soccer gear with the trademark of the AXA financial group emblazoned across their jerseys. David Beckham, who makes a brief cameo appearance as himself, a celebrity being chased and photographed by a frenzied media throng, is the perfect picture of this vision of globalization. Or at least that's what I think, but I admit there are differing views.

I believe that David Beckham is the perfect symbol of postmodern globalization—he is everything that Michael Jordan is and much more. His game is more global, his importance to it perhaps even more frankly commercial, his role and his existence even more media-driven, and his image sells, sells, sells. Plus, of course, he is a rich white male from an imperialistic country who models a high-end, cosmopolitan, metrosexual postmodern lifestyle.[5] What more do you want in a postmodern globalization poster boy?

Some people disagree, however—a true soccer fan would probably say that Beckham cannot be the symbol of soccer globalization because, unlike Michael Jordan in his prime, he is not the most skilled player in his game. Or at his position. Or on his team. If skill on the field counts (and soccer fans can be excused for imposing this requirement, which others of us might not), then Beckham's name should be replaced with one of these: Zinedine Zidane, Thierry Henry, Ronaldo, Pavel Nedved, Roberto Carlos, or Ruud Van Nestelrooy.[6] These are the players who finished ahead of David Beckham in the 2003 FIFA[7] player of the year poll. Zidane, Ronaldo, and Roberto Carlos play for the same team as Beckham, Real Madrid.

Fans say "no," but I'm going to interpret their answer as "probably not," because it seems to me that the reasoning behind their "no" is in fact strong evidence for the opposite argument—that Beckham really *does* embody the spirit and image of authentic postmodern globalization. Whereas Michael Jordan's great popularity and the power of his image was built on the foundation of his unmatched excellence as a player, Beckham's celebrity is due much less to his sports skills and much more to image creation and media manipulation—to his ability, in short, to extend the influence of global sports to people who are not sports fans.

Indeed, Beckham is perhaps as famous for his on-field errors in critical moments as for his outstanding performances. These would be damning errors for an ordinary soccer player, but they are just another part of the endless highly publicized saga for a tabloid media celebrity. We demand perfection from athletes, but celebrity misdeeds are not just tolerated, they are expected. The tension between athletic value and market value is inevitable. "The Spanish sports press and many of the players are fearful of the impact Beckham, his entourage and the media circus that follows him may have," Lowe reported. "His off-pitch lifestyle may encourage press intrusion into areas that are traditionally left alone; it simply isn't accepted practice for journalists to camp outside players' homes or follow their wives out shopping. With David and Victoria, that could all change."[8]

There is a third answer to the question of Beckham's global celebrity. Is he the perfect symbol of globalization? "No" is the answer that you would probably give this question if you lived in the United States. David Beckham? Globalization? No, of course not. *Who* is David Beckham? How can he represent globalization (and Americanization) if I have never heard of him?

America is the exception to the rule that soccer is the global spectator sport. Soccer is certainly played in the United States, but despite several attempts and millions of dollars, it is a sport that only a relatively few follow and those few are generally either immigrants or highly paid and educated elites. Americans, who *define* globalization in many eyes, are just about the least likely people on earth to know the name David Beckham.

I hope you appreciate the elegant irony of this situation. If globalization is Americanization, then the David Beckham image of globalization embodies even more of the stereotypical "American" elements than does the iconic Michael Jordan. Yet America is the one part of the world where Beckham's sport is not wildly popular because, as we will see, it is considered so un-American. The paradox that Americanization is un-American, if it holds up to closer scrutiny, is just one interesting insight we will encounter as we examine soccer, the self-proclaimed "beautiful game," and the American exception.

How Soccer Became the Global Game

People have probably fooled around kicking round objects for as long as *Homo sapiens* has stood upright. Ball, feet, and goal seem to have first come together in an organized game (called *tsu chu*) about five thousand years ago in China.[9] Players tried to put the ball through a net in the center of the field, using their feet, never their hands, to keep it from touching the ground. References to other soccer-like games, with teams, ball, kicking, and running, can be found around the world: Greece, Japan, Persia, Egypt, Italy, and among North American Native Americans, among others. "The comedies of Antiphanes contain telling expressions like *long ball, short pass, forward pass*," according to Uruguayan author Eduardo Galeano. "They say that Emperor Julius Caesar was quick with his feet and that Nero couldn't score at all."[10]

Early soccer was not the Beautiful Game that we know today. The balls were typically heavy, stuffed with rags, hemp, or horsehair or an inflated animal bladder; the teams, which were sometimes gangs and sometimes whole towns, were large, and the games lasted indefinitely—until the decisive goal was scored (no shoot-outs!). Play was physical, tough, and sometimes violent; soccer was banned more than once by medieval British monarchs for this reason. Soccer was almost war and, at least sometimes, it was probably a substitute for war. The fact that soccer was often played by soldiers may indicate that its combination of violence and individual responsibility within a framework of coordinated team strategy was good training for soldiers. British soldiers in the Roman era are said to have started playing using the skulls of defeated enemies as balls.[11]

Soccer has experienced four waves of "globalization": the Roman Empire, the British Empire, the FIFA empire, and the current era, the winner-take-all age. Soccer spread throughout Europe during the Roman Empire and then spread virtually throughout the world during the British Empire. The FIFA empire created global soccer competitions and a global *audience* for them, which has become a global winner-take-all *market* for soccer players, products, and images in recent years.

Roman Soccer Conquest

Rome's legions spread their version of soccer, which was called *harpastum*, wherever they went, from Egypt to Scotland. The game evolved in the context of indigenous culture and institutions (and of course, existing local foot and ball games)—*harpastum* was "glocalized" in the current parlance. Soccer terms and metaphors entered common usage; William Shakespeare used them in both *The Comedy of Errors* and *King Lear*.

Local and national games naturally evolved in different ways in different places. Modern soccer is said to be most directly derived from the French game called *soule* and the Florentine *calcio*. *Calico* is still the name given to soccer in Italy (football, futbol, or soccer are used pretty much everywhere else). Because it developed in Renaissance Florence, where civic humanism has been studied and documented, we know quite a lot about *calcio*. It was played by large teams, twenty-seven or more players on each side, and was one of several tools used by the commune's leaders to generate civil pride and identity. Leonardo da Vinci is said to have been a fan. Players included Machiavelli and Popes Clement VII, Leo IX, and Urban VIII.[12] Unlike today's game, which popes mainly watch, not play, use of the hands was allowed, both to manipulate the ball and to abuse opponents. *Calcio* was sufficiently popular and organized that its rules were published in 1580.[13]

Two different types of ball games emerged in nineteenth-century Britain. One, rugby football, retained more of the violence and gang warfare aspects of the earlier games; rugby is said to be a crude sport played by well-educated gentlemen. It evolved into American football in the United States through intercollegiate play. The other version, called association football, became the game we know today. Soccer is a more refined sport than rugby, it is said, but one that was in Britain more popular among the working masses than the educated elites. The division of football games along class lines in class-conscious Britain shows how games are shaped by specific local social context and why the globalization of any game is problematic. Even when the same game is played, it will often have a unique local social meaning. In apartheid South Africa, for example, rugby was the white sport and soccer the black sport, reflecting racial rather than strictly class divisions. In the United States, rugby-derived American football is today the sport of the masses while soccer is often viewed as a game followed by elites. Same game, different meaning.

Soccer became more than just a game in Britain in the nineteenth century—it developed into a sports culture. A sports culture includes players, spectators, and those who "follow" the game and become avowed fans of one team or another. Sports cultures allow individuals to create distinct identities based upon the perceived qualities of teams, localities, and their relationships with other teams and fan groups. The emergence of soccer sports culture in nineteenth-century Britain can be linked to Britain's early industrialization and the urban environment it created. "Sports in its organized form of regulated leisure and, subsequently, commodified culture, has proceeded hand in hand with such major components of 'modernization' as urbanization, [and] industrialization," according to Andrei S. Markovits and Steven L. Hellerman. Sports became

> inextricably linked to the most fundamental aspects of modernization: discipline exacted by regulated industrial life, the strict separation of leisure and work, the necessity of organized and regularized recreation

for the masses, cheap and efficient public transportation . . . and widely available mass communication via the press (introduction of the sports pages in newspapers and the establishment of sports journalism).[14]

It is unsurprising that in Britain, where the urban industrial working class first developed, an urban industrial sports culture also developed. And, for class reasons, its distinctive game was soccer.

Soccer became more than a game; it became a mechanism of social control. Soccer was probably encouraged in Britain as a way to keep young workers out of trouble, or at least in less trouble than if they roamed the streets in gangs or attended radical political rallies. Anyone who is shocked by violence at some soccer matches today should consider that earlier social leaders found such controlled conflict preferable to uncontrolled rioting on the streets!

The Cambridge Rules of football were published in 1848 (the same year that Marx and Engels published *The Communist Manifesto*), and the Football Association established in 1863. City teams were playing each other by the 1870s, and there were also international competitions (England versus Scotland in 1872 was the first international game). Professionalism was introduced in 1885.[15] As other countries industrialized, urbanized, and modernized, they became fertile ground for emerging sports cultures, too, including soccer. The first meeting of the International Football Association Board took place in 1883.

British Soccer Empire

With soccer established as a "hegemonic sports culture" in Britain, to poach a term used by Markovits and Hellerman, it is not hard to imagine how it spread around the world at the zenith of the British Empire. British soldiers and sailors introduced soccer wherever they went. British colonial administrators encouraged play, too, despite their own preference for "gentlemen's games," such as rugby and cricket. Bill Murray reports the extreme case of a British colonial schoolmaster in India, a Mr. Tyndale-Biscoe, who in 1891 literally beat his students with a stick to make them play soccer. The students, Hindu Brahmins all, could not touch the cowhide football without becoming "unclean," but he whipped them until they did. Perhaps it is not surprising, then, that the most famous game in Indian soccer history was the 1911 triumph of an Indian team, Mohan Bagan, over a crack Middlesex Regiment squad.[16] Revenge is sweet.

94

"Football in Brazil has its Year Zero," writes Alex Bellos. "In 1894 Charles Miller disembarked at the port of Santos with two footballs, one in each hand."[17] The son of a Scottish rail engineer who migrated to Brazil in search of opportunity, Miller returned from his Southampton boarding school with soccer fever. The game spread through the British immigrant community and then generally throughout Brazil. A street in São Paulo today bears Miller's name to commemorate his seminal contribution to contemporary Brazilian culture.

The fact that Miller's father was a railway engineer is particularly significant because it helps explain why this second era of soccer globalization was so widespread. As Lenin famously noted in his book *Imperialism: The Highest Form of Capitalism*,[18] Britain's effective empire in the nineteenth century was larger even than its administrative empire. Britain exported financial capital to politically independent countries such as Brazil and Argentina, which they used to purchase British industrial products, such as railroad equipment. This rendered these independent states economically dependent upon Britain both for money and technology. Thus British influence and even its sports culture penetrated not only its colonial possessions, which might be expected, but its financial and technological dependencies as well. The fact that South America became a virtual hotbed of soccer culture attests to how deeply Britain's finance-driven influence penetrated these countries. First they imported British money, then its industrial products, then balls, nets, boots, jerseys, and soccer language.

Eduardo Galeano's *Football in Sun and Shade* paints an especially clear portrait of how soccer spread through British economic imperialism in South America in the late nineteenth century. In Argentina, he explains, "the first popular clubs were organized in railway workshops and shipyards. Several anarchist and socialist leaders soon denounced the clubs as a maneuver by the bourgeoisie to forestall strikes and disguise class divisions. The spread of soccer throughout the world was an imperialist trick to keep oppressed peoples in eternal childhood, unable to grow up."[19] Such hundred-year-old criticisms of global sports are distant echoes of similar comments heard today. In Argentina many of the clubs took English names (River Plate, not the Spanish Rio Plata, and Boca Juniors, for example), and some required that English be spoken at club events. Some clubs were even organized as symbols of proletarian protest, an attempt by anarchists or socialists to use sports imperialism against itself.

The two key points about soccer's British Empire globalization are these. First, essentially identical versions of the game were introduced around the world at about the same time, through transportation and trade, driven by British education, administration, and finance. British sailors in Genoa, for example, introduced association football into the home country of *calcio*, where it quickly spread. The globalization of the sport was borne on the back of economic globalization in the case of soccer to a far greater extent and for different if related reasons than is true of basketball. (Basketball's initial globalization, as we have learned, was due to Christian missionary activity.) Thus the real story of sports and economic globalization—a story that is more than one hundred years old—is better told through soccer.

The second key point is what I call the American exception. While soccer filled a need in societies around the world that were becoming urbanized, industrialized, and modernized, the game did not catch on in the United States, the presumed home of globalization today. Soccer generally has been adopted by different countries and its meaning tailored to fit local social patterns. In the United States, however, this process has so far meant the rejection of soccer as a mass spectator sport. More on this to come, but now on to the third era of soccer globalization.

FIFA's Global Soccer Stage

FIFA is soccer's global governing body. Its initials stand for Fédération Internationale de Football Association or the International Federation of Association Football.[20] FIFA was founded in Paris a hundred years ago, in May 1904, by agreement of the national soccer associations of France, Belgium, Denmark, the Netherlands, Spain, Sweden, and Switzerland. FIFA now has 204 national members, thirteen more than the United Nations. FIFA was, of course, an official rule-setting body, but it is interesting that it evolved into a much stronger institution, sanctioning play within nations and between nations, and forbidding games with unsanctioned teams. In other words, FIFA is noteworthy for its clout. It is to global soccer far more of a "world government" than the UN, World Bank, and International Monetary Fund added together are for the global political economy. As such, of course, it was FIFA that became the driving force of the third wave of soccer globalization, which began in Montevideo, Uruguay, in 1930, with the first World Cup competition.

Before the 1930 World Cup, international soccer competition was more national (reflecting FIFA's nation-based structure) and regional than it was global. The only venue for global competition before 1930 was the Olympics, but no South American soccer team participated in Olympic soccer until 1924, when the team from Uruguay came and soundly defeated the competition. More South American teams came to the 1928 Olympics, where Uruguay won again, defeating Argentina in the finals.

Uruguay was, in effect, the reigning world champion of soccer when FIFA conceived of a global competition. Montevideo sought to host the competition to honor its team and to commemorate the hundredth anniversary of its independence. It even offered to pay the expenses of European teams. Just twelve nations participated in the 1930 World Cup, however. Although they all received invitations, only four European teams thought the event worth the long Atlantic crossing. When Uruguay beat Argentina 4–2 in the final it was hardly newsworthy at all, except within these two countries—the event "did not merit more than a twenty-line column in the Italian daily *La Gazzetta dello Sport*," Galeano reports.[21]

FIFA and the World Cup were instrumental, especially in the postwar period, in making soccer a global sport. Joining FIFA and fielding a World Cup team was, along with joining the international Olympic movement, an obvious way for countries emerging from colonial rule to establish their international identity and to help build domestic solidarity. FIFA opened up Africa and Asia through sport more quickly and permanently than corresponding economic or political efforts. North Korea and Myanmar, two countries notoriously closed to other "Western" organizations and influences, maintained solid ties with FIFA. (Korea is a strong soccer nation: North Korea advanced as far as the quarterfinal round in the 1966 World Cup before losing to eventual third-place finisher Portugal. South Korea was cohost with Japan of the 2002 World Cup.)

When the 2006 World Cup begins in Berlin, thirty-two of the 204 FIFA countries will have qualified for the final competition. Brazil, as the reigning champion, and host country Germany are the only teams guaranteed places. All the rest must move through preliminary competitions for the places set aside for Europe, Asia, Africa, North America and the Caribbean, South America, and Oceana. There will be a lot more than national pride at stake, however.

The World Cup is the most watched television event in the world; about 1.5 billion people watched the 2002 final between Brazil and Germany, for example. FIFA estimates that three hundred million viewers in China watched the preliminary game where that country qualified for the finals for the very first time.[22] FIFA's contract guarantees it at least $1.7 billion for the television rights to the 2002 and 2006 games.[23] Billions of dollars more in media promotion, advertising, and product endorsements will be at stake along with further millions in travel and sport tourism spending.

Soccer's Global Market

The commercial success that the World Cup achieved has paved the way for even greater commercialization of the sport in general.[24] The World Cup created a truly global audience for soccer and provided global exposure to top-level international players. It is, however, contested just once every four years by national teams called together from the professional clubs. The vast audience that the World Cup created was an obvious target for sports entrepreneurs who have sought to exploit it through the creation of super-clubs, such as Manchester United, Chelsea, Juventus, Bayern Munich, AC Milan, and Real Madrid, and through the creation of an elite international super-league competition, the Champions League. (If you wonder why there are no South American teams on this list, read on!) Both of these developments, and their effect on the business of soccer generally, are of interest to us here.

The teams that I call the super-clubs are more transnational enterprises than soccer clubs. Although they are very successful on the field, winning games is best viewed as less an end in itself than a means to establish an image and a marketable brand that can be sold, in the best cases, to consumers generally, not just to soccer fans and not just to local or regional customers.

Real Madrid was the world's richest soccer club in fiscal year 2002, according to *World Soccer* magazine, with total revenues of €252 million not counting revenues from player transfers.[25] Manchester United was second (€207 million), followed by Juventus (€195 million), Bayern Munich (€176 million), AC Milan (€161.7 million), and Chelsea (€161 million).[26] The money comes from

- *Ticket sales.* Average attendance for this group is 50,000 to 70,000 tickets per home game. Manchester United takes in about €900,000 from ticket sales for each home game.
- *Sponsorship.* Payments from team sponsors (the corporate names

that decorate the jerseys)—figure €10 to €20 million per year for the main sponsor, and there can be several secondary sponsors of one sort or another.

- *Home TV.* Sales of home country television rights vary greatly among the teams depending upon league revenue sharing provisions. (Juventus reportedly received €84 million in 2002.)
- *International TV.* A share of the television earnings from UEFA[27] Champions League games. (Real Madrid received €42 million from this source alone in 2002.)
- *Other revenues.* The list here goes on and on, from image rights to replica jersey rights to logo wear generally, and so on. Chelsea, which is sponsored by Air Emirates, even operates a travel agency.

Bear in mind that these figures list revenues, not profits. Real Madrid's revenues of €252 million in fiscal 2002 (exclusive of transfer fee net revenues if any) must be set alongside their costs, which included a player wage bill of €140 million. Super-clubs, as I have called them, are not necessarily super-profitable, although some are. Lazio (one of two teams from Rome) was number thirteen on the rich club list, but paid out more in player wages (€123.7 million) than its total revenue (€112 million). I will have more to say about soccer club profits shortly.

The super-teams are very global indeed. Each year, it seems, Real Madrid acquires the reigning FIFA world player of the year, a practice designed to generate hype and sometimes to raise the quality of team play. They paid Juventus a world record transfer fee of $64.5 million for Zinedine Zidane in 2001, for example, and a salary estimated at $150,000 per week on top of that.[28] In 2003 the squad included three former world player winners—Luis Figo, Zidane, and Ronaldo—as well as famous nonwinner David Beckham.[29] Manchester United has signed a joint marketing agreement with the New York Yankees baseball club to further develop both global brands. Manchester and all of these clubs also tour abroad in the off-season, developing their brand names in emerging markets such as China (Real Madrid, summer 2003) and the United States (Manchester United).

One of the most interesting recent developments among the super-teams has been the emergence of Chelsea, previously a somewhat down-and-out London team, as a potential global brand name. Thirty-six-year-old Russian oil billionaire Roman Abramovich purchased Chelsea in 2003 and began to spend lavishly to build a super-team. The 2003 squad roster reads like a world atlas: Russian owner; Italian coach;

players from Italy, Austria, Nigeria, the Netherlands, France, Germany, Denmark, Cameroon, Croatia, Argentina, Ireland, Iceland, Romania, Portugal, and, oh yes, England.[30]

The problem that all soccer clubs face is how to make a profit. Although soccer is a fairly large global industry (£150 billion estimated global turnover), it is not necessarily a very profitable one.[31] It is difficult to compile a profits table for professional soccer, in part because most clubs are as secretive about their finances as the law allows and some adopt accounting practices that distort reported profits. The fundamental problem, questionable accounting aside, is that the super-clubs form a winner-take-all market that benefits the top clubs disproportionately. Elite clubs can make high profits, but the costs that lesser clubs must pay for skilled players is driven up far more than their share of the total revenues, so losses among these clubs are common. "The big money in international soccer is concentrated on the elite European clubs, but some of them are also suffering serious losses," wrote Gideon Rachman in a 2002 *Economist* survey of the world soccer industry. "In Italy, top clubs such as Fiorentina and Lazio have had trouble paying their players this year. The English Premier League is widely regarded as admirably businesslike, yet almost all Premier League clubs will lose money this year."[32] Real Madrid, the club with the highest gross revenues, ran up a debt of perhaps €400 million to get there and was forced to sell club property for development to get out from under the overhang.[33] The globalization of professional soccer may in fact be a "race to the bottom" in financial terms, except for a few super-clubs.

One problem that the super-teams face is the fact that they exist within the FIFA-sanctioned system of clubs, which means that they must be members of national soccer leagues, such as the Premier League in England, play most of their games in the league, and earn a place in any international competitions the same as any other team. This is a problem because super-teams make the most money when they play other super-teams. How can Manchester United advance its brand name playing Sheffield Wednesday, which is a perfectly good ordinary team, but not the financial draw that Chelsea or Juventus would be? The top teams have tried to break free and set up their own super-league, but so far FIFA's power has resisted this challenge. Global soccer thus displays the classic tension of state (FIFA) sovereignty versus market (super-league) dynamism that is cited so frequently in the globalization literature.

But the market-driven evolutionary path toward a global soccer super-league is fairly clear. In England, for example, the old ninety-two-team Football League was split in the 1990s into an eighteen-team Premier League and a seventy-four-team Football League (itself further divided into a first division, second division, and so on). The Premier League is essentially the English super-league. The total operating profit of the ninety-two teams in 2001–2002, according to Deloitte & Touche, was £39 million. This total was divided as follows: Premier League teams earned operating profits of £84 million and Football League teams earned aggregate operating *losses* of £45 million. If we take into account full costs, not just operating expenses, even the Premier League was a loss maker—the total loss for all ninety-two teams was £204 million.[34] I think that Manchester United may be the only team in England that has been profitable over the last ten years. That's really a winner-take-all game!

The UEFA Champions League has evolved into something of a super-league, too, even if its membership is not as elite as the top teams would probably prefer. (The 2004 championship match was played between Porto and Monaco, excellent soccer clubs but not members of the financial elite.) Super-club AC Milan won the Champions Cup in 2003. Previous winners included Real Madrid (several titles), Bayern Munich, Manchester United, Juventus, and so on—the super-clubs. It seems to me that the only teams that can afford to compete with these super-teams are other super-teams.

The sorry state of club finances in 2003 accounted for the relatively low price that Real Madrid paid for David Beckham, although this was not a serious problem for either Beckham or the selling team, Manchester United, because of their many other sources of income. But falling player transfer fees are a significant problem for many of the lesser teams, those who export their rising stars to super-leagues and super-clubs, both in Europe and around the world, that count upon a steady income from player sales.

The fourth wave of soccer globalization, then, has commercialized professional soccer and intensely stratified the competition. So tightly connected are the business of soccer and the game of soccer today that it is sometimes difficult to tell which are the sports pages of the newspaper and which are the business pages.

Three Images of Global Soccer Today

I am struck by how much the history of the globalization of soccer mirrors the history of globalization more generally. Like globalization generally, global soccer was initially the product of imperialism, military and then economic. Soccer hegemony and economic hegemony were both centered in Great Britain during the Victorian era. When nationalistic forces swept the world in the 1930s, overcoming global market forces, FIFA and its strongly nationalistic structure became increasingly significant. The World Cup reinforced the authority of the nation-state and gave tangible form to nationalistic rhetoric through international competition. And now, as economic globalization proceeds, creating global markets and weakening the nation-state, the same pattern is clear in soccer. Basketball cannot compare to soccer as a metaphor for globalization's ebbs and flows.

As I look at global soccer today, I see three patterns (and certainly relationships among the patterns) that seem interesting enough to include in this chapter. I wonder if they are just patterns that are unique to soccer or if they reflect the world more generally? Let me tell you about them and then see what you think.

First, the global soccer player market seems to display a classic core–periphery structure, which is often associated with exploitation in political economy. But, second, if we look closely at the periphery, it appears that there is something else going on besides simple exploitation. Soccer seems to be used as a tool to build local identity in resistance to globalization and exploitation. So this relationship seems complex and interesting. And, finally, there is the American exception to consider—what should we make of soccer's persistent inability, even during this era of strong market forces, to penetrate the United States as a spectator sport? The remainder of this chapter tries to understand the causes and consequences of these three images of globalization and soccer today.

Core and Periphery

If you look at the top five professional soccer leagues in the world—England, Spain, Italy, Germany, and France—you will see the top players in the world at work. Not just the top English, Spanish, Italian, German, and French players, but the top players from everywhere: Africa, Asia, North America, South America, the works. The top teams in the top leagues bid talent away from the countries and teams in the soccer periphery and then sell the finished products—games, shirts, images—back to them. This pattern has all of the qualities of a classic core–periphery relationship in political economy. The core of the system controls the key elements of economic power (in this case, it is the privileged position within the winner-take-all system) and uses its advantage to purchase cheap natural resources from the periphery, selling back finished products at advantageous prices. That is a basic core–periphery relationship, considerably oversimplified, as originally conceived by Immanuel Wallerstein.[35]

The intensity of the core–periphery relationship in soccer is quite amazing. Here is some information that I collected about some of the players from four teams in the 2002 World Cup finals.[36] I have put together some representative segments of the rosters of four teams from the economic periphery of soccer so that you can see where the members of Turkish, Nigerian, Argentine, and Brazilian teams play during the professional league seasons (see table 4.1).

Let's begin with Turkey, a team that made it to the World Cup semifinals, where it was defeated by Brazil, the eventual champion. Turkey is clearly *not* in the periphery in terms of soccer skills and strategy, but in economic terms its position is much different. Of the first eleven players on the roster of the national team, only one earned his living playing for a Turkish league club. All the rest but one played for clubs in one of the five super-leagues: England, France, Spain, Germany, or Italy. The story is essentially the same in the case of Nigeria. Of the first eleven players listed on the roster, all played at clubs outside of Nigeria (outside of Africa, in fact).

The power of economics in shaping the pattern of soccer imports and exports becomes even clearer when we look at Argentina and Brazil, countries that are solidly the core in terms of soccer skills and competition, but still peripheral from a strict economic standpoint. Almost all of Argentina's best players are "guest workers" for foreign clubs. At the highest level, Argentina's national team players are much more likely to confront each other in Italian Serie A competitions or in Champions League games than they are to meet in Argentina.

Finally, consider the 2002 World Cup champions, Brazil. As of 2002, two of the players listed here came from Brazilian sides; the rest played in Europe with one of the super-teams. The number of Brazil-based players fell dramatically after the finals, of course, as the result of the international publicity they all received. Dida was transferred to AC Milan, for example, and many of the players already in Europe were transferred up the soccer food chain, to even better and more prosperous clubs. Brazilian soccer is still a joy to watch, but the very best players are seldom seen at home (except via satellite sports television).

Table 4.1 Club Affiliations of Selected World Cup Players

Turkey		Nigeria		Argentina		Brazil	
Player	2002 Club	Player	2002 Club	Player	2002 Club	Player	2002 Club
Boukar Alioum	Samsunspor, Turkey	Ike Shorunme	Lucerne, Switzerland	Roberto Ayala	Valencia, Spain	Dida	Corinthians, Brazil
Bill Tchato	Montpelier, France	Joseph Yobo	Olympique Marseille, France	Walter Samuel	Roma, Italy	Cafu	Roma, Italy
Pierre Wome	Bologna, Italy	Celestine Babayaro	Arsenal, England	Hernan Crespo	Lazio, Italy	Roque Junior	Milan, Italy
Rigobert Song	Cologne, Germany	Nwankwo Kanu	Arsenal, England	Javier Zanetti	Inter Milan, Italy	Edmilson	Olympique Lyonnaise, France
Raymond Kalla	Extremadura, Spain	Isaac Okoronkwo	Shakhtar Donetsk, Ukraine	Gabriel Batistuta	Roma, Italy	Roberto Carlos	Real Madrid, Spain
Pierre Njanka	Strasbourg, France	Taribo West	Kaiserslautern, Germany	Ariel Ortega	River Plate, Argentina	Ricardinho	Corinthians, Brazil
Joseph Ndo	Al Khalees, UAE	Pius Ikedia	Ajax, Netherlands	Juan Veron	Manchester United, England	Gilberto Silva	Atletico Mineiro, Brazil
Geremi	Real Madrid, Spain	Mutiu Adepoju	Salamanca, Spain	Diego Placenta	Bayer Leverkusen, Germany	Ronaldo	Inter Milan, Italy
Samuel Etoo	Real Mallorca, Spain	B. Ogbeche	Paris St Germain, France	Kily Gonzalez	Valencia, Spain	Rivaldo	Barcelona, Spain
Patrick Mbomba	Sunderland, England	Jay Jay Okocha	Paris St Germain, France	Pablo Aimar	Valencia, Spain	Ronaldinho	Paris St Germain, France
Pius Ndiefe	Sedan, France	Garba Lawal	Roda Kerkrade, Netherlands	Claudio Husain	River Plate, Argentina	Denilson	Betis Seville, Spain

Pelé is a great exception to the rule that the top Brazilian soccer players are always exported to Europe. Why didn't he leave Brazil during his playing days? Because it was against the law! He was declared a national treasure by the Brazilian parliament and forbidden to play for a foreign team. (Pelé did eventually play abroad—for the New York Cosmos in the United States—but only after he retired from the Brazilian national team.)

The same winner-take-all forces that draw the best Argentina and Nigeria players to the top European teams also affect players from England, Italy, Spain, France, and Germany, of course, but differently. The best English players (Beckham aside) tend to play in England and the best Italian players in Italy. All the 2002 World Cup team members from these countries stayed at home, more or less. They played in the super-leagues, which have a relatively strong home country bias that is strongest in the richest markets, England and Italy, and weakest in France. Fans from these countries are able to see many of their countries' best players on a regular basis, either in league games or Champions League contests. Fans on soccer's periphery must maintain a long-distance relationship.

To restate my point, the economic core of soccer is in Europe's super-leagues, even though the playing core is centered in South America, with emerging pockets of excellence in Africa, Turkey, and Eastern Europe. The economic forces of winner-take-all markets mean that clubs in Brazil, Argentina, Nigeria, Turkey, Croatia, and other countries cannot possibly compete with the super-clubs for the services of their own players. So, to a certain degree, they assume the role of minor leagues or youth leagues. Players with outstanding potential are identified and trained and then sold to European clubs. Sales of players take the place of ticket or television rights sales in their economic structures.

In fact, it is possible that formal "major league–minor league" links between core and periphery teams may be developing, a process that could institutionalize the dependency condition we have observed. Ajax of Amsterdam, long a powerful European club, has negotiated such arrangements with at least two teams. One, now called Ajax Orlando, will use its Florida base to develop New World player prospects. "Internationally, there are good players coming from places like Iran and Egypt, and we're even starting to see it from the U.S.," according to Mark Dillon, the Ajax Orlando founder. "In some ways the U.S. is the new Africa: a lot of relatively inexpensive players."[37]

The very best periphery teams can be remarkably successful, although not in the same way as the European super-teams. Boca Juniors of Argentina, for example, enjoys both economic and soccer success. In 2003 it won the Argentine league championship, the South American club competition, and beat European Cup champions AC Milan in Tokyo to claim the world club title. All this success on the field, with corresponding television rights earnings, meant that Boca was able to hang onto some of its best players for perhaps an extra season before selling their contracts to European clubs. But Boca Juniors is the exception. In 2003 it enjoyed its own version of the winner-take-all payoff. Boca's situation as the number one team was miles ahead of the average team in the Argentine league, which leaks money like a sieve, like most clubs in most countries.

Brazil is perhaps the world's leading exporter of soccer players. Brazilian players are said to have a particularly fluid and creative style and it seems like every team wants to have one. About five thousand Brazilians play professional soccer outside of Brazil, according to Alex Bellos, author of *Futbol: Soccer, the Brazilian Way*.[38] He explains Brazil's position as a huge net exporter in simple supply and demand terms. Many Brazilians, inspired by the success of Pelé, Ronaldo, and others, want to play soccer (a predictable problem in a winner-take-all market). There are too many for Brazil to absorb, even with its five hundred professional clubs employing about twenty-three thousand players. With so many teams, the individual club economic markets are small for all but the top teams and the pay low. (Bellos says that 90 percent of Brazilian players earn less than £100 per month.) Poor clubs, poor pay—and a high demand abroad. No wonder Brazil exports soccer players to the world.

Argentina's situation is of particular interest to me because of the way soccer reflects life and globalization more generally. Argentina experienced a severe economic crisis in recent years—a currency crisis, a banking crisis, and an international debt crisis all in one. Deteriorating domestic economic conditions affected the country's soccer clubs, too. Ticket and television revenues dried up, and even sponsorship funding fell. The two best teams, River Plate and Boca Juniors, were able to switch to international sponsors (Budweiser and Pepsi respectively) to shore up their revenue base, but most other teams did not fare so well. Desperate for funds, they flooded the world transfer market with players, pushing up supply at the same time that financial problems in Europe were cutting demand. The result: even their most valuable assets, the players themselves, could not be sold for enough money to make ends meet (Boca Juniors aside).[39] The plight of Argentine soccer mirrored in this case as in many others the sad economic situation of the country itself.

Soccer and Local Identity

If exploitation of the periphery were the whole story of soccer globalization it would be a sad story indeed, but it is not. Soccer is more than global capitalism acting upon countries like Argentina and Brazil; it is also a tool that people use to define themselves and, implicitly at least, to resist the forces of globalization.

The relationship between soccer and national or local identity has many layers, and my brief discussion here can only scratch the surface.[40] It begins, I suppose, with styles of play. Although soccer is a simple game, there are endless variations in styles and strategies. "The Brazilians play like they dance; the Germans play like they make cars, with lots of technical efficiency and not much left to the imagination; the English run hard all the time, maybe because of the weather; the Spanish are a mosaic of regional styles, which has yet to find a national pattern," according to Jorge Valdano, a member of Argentina's 1986 World Cup champion team. "And the Italians, they are a paradox. In every other area they export style and flair to the world; but in football they've allowed the ideal of collective organization to crush individual talent."[41] The way a player or team approaches the game makes a statement about their identity, or at least it can seem to do so.

The next layer is this: soccer can be used to establish or reinforce a national or local identity. Soccer is not unique among sports in this regard—Hitler famously tried to use the 1936 Berlin Olympics for particular nation-building purposes. FIFA's World Cup was, as previously noted, inaugurated during an era of growing nationalism and has been used ever since as a way to reinforce national identity. Soccer is an "us versus them" game and therefore can be an especially effective way to define identity, both who we are and who and what we are not.[42] The case of the Brazilian Pelé is an especially interesting one in this regard.

Pelé was the greatest soccer player of his generation, perhaps of any generation. He was born in 1940 and played for most of his career with Santos, Sao Paulo's richest team. A personal sponsorship contract from the Brazilian Coffee Institute allowed him to resist the financial incentives to play in Europe.[43] Pelé was a black player at a time when Brazilian teams still discriminated against blacks. Pelé's amazing skill and creativity changed that and, to some extent, changed Brazil, too.

Brazil's government quite purposefully used Pelé to shape the country's identity and to legitimize its own hold on power. When a military regime seized power in Brazil in 1964, it immediately turned its attention to the most famous Brazilian, Pelé, the man who defined Brazil to many people. "For the generals," Bill Murray writes, "Pelé became a resource to be shamelessly exploited in their own interests. He was encouraged to speak on behalf of their dictatorship, claiming that Brazil was not ready for democracy, and in a country with more soccer pitches than schools pointed to himself as an example of how the poor and blacks could do well."[44] Race was an important issue. When Pelé married a white woman it was promoted as a symbol of racial harmony and integration. Pelé was an especially powerful symbol because he was, like Michael Jordan in the 1990s, a ubiquitous presence. Media and commercial interests made sure that his face was everywhere, and his image was designed to sell more than just soccer and coffee—it was designed to sell a particular view of Brazil's government and a very particular image of Brazil itself: the harmonious multiracial land of opportunity.

We know that governments will use whatever tools they can find, soccer included, to advance their interests and shape national attitudes, but I am most interested in how people themselves use soccer to create or reinforce their identities. There has been a good deal of scholarly work written about how fan groups have used their association with soccer to build distinctive local identities.[45] One very interesting personal account is *A Season with Verona* by the novelist (and literature professor) Tim Parks.[46] Parks is a fan of Hellas Verona, his local team, and spent one season attending every home and away Verona game in the company of a group of *ultras* or extreme fans. Parks's book obviously lacks scholarly distance and objectivity, but it does provide an interesting perspective on this identity-creation process as seen from inside. The particular case that Parks reports is also interesting because Hellas Verona fans were thought to be especially racist and for a time Verona was forced by the Italian league to play its home games on neutral grounds due to the alleged racist environment. Soccer identities can be negative as well as positive ones and Parks helps us understand that the meaning of soccer within an *ultra* group may be different than the meaning assigned by outside observers.[47]

The basic "us versus them" structure of soccer seems to enable team followers to assign many different meanings to the teams they support. We might expect national identities would be at stake (France versus Germany), but it is more complicated than this. A game between the English teams Aston Villa and Birmingham City, for example, assumes the identity of a class war. Both teams are based in Birmingham, but City's fans identify themselves as blue-collar working class—gritty and hard-working—versus the bourgeois suburban Villa fans. Marx's class war is played out in surrogate form inside the stadium (and sometimes in real form outside it) each time these teams play.[48]

The rivalry between Glasgow's two Scottish Premier League teams, Celtic and Rangers, is even more complicated. The identities of these two Scottish teams reflect Irish religious tensions as transferred to Glasgow through industry and immigration![49] Rangers is the team of anti-Catholic protestants and Celtic is the pro-Catholic team. Rangers are "closely tied to the Unionist majority of Northern Ireland, whose livelihood was strongly associated with the shipyard industries of Belfast and Glasgow," according to Richard Giulianotti. "Celtic were founded in Glasgow's east end . . . as a benevolent club for poor Irish Catholics immigrants. It soon became a symbol of sporting and cultural success of the disadvantaged minority."[50] If Catholic–anti-Catholic sentiments define Scottish soccer at its highest level, you need only imagine what goes on in Ireland! Fortunately, religion and soccer do not *always* mix in conflictual ways. Giulianotti also reports a belief held by some Greenland Inuit people that the "northern lights" (aurora borealis) appears when the spirits of the dead play soccer.[51]

One of my favorite movies is all about how soccer can be used to construct an identity among oppressed peoples. It is *The Cup*, a 1999 film by Khyentse Norbu, a Bhutanese writer and director.[52] It was filmed in Nepal. All of the dialogue is in Tibetan (with subtitles, of course). It was the first Bhutanese film ever to be nominated for an Academy Award. It is the story of Tibetan refugee children who are smuggled into a monastery in Nepal. Separated from their families and friends, some of the boys get it in their heads that they need to watch the 1998 World Cup being played in France so that they can root for the French team (lead by Zinedine Zidane). Why? Because France is the only country that recognizes Tibet as a sovereign nation. A victory by France is, in their minds, a victory of their own and validation of their identities as Tibetans. The movie is the tale of how they found a way to watch the game and what, if anything, France's actual victory meant to them.

Soccer's ability to help nations and individuals construct their own identities is a very hopeful sign. We hear constantly that globalization destroys local culture, replacing it with the meaningless consumption culture of the American suburb, and if soccer is part of the globalization process, you'd expect it to do the same. But if soccer also builds distinct local identities, then it is also a force opposed to homogenization and commodification.

Thus, for example, when the great Diego Maradona left to play in Europe, one effect of his transfer was to actually strengthen the identity of the fans of his Argentine club, Boca Juniors. As far as the fans were concerned, or at least some of them, he was still their Boca player and his successes and failures were theirs as well as his. To the extent that this effect holds more generally, and I don't think that it can be as true for most exported players as it was for a famous player like Maradona, then I think the net effect of soccer globalization may be to strengthen local identity in opposition to whatever global forces may be weakening it.

That said, I also think that the relationship between global economics and local culture is a like a mousetrap, delicate and dangerous. I find it difficult to be confident about causes and effects, even when operating within a relatively simple framework such as soccer globalization. I'd like to say that global soccer strengthens local identity, but I worry that it just isn't so.

The economic tension between the professional clubs and the national teams seems to make this problem even worse. Players are paid by their clubs, of course, who are expected to release players for international competition (World Cup qualification games, for example) during league seasons. The clubs and their leagues are creatures of FIFA, the sanctioning body that organizes these competitions, so their cooperation is expected. But FIFA's interests and the interests of a club are often at odds when, say, an important league match coincides with an international game. The players are often caught in the middle between their clubs and fans in the super-leagues and their national teams and fans back home—a difficult situation either way. Some European-based players declined to join their national teams for the 2004 African Cup competition, for example, actions that caused many reactions—none of them good—in the home countries and teams.[53]

If you want to see the power of soccer to define local communities but also perhaps to destroy them, come to Buenos Aires. A city of twelve million, Buenos Aires is home to literally dozens of professional soccer clubs. Thirty-six clubs, each with its own stadium, are found in the city proper, and the suburbs are home to another thirty-seven clubs (with thirty-seven stadiums).[54] Taken together, the seventy-three teams divide up the territory and population into large and small pockets of soccer identity. If local identity is an asset, then Buenos Aires fans are perhaps the wealthiest soccer fans on earth, wealthier even than the residents of London, who have twelve professional teams from the top three divisions to choose from, not counting teams from the outlying suburbs.

The sad fact of this is, however, that a population that could support three or four teams adequately in this winner-take-all world is spread too thin. Each club has its own stadium, so none of them are very good facilities (none of them would meet the standards for a World Cup match, for example). Many of the stadia are shoddy, some dangerous. Most of the clubs are financial basket cases, a fact partly due to their organizational structure: Argentine clubs are really clubs, which sponsor youth teams, women's teams, and teams in other sports such as basketball. Fans join and pay monthly dues, which give them the right to attend home matches for free. (This practice is not uncommon in Europe, which accounts for the low gate receipts they receive.)

The logical thing for the Buenos Aires clubs to do would be to consolidate, share facilities, share costs, and in this way evolve into an economically sustainable structure. But such changes—even sharing a stadium—are intolerable ideas because they challenge what it means to be a local club member. They threaten the identity that these soccer teams have helped their fans and supporters create. They would rather that the stadium be a shambles and the best players quickly sold than compromise the identity of the team.

In winner-take-all markets like soccer has become, team loyalty fragments the market and may doom the very clubs with which the fans identify. Or, if not doom them exactly, keep them firmly in the economic periphery of the game, despite their place at the core of the game of soccer itself.

The American Exception

Globalization is seldom really global. Africa, for the most part, was left out and left behind in the hot money investment-fueled, technology-driven rush to profit from economic globalization. It is the huge hole in the globalization ozone. If we look at globalization through soccer, however, Africa is right in there, and it is growing in significance (the 2010 World Cup will be played in South Africa). But the United States is missing. It is the "Africa" of soccer globalization.

This is not a trivial fact. There is a lot of money behind professional soccer, lots of commercial interests and media stakes. In the super-leagues, soccer has been thoroughly commercialized and tailored to a high-end consumer market. All these factors are supposed to be ones that distinctly appeal to Americans—that define Americanization, in fact. So what gives? Why the American exception?[55]

Before I try to answer this question, let me remind you what is at stake. Globalization-Americanization is supposed to be an unstoppable force, but if Americans, who are most comfortable in this environment, and presumably most susceptible to it, are immune in this case, then perhaps other people in other countries may be immune as well. That is, perhaps the idea that globalization-Americanization is inevitable is, you guessed it, globaloney. Briefly, here are five ways to try to explain the American exception to soccer globalism.

Explanation One: There is no American exception. Soccer has been thoroughly embraced by America and Americans (even if most of them could not pick David Beckham out of a lineup). Soccer is, indeed, the most played sport in America. More school-age Americans play soccer than baseball, football, or anything else. But whereas young people who play baseball in school tend to follow the professional teams as spectator or fan (and many who do not play do also), young people who play soccer grow up, for the most part, to be followers of other sports. Soccer is a game to be played by the young in the United States, not an adult spectator sport (apart from the ubiquitous soccer moms and dads who loyally attend their children's games). Americans seem to identify with soccer as participants, not observers. This answer has accuracy in its favor—soccer really is number one—but it really raises more questions about why this is so than it answers.

Explanation Two: Soccer is not currently a major American sport, but it will be. And soon. Nike will see to it! This answer returns to the Nike theory of globalization—anything that Nike and the media moguls want, they can get. The argument runs like this. Nike intended that basketball, Michael Jordan, and the new global capitalism would sweep (or maybe "swoosh" is a better verb) the world, starting from the United States and expanding steadily outward. But they did not take into account the strength of soccer, which steadfastly held onto its position as the world's number one sport. So, it is argued, Nike decided to reverse its strategy. It signed major soccer stars and teams to lucrative contracts and then set about both conquering the soccer world and extending that domain to include the United States. Having failed to conquer the world with basketball, Nike aims now to conquer the United States with soccer—an inside-out conquest.

Any argument set in the future is impossible to prove or disprove, but Nike certainly seems to be taking soccer seriously. One building on the Nike corporate headquarters campus is named for Michael Jordan, but another honors Mia Hamm, the best U.S. female soccer player. Nike has indeed vigorously entered the world soccer market, signing its share of the super-teams and super-players in the super-leagues. It does have competition in this, however, from companies with longer histories in soccer such as Adidas, Umbro, Puma, Lotto, and Kappa. So Nike's success abroad, although likely, is not assured.

It is also clear that Nike is trying to build a U.S. market for soccer. In summer 2003, for example, it sponsored a U.S. tour by Manchester United, its most famous team, which played a series of matches around the country against other super-league teams. (The tour was repeated and even expanded in 2004.) Several stadiums set attendance records, an indication of the power of the best to attract an audience for a one-off event even in an otherwise unpromising market. More significant, to my mind, was what went on at the Nike campus in Beaverton, Oregon. Elite youth teams from around the country and around the world came to rub shoulders with the "swoosh"-emblazoned Manchester United players, to train and to play in tournament games. The top-down strategy of the touring super-teams was matched by a bottom-up strategy to develop American players who can attract American fans.

Explanation Three: The third explanation for the American exception suggests why Nike's initiative might work where previous attempts to inject soccer into the American sports culture have failed. Answer three is taken from a book called *Offside: Soccer & American Exceptionalism*, which was written by a politics professor (Andrei S. Markovits) and a former sports journalist turned political economy student (Steven L. Hellerman).[56] Markovits and Hellerman explain that there have been several attempts to introduce professional soccer in America and all have failed, at least so far. One reason they cite for the failure (there are many) is that soccer has generally been presented as a foreign sport and professional leagues, at least at the beginning, have relied upon foreign players. This strategy was effective in attracting an immediate audience of immigrants from soccer-playing countries and some well-educated Americans who sought status and elevated self-esteem by identifying with an international sport (that would be me, I suppose). But a focus upon foreign players to appeal to immigrant fans did little or nothing to develop a distinctly American constituency for the game. The teams and leagues just died away.

My personal experience as a fan of North American Soccer League (NASL) and Major Indoor Soccer League (MISL) soccer teams in the Pacific Northwest bears out this point. I remember the 1977 NASL championship game between the Cosmos, with Pelé and a squad of mainly aging European internationals, and the Seattle Sounders, which featured a number of players from the 1966 England World Cup squad. Each team had a several American players besides the "internationals," but the fans clearly came to see the exceptional skills of the foreign players, even if they were a little past their prime. The NASL folded relatively quickly, despite substantial financial backing, in part I think because the fans identified with the foreign players, who inevitably had to move on or out, not with their "home" teams themselves. How many fans came to see a Cosmos game? How many came just to be able to say that they had seen Pelé play?

Perhaps because the Pacific Northwest is soccer-mad, at least compared to the rest of the United States, interest remained after the Sounders faded away with the rest of their league. Indoor soccer (soccer played, basically, on an Astroturfed hockey rink) caught on, at least for a while, and I attended the finals series between the Tacoma Stars and the Dallas Sidekicks. There were many more American players on these teams, but the stars were still foreigners. Steve Zungul, from Yugoslavia, was the most famous and productive player in the league, followed by another young Yugoslav named Preki. (Preki later acquired U.S. citizenship and played on U.S. World Cup teams.) Only one player on the top ten all-time MISL points scorers (Dale Mitchell of Tacoma) was American, for example.

If you want an audience to embrace a sport as their own, it seems that the worst way to do this is to present it as a foreign game played by foreigners, yet this is what soccer promoters did in the United States until very recently. It is interesting how careful the National Basketball Association (NBA) has been about this as more and more non-U.S. players have arrived in the league. The NBA calls them international, not foreign, players (at least in that part of their publicity focused on the U.S. audience). But there are other problems. The structural organization of soccer is, in many respects, foreign to America audiences. Most American professional sports leagues are organized in a very simple way. Teams play each other within roughly geographical divisions (designed to minimize travel costs) to determine a play-off field. Several play-off rounds determine a league titlist. The more games a team plays, the more money it earns, which exacerbates the "winner-take-all" element of the business.

Soccer in other countries has a much more complex structure. Most soccer countries have a multiple hierarchy of leagues (in Italy the leagues are A, B, C1, C2, etc.). Teams compete to be at the top of their leagues, of course, but there is also interest at the bottom because the worst teams in league A, for example, are relegated to league B and replaced by the best teams from league B, with similar movements from leagues B to C1, C1 to C2, and so forth. So there is something at stake in games at both ends of the league table, which of course gives all of the games more meaning. Good teams want to advance and be promoted; bad teams try to avoid relegation. In theory it is possible for a team from a lowly C2 league town to advance via several excellent seasons to one of the super-leagues. This actually happened in Italy in the 1990s, a story that was documented by Joe McGinnis in *The Miracle of Castel di Sangro*.[57]

Teams in the middle may also compete for positions in international competitions, giving their fans a reason to care. In Italy, for example, the very top teams qualify for the Champions League competitions, but others who finish in the top half of the league table may enter the UEFA Cup competition or earn the right to compete with teams from other countries for a spot in these competitions.

Each soccer nation also features a national cup competition that includes teams from several of the national leagues, providing a C1 team the opportunity, in theory at least, to play an A team and win a major trophy (and a place in the next year's international competitions). The result of this is that fans of most teams always have something to hope for or to fear with each game. In a given week a team may play one league match plus an international or national cup game, and in general competition proceeds on several different levels at once. This system is confusing to the outsider and represents another "foreign" barrier to American acceptance.

If Markovits and Hellerman are right, then the current Nike strategy is trying to have it both ways—to get attention through international super-teams and star players while also developing a distinctive American soccer identity. Perhaps it will work. But maybe it is too late.

Explanation Four: Markovits and Hellerman are optimistic about the chances of soccer finally catching on in America (see answer five below), but the timing is bad, they say. They note that the major spectator sports cultures around the world emerged during the period of the 1890s through the 1930s. This was the period when the urban middle class emerged in the industrial democracies and when the "space" of sports culture was created and filled. In the United States, they argue, this space was occupied by "the big three and a half" sports—baseball, basketball, American football, and, to a certain extent, ice hockey. Together these sports spanned the four seasons and provided a year-round outlet for the sports consumers' interest, enthusiasm, loyalty, and money. It is very difficult, they argue, for new sports to invade this space either in the United States or elsewhere around the world. What about basketball, you might ask (thinking about the theory that Michael Jordan and Nike have created a world hoops culture)? It was already there, as we learned in the last chapter, thanks to YMCA missionaries. What about baseball in Japan? It was introduced in the 1940s and 1950s. Yes, but it was introduced through the forces of U.S. military occupation, which perhaps indicates how unusual the circumstances must be for a new sport to enter the arena.

Why didn't soccer take a place in the U.S. sports space a hundred years ago? Markovits and Hellerman suggest that it could have done so, but didn't. The "foreign" element worked against it, of course, but there is a better reason. American football emerged during this period instead. Elite colleges in the Northeast began to play a form of soccer in the nineteenth century, but it was the rough rugby-type game that was popular in England. It could have developed either way—into the Beautiful Game of association football or into the more violent game of rugby. Harvard seems to have been the key here. Just when it looked like Harvard would adopt rules like those in soccer today, the team played a series with McGill University in Canada, which played the rugby-style game. The team preferred this approach and published rules that evolved into American football. Ironically, American football, like "American" basketball, owes its emergence to Canadian influence. Professional football leagues eventually developed, building on but not replacing the college game, and the space that could have been occupied by soccer in the United States was filled instead by American football.

Explanation Five: Is it too late for soccer in America? Answer five is: maybe not. Markovits and Hellerman are optimistic that soccer can succeed as an important spectator sport this time around by developing a homegrown product and finding ways to span the gaps between youth, college, and professional strata. They are hopeful that current attempts to develop domestic soccer leagues that feature and develop American talent will be successful. A new professional league structure was launched in the mid-1990s, shortly after the successful U.S. World Cup. Major League Soccer (MLS) is the top U.S. league with ten teams at this writing (New York/New Jersey; Columbus; Chicago; New England; Washington, D.C.; San Jose; Dallas; Los Angeles; Colorado; and Kansas City), all owned by the league itself, which limits competition for player rights as a way of controlling costs. It will begin its eighth season in 2004. Just below the MLS is the A-League, with sixteen teams, in Calgary, Edmonton, Vancouver, Seattle, Portland, Milwaukee, Minnesota, Atlanta, Charleston, Montreal, Puerto Rico, Richmond, Rochester, Syracuse, Toronto, and Virginia Beach. Several lower layers of developmental leagues also exist. Taken together MLS and A-League include many cities with relatively strong local soccer traditions (former NASL cities such as Seattle, Portland, and Dallas), strong college soccer traditions, or relatively high foreign or international fan bases. (Virginia Beach has a large military-related population, for example, and San Jose's potential fans include both Hispanics and people from many nations attracted to nearby Silicon Valley.) Competition with the MLS and A-League is strictly American-style: no relegation and promotion.

If it is to be successful, the MLS must master several delicate balances. One goal is to develop American players and create a following for an American game, but foreign players are useful both on the field and to attract fans. Teams are therefore limited to three senior international players and must include some American developmental players on their rosters. Salaries are controlled by the league (so many of the best players leave the U.S. to play in the European super-leagues). Audiences have been slow to build, but the MLS does now have an ABC/ESPN television contract, which is a positive sign.

The future of the MLS is perhaps best represented by Freddy Adu, who was fourteen years old when signed by D.C. United to the highest contract in MLS history. Born in Ghana, Adu migrated to the United States with his parents, the happy winners of a green card lottery. He became a U.S. citizen in February 2003 and quickly became the star of the U.S. Under-17 team and, in November, a member of D.C. United. Interestingly, Adu did not play organized soccer in Ghana, it seems. Classmates in Virginia were impressed by his schoolyard skills and talked him into joining their local team.

Adu will likely be a star on the U.S. national team in a few years, and the MLS has made a commitment to pay enough to keep him out of the European super-leagues, at least for a while (Inter of Milan was also interested). I think MLS would like Adu to become the Michael Jordan of American soccer (or perhaps its Tiger Woods) and to use him to raise the league from the periphery of American sports culture into its core. This will be a delicate undertaking, however. It remains to be seen if economic imbalances can be avoided and if the foreign versus American versus "international" issues can be dealt with successfully. Perhaps Markovits and Hellerman are right: the time is ripe and the MLS can avoid the problems that have doomed earlier attempts.

But I have my doubts. People thought that the 1994 World Cup, which was played in the United States, would give this process a jump start, and it did not. And then there is the core–periphery factor. If the new American leagues are indeed successful in developing local talent, it seems inevitable that they will be swept away into the super-leagues, depriving the U.S. teams of their feature players.

Perhaps, however, there is hope—for women's soccer. The U.S. women's soccer team competes at the highest level internationally, a statement that cannot be made about the men's side. There are professional women's leagues in other parts of the world, but they have not yet formed anything like a global winner-take-all market. Perhaps the United States could embrace women's soccer and be the center of the professional women's game? Perhaps, but that would require a greater change in U.S. sports culture than just accepting a foreign game with foreign players. It would require U.S. society to accept female athletes on the same terms as it does males. That may be a challenge even greater than globalization.

Sports Globaloney

What have we learned by looking at globalization through the case studies of basketball and soccer? Answering this question is necessarily an exercise in globaloney, if only because any attempt to generalize from just two examples is an obvious distortion of the truth. That said, here goes.

Although both sports are *global* in the sense that the term is commonly used, there seem to be as many differences as similarities in the globalization stories they tell. Globalization theories should not be one-size-fits-all because globalization itself is highly variable.

History matters. The shape of global soccer and global basketball today was determined, to some extent, by century-old events and processes. Globalization is path dependent, to use some economics jargon; where you are depends upon where you've been. If the past had been different (if Harvard had rejected McGill's rules or if volleyball had been invented before basketball in the Springfield gym), the present would be different too. There is no single line of globalization.

It is commonplace to assume that globalization is Americanization, but neither of these examples seems to support that notion very well. I am not saying that America or Americanization is not a factor in globalization, but rather that there is more to it than that and some globalization may be unrelated to Americanization or even antithetical to it.

To the extent that globalization creates winner-take-all markets, it is a real problem. It is very difficult to take an optimistic view of the effects of winner-take-all markets in either sport. These markets do not seem to be beneficial to the players, the teams, or the fans who support them (aside from the winners who take all, Michael Jordan and David Beckham). Not all global markets are winner-take-all markets, however, which suggests that globalization's effects will vary.

Resistance to globalization is certainly possible. It is too early to conclude that the new global capitalism will simply mow down any opposition. There is no better example of successful opposition than the United States. Local cultures can assimilate global influences and construct distinctly local identities from them.

So there is reason to be hopeful about globalization based upon this exercise in globaloney. Yet I do find it hard to be very hopeful because of what we saw in Buenos Aires. There the strong local soccer cultures—successful resistance!—fragmented the sports market, making teams too small to compete. Fan loyalty crippled their teams in the winner-take-all markets. Strong resistance, in this case, seemed to doom economically the local identity that it was trying to preserve.

* * *

Sports metaphors are powerful rhetorical tools, which is why they are used and abused so frequently. But no image in the globalization debate has more clout than that of a humble hamburger. The Big Mac: is it globalization or just globaloney? It's time to examine closely the McDonaldization of the world.

GLOBALIZATION AS McWORLD

Who invented globalization? The way you answer this question depends on how you think about globalization. If you think of globalization literally you might answer "Christopher Columbus" or someone else from the great era of (European) discovery. If you want to know who "invented" the world as a single geographic unit, all connected to the European center, there are several names you might give, but Columbus is as good as any of them.

If you think of globalization as the *idea* of an economic process that unites and transforms the world, creating a single global system, the inventors' names are Karl Marx and Friedrich Engels. They said it all in *The Communist Manifesto*, first published in that great year of revolutions, 1848. The bourgeoisie, Marx and Engels wrote,

> has through its exploitation of the world market given a cosmopolitan
> character to production and consumption in every country. . . . In place
> of the old wants, satisfied by the productions of the country, we find
> new wants, requiring for their satisfaction the products of distant lands
> and climes. In place of the old local and national seclusion and self-
> sufficiency, we have intercourse in every direction, universal interde-

121

pendence of nations. And as in material, so also in intellectual production. The intellectual creations of individual nations become common property. National one-sidedness and narrow-mindedness become more and more impossible, and from the numerous national and local literatures, there arises a world literature.[1]

Marx and Engels were writing about capitalism, of course, but they were really describing globalization in this passage. Like many visions of globalization, theirs was rooted in technology. The bourgeoisie, which we may think of as the masters of globalization, "by the rapid improvement of all instruments of production, by the immensely facilitated means of communication, draws all nations, even the most barbarian, into civilization."[2] Resistance is futile; globalization "compels all nations, on pain of extinction, to adopt the bourgeois mode of production; it compels them to introduce what it calls civilization into their midst, i.e., to become bourgeois themselves. In a word, it creates a world after its own image."[3]

Marx and Engels provide us with an analysis of the process of economic globalization that might have been written yesterday. Indeed, someone somewhere probably did write it yesterday, or something much like it, totally unaware of Marx's prior claim to the idea.

Marx wrote about globalization, but he didn't call it that. The term *globalization* (or *globalisation* if you are British) seems to have come into use in the 1960s, according to the *Oxford English Dictionary*. Many people credit the Harvard political economist Raymond Vernon for inventing the concept, even if he did not actually coin the term. Vernon was famous for two things. The first was his path-breaking research on multinational corporations from the 1970s to the 1990s, which made him the "father of globalization," according to Daniel Yergin.[4] His second great achievement? The Peanut M&M, which he brought to market in the 1950s while working for the Mars candy company.

There is one product that is so closely associated with globalization that it has become a symbol for the process that Columbus got started, Marx and Engels described, and Raymond Vernon studied. According to popular accounts, globalization was invented, more or less, by two brothers named Richard and Maurice when they opened a tiny drive-through restaurant in Pasadena, California, in 1937 and named it after themselves. Surely you have heard of "Richard and Maurice's"? No? Of course not; why choose an awkward name like that when your last name is McDonald. Perhaps you've heard of that? In 1940 they opened a larger operation—600 square feet!—in San Bernardino.[5]

The McDonald brothers did not invent hamburgers. In fact, their first store didn't even sell hamburgers—hot dogs and milkshakes were its specialties. Burgers were introduced in San Bernardino, but the Mc-Donald's innovation wasn't putting meat on a bun, it was turning bread and meat into dough—profits, that is. Drive-in restaurants like McDon-ald's were caught in a profit pinch, selling low-priced food using tradi-tional methods, which were labor-intensive and expensive. The brothers' contribution to globalization was their decision to rationalize the food production process. They stripped down their twenty-five-item menu to its core—hamburgers accounted for 80 percent of their sales—even though this meant dismantling their authentic hickory-fired pit barbeque. They closed shop for three months in 1948 and re-modeled the whole operation to be fast and efficient. Eventually the McDonalds designed new types of kitchen equipment for their maximum-efficiency operations.

McDonald's reopened with a product that was cheap but standard-ized. The old 30-cent burger now sold for half that amount, but it came just one way. "If we gave people a choice there would be chaos," Rich-ard McDonald said.[6] They were not an immediate hit, but eventually speed, consistency, and low price found a market.

The secret to the McDonalds' success was their mastery of Adam Smith's famous division of labor. In a traditional drive-in restaurant, one or two chefs might make the food from start to finish and some-times they would serve customers, too. The McDonald's system applied the division of labor: three countermen took orders at two windows and issued orders to the production crew: three grill men, two shake men, two fry men, and "dressers" who assembled and added condi-ments to the hamburgers. They could take and fill an order in 30 sec-onds—or less.[7]

Today McDonald's is a multinational corporation that operates 30,000 restaurants in 119 countries that serve 47 million customers each day. Its flagship product, the Big Mac, is so nearly universal that the *Economist* magazine uses it to calculate the relative purchasing power of foreign currencies.[8] Some people love McDonald's, and others hate it. In the 1990s McDonald's became the defining symbol of global-ization—the Golden Arches that "provoked" José Bové to violence. No McDonald's store is a safe harbor during an antiglobalization protest.

McDonald's place in the center of the globalization debate is due mainly to the work of three men: Thomas Friedman, Benjamin Barber, and George Ritzer. All three use McDonald's and its ubiquitous Golden

Arches as an icon or metaphor for the transformative force of contemporary globalization. Two of their versions of globalization-McDonaldization are globaloney pure and simple. One offers real insight into what globalization is today and where it may be headed. None of the three tells the whole story.

Golden Arches: The Good Globalization

New York Times columnist Thomas L. Friedman is a globalization optimist who uses McDonald's to motivate a hopeful American vision of globalization past, present, and future. Friedman's idea of McDonald's and globalization is a distinctly American view, one that only an American who constantly travels abroad might naturally develop. McDonald's appears with nearly numbing regularity in Friedman's book *The Lexus and the Olive Tree* (as it does in many books on globalization). The entry for McDonald's in the index looks like this:

> McDonald's, ix, 9, 169, 248–254, 258, 263, 268, 271, 274, 292, 294, 296, 301, 303, 305, 311–13, 344, 358, 374, 379, 382–84, 464 [9]

Why so much McDonald's? Probably because it is such a useful rhetorical device—McDonald's is an instantly recognizable symbol of America to Friedman's readers, who are mainly Americans living in America. Frame a foreign problem in terms of McDonald's and your audience connects the dots immediately. But it is probably also true that Friedman, like many Americans who spend months and months abroad, is always looking for reminders of home. And since his home is the United States, his eyes search for branded goods, which are the way Americans think of things: not hamburgers, Big Macs. Not beer, Budweiser. Not soft drinks, Coca Cola. And McDonald's has more than thirty thousand locations that display their trademark logos and designs, of which more than seventeen thousand are located outside the United States.

McDonald's is easy to spot—the company goes out of its way to be visible. And it is almost everywhere. McDonald's says that in 2002 its global restaurant system was arrayed across the world map as follows: United States, 13,491; Europe, 6,070; APMEA (Asia-Pacific, Middle East, and Africa), 7,555; Latin America, 1,605; and Canada, 1,304. The top five countries, ranked by numbers of stores, were the United States, Japan, Canada, the United Kingdom, and Germany.[10] So it is easy to understand why Thomas Friedman so often sees the Golden Arches in his travels and has a quiet little "globalization moment."

Looking at the world and seeing Golden Arches is a distinctly American kind of vision. It's not obvious that other people see globalization the same way. Imagine for a moment an Italian version of Thomas Friedman—call him Tomaso. For Tomaso, McDonald's restaurants are all but invisible. They are everywhere, you run into them all the time on the way to the airport, but they disappear into the visual noise of the background. They are unimportant because they are not what Tomaso is looking for, which is decent Italian food. Tomaso is looking for signs of home—good Italian restaurants—and he sees them everywhere. They are even more ubiquitous, if that's grammatically possible, than McDonald's. According to the Italian culinary magazine *Gambero Rosso*, there are about twice as many reasonably authentic Italian restaurants *outside of Italy* as there are McDonald's restaurants *in all the world*, including the United States.[11] So it's not hard to see them if that's what you are looking for.

Gambero Rosso estimates that there are about 15,000 decent Italian restaurants in the United States and Canada, which is about the number of McDonald's you will find there. Japan has more than 3,500 McDonald's and only about 2,000 Italian restaurants (both numbers insignificant, of course, compared to the number of Japanese food shops there). *Gambero Rosso* puts the number of Italian restaurants in Latin America at 7,000, in Africa at 1,000, 300 in the Middle East, and more than 28,000 in the European Union and Eastern Europe. McDonald's numbers are much less in each of these regions and especially in Africa, where McDonald's is all but unknown (except via satellite television commercials).

Except in Japan, Italian restaurants seem to be far more common than McDonald's stores. Surely you have seen Italian restaurants wherever you have traveled in the world? Yes, but you have not taken account of them the way that Tomaso Friedman would. Why is that? Branding is part of the story. McDonald's stores all have the same name, use versions of the same trademarked logo, and serve somewhat similar food items, so it is easy to use them to connect the dots that form a global pattern. McDonald's franchises are everywhere—must be globalization. But Italian restaurants have a stronger claim to globalization, even though their visual variety makes them blend into the background to American eyes. If Tomaso Friedman were writing a book about globalization, he would be having tagliatelle al ragù moments (not Big Mac attacks) and seeing Italian influences everywhere. It would be a different book, but it would be just as valid as Thomas Friedman's.[12]

Tommy Friedman's book (Tommy is British) would be filled with examples of British influence abroad, and he would have no trouble finding it, let me tell you. The legacy of Britain's global empire guarantees that Tommy would constantly encounter familiar people, places, and things, including the food. He'd run into Britain's signature fast food everywhere he went and build clever global metaphors from the experience. Do you doubt it? No, I am not thinking of fish and chips or bangers and mash or bubble and squeak, as you might assume. Britain's fast food of choice is "curry"—Indian food. Curry is the most popular food in Britain. Britain has taken Indian curry to its heart much as Americans have adopted hamburgers and hotdogs (frankfurters)—food with Germanic origins that are obvious to anyone who thinks even for a moment about their names (Hamburg, Frankfurt). The global Indian diaspora practically guarantees that Tommy Friedman would be able to find a familiar plate of chicken tikka masala nearly everywhere he goes.

For my money, Tao Friedman would write the most interesting book. Tao is Chinese, and I probably do not have to persuade you that she would be able to find familiar home-style dishes wherever she goes and the experience would raise important questions for Tao about Chinese influence abroad and about globalization's effect on China. Are traditional recipes and preparations preserved in foreign Chinese restaurants, or are they adapted to local tastes and ingredients? Is "authenticity" preserved? Are culinary norms maintained—or are they lost forever as regional Chinese cuisine is melded into international "fusion" foods? Tao Friedman is a fictional invention, but there are real scholars who study these questions and publish volumes with titles like *The Globalization of Chinese Food*.[13]

Thomas, Tomaso, Tommy, and Tao constantly encounter images of home as they travel the world, and they associate them with their particular visions of globalization. Their reactions to what they find are likely to differ, however, because, although they see the same world, they process the images through different cultural filters, which yield predictably different conclusions. Thomas assumes that the fast food he finds abroad is the same as at home and takes comfort from that.[14] But he's wrong. In fact, McDonald's menus are not all the same, although they tend to be as similar as local markets will allow. McDonald's tries to have each location carry some of the "classic" American items, but please remember that McDonald's really isn't about particular foods, although that's what the branding process leads you to believe. What made the original McDonald's distinctive was price and efficiency, and this is still true today.

McDonald's must compete with local retailers wherever it operates (and with local Italian, Indian, and Chinese restaurants), so its restaurants necessarily adapt to local tastes in terms of food recipes and preparations—only the efficiency remains the same. After trying and failing to sell all-beef burgers in India, a country where the majority of the population considers cows sacred, McDonald's now has a 100 percent vegetarian menu in Hindu regions, featuring items such as Pizza Mc-Puff, the McAloo Tikki spiced potato sandwich, Paneer (Indian cheese) Salsa McWrap, and McCurry.[15] Because Chinese food is popular in India, there is even a vegetarian Crispy Chinese burger. McDonald's menus in most other countries have not adapted to local taste to quite this degree, but all show the combined influence of local preferences and competition from local restaurants that know those preferences well. Interestingly, some Indian items have been earmarked for introduction in China, Hong Kong, Great Britain, and the United States.[16] That's globalization, I guess.

The world has become a culturally complex space, both in terms of food and more generally. As Tyler Cowen has noted, as local areas become more diverse (with more kinds of ethnic foods, for example), the discontinuities between places fade and the world as a whole feels less diverse.[17] What each of us makes of this depends on how we approach it. People who love America will see it and smile. People who hate America will see it and scowl. People who look for Italy or India or China will find them, too. Thomas Friedman's perspective, with McDonald's everywhere, is that of an American looking for America and finding it.

This is what makes Thomas Friedman's version of McWorld a globaloney theory. It presents as universal a view of the world that is strictly American, using American symbols to tell an American story. I call it The Good Globalization because it is an optimistic viewpoint. Friedman can at least appreciate why people would be happy to embrace the image of McDonald's and globalization that he creates.

McWorld: Globalization Gone Bad

McWorld is perhaps the most powerful image of globalization yet conceived. Significantly, it is a very negative image. Thomas Friedman's optimism aside, McDonald's has an image problem. If you want to express your informed disrespect for anything that the masses seem to enjoy, the best way is to make it a Mc, as in McMansions (suburban housing), McDoctors (HMO health-care providers), McWine (wine that lacks distinctive character), and volumes like this one (McBooks). Mass-produced, interchangeable, undistinguished—crap—that's what a Mc-prefix says.

So you don't need much imagination to guess that McWorld is a description of globalization gone bad. Benjamin R. Barber invented McWorld in a 1992 *Atlantic Monthly* article titled "Jihad vs. McWorld."[18] The article inspired a 1995 book, also called *Jihad vs. McWorld*, with the subtitle, "How the World Is Both Falling Apart and Coming To-gether—And What This Means for Democracy." A paperback edition appeared in 1996 with a different subtitle, "How Globalism and Tribal-ism Are Re-shaping the World," and a revised volume was released in 2002, subtitled "Terrorism's Challenge to Democracy."[19] McWorld is a flexible concept, apparently, equally relevant to the collapse of commu-nism in 1995, the rise of ethnic violence in 1996, and terrorism after September 11, 2001.

I fear that Barber's McWorld has become a McIdea—an undistin-guished product cynically crafted to appeal to an undiscriminating mass-market audience, which is a shame. The migration of titles gives it away: Barber's publisher seems to be trying to sell the book by appeal-ing to the market's "fear du jour"—tribalism, terrorism, whatever. Bar-ber's core *argument* is not crap, however, and it is worthwhile to separate the two and appreciate their differences.

Barber believes that globalization is a threat to democracy, which is a legitimate concern (the book's title should be *Globalization versus Democracy*, not *Jihad vs. McWorld*). The argument is that globalization twists the world in two ways at once. On one side it bends the world toward markets and business, which tend to organize along certain lines, guided by the ideology of globalism. This is McWorld, an America-centered, media-driven version of global capitalism. I don't even have to tell you what McWorld looks like—it is McDonald's and the culture, media, technology, and values that critics associate with it.

At the same time the world is twisting toward McWorld, however, it is also turning toward Jihad. Globalization magnifies ethnic, religious, and racial divisions, producing Jihad. Jihad is not literally an Islamic holy war in Barber's lexicon any more than McWorld is literally the global McDonald's empire. Barber doesn't intend to pick on Muslims when talking about "Jihad," and he is very careful in this regard in the book's text. Unfortunately the regrettable image of an apparently Muslim woman in full head-scarf holding a Pepsi can on the cover strongly reinforces at every glance the very Islamic Jihad connection that Barber says he wants to avoid.[20] Jihad, properly understood in Barber's argument, is the reaction to or retreat from globalization and back toward the security of tradition, religion, and tribe or nation.

Now the problem, Barber says, is that both Jihad and McWorld are essentially undemocratic and perhaps even antidemocratic. Therefore this global torsion is a threat to democracy. Jihad places tradition or religious teachings ahead of popular opinion and legitimizes autocratic rule. Hard to grow democracy on that rocky field. McWorld privileges money over people, replacing one-person, one-vote with one-dollar, one-vote. As neoliberal policies shrink the state and market forces expand, democracy becomes at best a meaningless ritual and potentially a threat to global competition. If the world disintegrates into Jihad and McWorld, Barber asks, what chance is there for democracy?

The future of democracy in a globalized world is a very important question, although I must point out that is a distinctly American question. Worship of democracy is America's civil religion—we are raised from the ground up to view the United States as a nation built upon democratic principles and to honor the Founding Fathers who symbolize a commitment to democratic ideals. A European might ask a different question, such as whether Jihad and McWorld are consistent with peace, not democracy. Americans, I believe, simply assume that democracy produces peace. Europeans worry that it might not. Others might be concerned with inequality, economic development, or environmental sustainability—there are many critical values potentially threatened by globalization. To privilege democracy in the pantheon of principles is not unreasonable, and I would probably do it myself, but we must recognize that it is a distinctly American thing to do.

Benjamin Barber is someone who takes democracy seriously. No wonder he is worried about it. Jihad and McWorld are not the only threats to democracy, however, nor perhaps even the most important threats. Jihad and McWorld are sexy concepts that quickly focus our attention on democracy and its discontents, and I think that's why Barber wrote the original *Atlantic Monthly* article. In a world where people don't worry very much about democracy, Jihad and McWorld made a lot of people think about it more seriously, which is a good thing. The book that packages the argument is another matter. In order to gather sympathy and support for democracy, Barber seems to try to make McWorld and globalization as evil as possible—a force that doesn't just destroy democracy, but everything else of value in modern and traditional societies, too. This is where the globaloney comes in.

If you read it uncritically, *Jihad vs. McWorld* is very persuasive—nearly as persuasive as Adam Smith's argument in the first chapter of *The Wealth of Nations*. Like Smith, Barber uses the "Newtonian" principle of the New Rhetoric—he states a grand principle, provides a few memorable and well-chosen examples, then leaps to a universal conclusion. The readers, you and me, are pleased to connect the dots. Soon we see examples of the argument all around us and we notice that they fit the rule even as we ignore everything that breaks it. Thus does unscientific observation make believers of us all.

Democracy has lots of problems, as I have said, and the globalization of the infotainment telesector is probably one of them, but not the only one or perhaps even the most important one. And many people (ask Thomas Friedman) think that markets might even promote democracy by undermining undemocratic authority. So I am suspicious that the threat to democracy is as simple as this or that saving it is just a matter of stopping globalization.

One of the best ways to understand why McWorld is more about globaloney than globalization is to look at what it has to say about its most representative component: McDonald's. McWorld is named for McDonald's, of course, and the Golden Arches show up almost as regularly in *Jihad vs. McWorld* as in *The Lexus and the Olive Tree*.[21] Here's the story, pieced together from Barber's book.

- McDonald's (and McWorld) stands astride the globe like a Colossus, more powerful than modern nation-states. "McDonald's serves 20 million customers around the world every day," Barber tells us, "drawing more customers daily than there are people in Greece, Ireland and Switzerland together."[22]
- McDonald's ideology is more powerful than even the great revolutionary thinkers. "The McDonald's way of eating is a way of life: an ideology as theme park more intrusive (if much more subtle) than any Marx or Mao ever contrived."[23]
- McDonald's is the vanguard of global capitalism. "Following McDonald's golden arch from country to country, the market traces a trajectory of dollars and bonds and ads and yen and stocks and currency transactions that reaches right around the globe."[24]

- Resistance is futile. "We have seen . . . how McDonald's 'adapts' to foreign climes with wine in France and local beef in Russia even as it imposes a way of life that makes domestic wines and local beef irrelevant."[25]
- We have sold our souls to McWorld . . . "When McDonald's sells *Dances with Wolves* and *Jurassic Park* videos with sundry movie tie-ins in a vague celebration of multiculturalism or environmentalism or extinct reptile preservation, or hires Michael Jordan to link its products to celebrity sport, simple service to the body . . . is displaced by complex service to the soul."[26]
- . . . and destroyed democracy in the process. "If the traditional conservators of freedom were democratic constitutions and Bills of Rights, 'the new temples of liberty . . . will be McDonald's and Kentucky Fried Chicken.'"[27]
- And if you think otherwise, you are just wrong. "There are stylistic differences between McDonald's in Moscow, in Budapest, in Paris and in London by which they all can be distinguished from the first McDonald's," Barber says. "But squint a little and all the small differences vanish and the Golden Arch is all that remains, a virtual ghost haunting our retinas even on Champs Élyseés in Paris, where the actual display is no longer permitted. . . . [The] 'world where there is only one image' has already come to pass."[28]

What is wrong with this argument? Well, you already know. Almost everything.

McDonald's has more customers than whole nations have citizens? That's comparing apples and oranges. It is wrong to compare lunch counters with nation-states—unless you think that national citizenship is the patriotic equivalent of pulling into a restaurant's drive-through line.[29]

McDonald's has a more subtle and intrusive ideology than Marx or Mao? Doubtful, although I see Barber's point and expand upon it in the next section. This seems overblown, however. I wonder how many people have gone to their deaths with the words "Big Mac" on their lips? Some, probably, but nothing compared with the effect of Marx and Mao.

McDonald's is the Trojan horse for global capitalism, clearing the way for bond markets and advertising agencies? Sorry, but McDonald's is a business, not an economic evangelical organization. McDonald's comes in *after* the property rights, markets, ads, and money, not before. McDonald's needs those things to survive.[30]

McDonald's *imposes* a way of life that makes local products irrelevant? That's strong language, and strong language invites abuse. To impose a way of life is to take away choice, but it seems to me that McDonald's actually does the opposite. I don't see how McDonald's *imposes* anything. I suppose there is one case: if you believe that people should have no options and make no choices, then adding McDonald's *does* change everything—it *imposes* the necessity to choose. It seems to me that an argument that is rooted in a concern about democracy ought to lean on the side of the right to choose, the McDonald's side, not against it, even if the choices made are sometimes poor ones.

McDonald's customers are seeking a soulful experience, not just a quick meal? Yes, I agree, but so what? We shouldn't be surprised that the people who eat at McDonald's think about their meals as more than just food. "Unlike other species," anthropologist Sidney W. Mintz notes, "human beings invest their food with secondary meanings that transcend nourishment. We eat to live, yes, but hardly ever *only* to live."[31]

"Temples of Liberty?" Is it even possible to compare McDonald's to the Bill of Rights? And the final straw—if you see anything that seems to contradict this argument, just squint and it will go away. This lacks the elegance of Adam Smith's solution to the problem of inconvenient counterexamples. Smith would have covered his tracks like this: "What is true of a single McDonald's cannot be false about the entire system, so tightly 'twined are branch and root, and what is true about McDonald's cannot be false about McWorld, its logical extention."

Benjamin Barber's argument about democracy deserves better than this. You don't need to use globaloney to argue his point about democracy and the forces that threaten it. That globaloney is useful, however, is clear because it covers over the fundamental flaw in *Jihad vs. McWorld*: that it is, like Friedman's argument, an argument about America, not the world. It is based upon American values and is concerned, ultimately, that America is not true to its uniquely American principles.

One particular problem with the McWorld scenario is its reliance on the power of the media—the "infotainment telesector." The working assumption seems to be that this sector has such power over people that it is virtually irresistible. Once the infotainment telesector has local consumers in its crosshairs, indigenous culture is dead meat. And, of course, it is under the command of American multinationals like McDonald's.

There are several reasons to doubt that the world really works this way and to believe that the infotainment telesector is globaloney. The first is that many multinational firms fail to penetrate foreign markets even with the help of their evil media persuaders. Even the McDonald's record is blemished.[32] These failures are invisible of course, because they have failed and so disappeared. You only see the success stories, so that's what is reinforced. The failures can be found, however, in MBA case-study books.[33]

McWorld believes that foreign consumers cannot resist these forces—it denies them agency and assumes that, absent media coercion, their own cultures would remain permanently fixed. They indiscriminately absorb the products and values that are pushed in their direction. This is a sad view of humanity, which is sadder still because it may be based on the belief that this is true about American consumers, too. If people are really such hollow vessels as this, then it is unclear why we should care about them. The world would be better off without them. We should fill them with large orders of fries until they explode!

But when you look closely at these people, they are not at all like their globaloney image. A group of anthropologists took a careful look at McDonald's customers in Asia, for example, and what they discovered didn't look anything like McWorld. The results were published in a fascinating 1997 book called *Golden Arches East: McDonald's in East Asia*.[34] The authors looked carefully at how McDonald's customers related to the products and brands and to each other over time and compared results across countries. Here is a small smattering of their findings.

McDonald's has induced (*imposed* is too strong a term) small changes in foreign cultures. In Japan, for example, few people ate food with their hands before McDonald's came along.[35] McDonald's and other fast-food stores are displacing local "street foods" to a certain extent, but research indicates that this is due in part to greater concern, especially by parents, over sanitation and food safety. As incomes rise, these factors become more important and restaurants with better sanitation gain market share.

On the other hand, there are many examples of how local consumers have transformed McDonald's, shaping it to play particular roles in their societies. In Beijing, Seoul, and Taipei, for example, many people use McDonald's as a refuge from urban chaos. Middle school students in Hong Kong hang out at McDonald's for hours, talking and doing homework. Both of these uses are diametrically opposite to the McDonald's system, which stresses efficient production and consumption of food, "turning" tables over to new customers every few minutes.[36] "Suffice it to note here," James L. Watson says, "that McDonald's does not always call the shots."[37]

McDonald's is given many meanings by its patrons, who seem to have the ability to do this (they are not *all* empty vessels, it seems). Some women in East Asia, for example, seem to use McDonald's stores as a "sanctuary" from male domination. As the multigeneration nuclear family has disintegrated into separate households, McDonald's has become a gathering place where children and grandchildren are especially celebrated. (McDonald's plays this role in the United States, too.)[38] McDonald's is the home of "conspicuous consumption" for some, who flaunt their wealth and foreign tastes, but it is also a great leveler. Low prices and restricted menu choice mean that everyone eats about the same food and pays about the same amounts, so no one is likely to "lose face" in McDonald's. Eating a Big Mac can even be a political statement. In Taiwan, for example, the choice of McDonald's (versus a restaurant owned by a mainland Chinese family) makes a statement about independence from mainland influence.

McDonald's in East Asia doesn't seem to be very much like McWorld. But maybe it was a bad idea to use McDonald's as a model for McWorld. McDonald's may be much more local than most multinational firms. McDonald's restaurants in East Asia are at least partly owned by local firms and families; they are run by local managers and staffed by local people. They mainly buy their supplies from local businesses. A good deal of their profits stay at home, too, and are reinvested. As already noted, local food tastes and dining habits are accommodated, at least in part, within the overall burger and fries framework. It's ironic, but McDonald's might be one of the worst examples of the McWorld model—if McWorld were really about the world and not, at its core, a commentary on the United States.

But is McWorld even a true representation of America? If we use McDonald's as our analytical guide, I believe the answer is probably no. I really don't believe that a big media push—the dreaded infotainment telesector—accounts for McDonald's success even in the United States. In support of my position I cite recent evidence on obesity in the United States. The fact that Americans are gaining weight quite rapidly is well known and often associated with fast-food consumption. McWorld is McFat. The same infotainment telesector forces that push McWorld down our throats are to be blamed, it is said, for our McFat. It's not just the same principle, it is literally the same thing.

Recently, however, Harvard economists David M. Cuttler, Edward L. Glaeser, and Jesse M. Shapiro have asked the question, "Why Have Americans Become More Obese," and their findings are indeed revealing.[39] They test a number of hypotheses using data for the United States and other countries. They conclude that the best single explanation of rising obesity is that technological change—increased efficiency—has reduced the cost of food in terms of both the money it takes to buy it and the time it takes to prepare and consume it. Time and money are the two main constraints upon economic behavior. Fast food is both fast (time) and cheap (money)—and has only become faster and cheaper over the years. No wonder there has been a shift in favor of such products as their relative prices have fallen.[40]

Now what is most interesting to me about these findings is that they point *away* from clever marketing and media power as the driving forces behind McFat, McDonald's and, by extension, McWorld and instead highlight the principle that the McDonald brothers recognized in their little San Bernardino store: efficiency, technology, and the division of labor. Cheaper. Faster. More. To understand the implications of this fact, we need to leave McWorld behind and move on to a simpler, but far scarier vision of globalization.

Rationalization: The Ugly Globalization

Capitalism's tendency to reward and therefore promote efficiency is well known. It is the secret behind Adam Smith's pin factory and invisible hand. For Marx and Engels, it is the force that enables global capitalism to transform foreign countries, not simply penetrate them. Capitalism's drive for greater and greater efficiency causes it to do for society in general what it did for Adam Smith's pin factory in particular: break it down into basic components and reassemble it in the most starkly efficient fashion. There is not much harm done (and much benefit produced) when the division of labor is applied to the manufacture of pins. The stakes are higher when whole societies are involved, as some have suggested. *This*, not the superficial influence of advertising and electronic media, is the truly ugly side of globalization.

Efficiency, and the process of rational calculation that is necessary to achieve it, reaches its zenith inside a McDonald's restaurant. The American sociologist George Ritzer observed this fact in his 1993 book,

The McDonaldization of Society: An Investigation into the Changing Character of Social Life.[41] If you make even a casual study of a McDonald's restaurant you will see Ritzer's point. McDonald's makes efficiency the top-most goal and consciously organizes its assembly line accordingly. This is not news, of course, since the McDonald brothers began doing this way back in the 1950s, even before they sold their name and business to Ray Kroc. What is interesting, however, is how McDonald's has managed to rationalize both sides of the counter. This is where Ritzer comes in.

It is easy to see the production side of McDonald's efficiency. Specialized technology and a highly organized division of labor produce standardized menu items quickly and efficiently. Service may not be quite as fast as in the San Bernardino store, where orders were filled in 30 seconds, but the menu is much larger and competitive factors have forced McDonald's to permit customers to make some special orders. All in all, it is a highly structured, very efficient production line for food of reliably consistent quality and relatively low price.

What may be more significant, however, is how McDonald's has transformed the way that its customers behave. In traditional restaurants, customers are relatively passive participants in the food service operation. They arrive, are seated, and given menus. Wait staff deliver water and other beverages, take the order and deliver it, assuring that everything is exactly as requested. Staff typically check on the customers at several points during the meal, which may be multicourse and require changes in cutlery, glassware, and so forth. Finally, the bill is delivered and paid, change given, and table cleared and reset before it can be turned over to the next group of customers.

Compare this to a typical fast-food experience. Customers arrive and queue to give their orders at the counter, choosing from the standard items listed on the backlit overhead display. The order is given, payment made, and the customer waits for the food to arrive at the counter. (In fast food, customers, not staff, do the waiting.) The customer gets her own condiments and eating utensils, fills her own cup, finds her own table, and then clears it when finished. Customers do much of the work of running the restaurant, work that would otherwise be performed by paid staff. (Over at the drive-through window, customers are actually making their own home and office deliveries!) And they do this work rapidly, efficiently, and without apparent displeasure. Actually, customers don't seem to be aware that they are doing McDonald's work; they just go through the paces automatically. The miracle

136

of the modern McDonald's is that its customers work for the firm but draw no wages. The experience of cooking a meal and eating it is thus transformed from an art to a highly engineered, precisely coordinated production process.

McDonald's is an excellent example of the process that the great German sociologist Max Weber (1864–1920) called "formal rationalization." According to Weber, Ritzer explains, "*formal rationality* means that the search by people for the optimum means to a given end is shaped by rules, regulations, and larger social structures. Individuals are not left to their own devices in searching for the best possible means of attaining a given objective. Weber identified this type of rationality as a major development in the history of the world."[42] Weber's analysis of formal rationalization focused on bureaucracy as an institution that organized a certain segment of society to achieve certain goals quickly and efficiently. A successful bureaucracy is able to process large numbers of people relatively quickly and in a highly predictable manner. Individual variations are tightly controlled, with rules and regulations generally relied upon rather than variable (and therefore unreliable) human judgment within a tightly defined division of labor. There are few "surprises," especially unpleasant ones.

A successful visit to a modern health maintenance organization clinic illustrates a bureaucracy at work. The division of labor, both within offices and among specialties, is obvious. The steps of making appointments, gathering information, making diagnoses, planning treatment, performing tests, filling prescriptions, etc., are all discrete and handled by specialists. Information technology is used to share information and coordinate the stages. The patient (you) moves efficiently through the production line, through various locations, until you are discharged, instructions in hand, into the parking garage. The term *patient* is well chosen because, as in the fast-food restaurant, the customer does all of the waiting, while the assembly-line workers are kept in constant, efficient motion. Other public and private bureaucracies, including income taxation and pension and insurance systems, work much the same way.

George Ritzer gave the name *McDonaldization* to the way that formal rationalization organizes contemporary society, especially in the United States, I think. McDonaldization is characterized by efficiency, calculability, predictability, and the use of technology to control human behavior. McDonaldization is not about McDonald's, Ritzer says, it is about the transforming force of rationalization.[43] Rationalization has many advantages, Ritzer notes.[44] More goods and services can be made available to a larger segment of the population with greater convenience with respect to time and place. Lower cost increases affordability. Workers and customers alike confront a standardized process that is therefore stable and familiar. Uniform treatment means that discrimination due to gender, race, age, or ethnicity is reduced.[45] Standardization means that many products are safer. A high degree of coordination means that technology is rapidly diffused.

McDonald's is a good example of each of these characteristics. When you go to McDonald's you know that there is little chance that you will have an unexpectedly good meal. The sandwiches, fries, and drinks will be just what you expect and no better. But no worse, either. The flip side of standardization is that bad surprises are systematically reduced (although the certainty of occasional human and equipment failures mean they can never fully be eliminated). If you've ever had an expensive meal with poorly prepared or unsafe food served (slowly) by a surly waiter, you know what I am talking about. There are few high points in a Big Mac value meal, but few lows, either.

I think this is why McDonald's is so popular in formerly Communist countries, despite prices that are high relative to weekly income. Under communism, people could be pretty sure of poor food and worse service in most cases, but sometimes they were pleasantly surprised. McDonald's is the other way around. The food is consistently decent. You provide most of the service yourself, so you are not dependent on the whims of a surly waiter. Not a bad deal, compared to the alternative.

If formal rationalization and McDonaldization were limited to McDonald's I don't think we would have very much to complain about. Ritzer's concern, which is shared by many others, however, is that what is true about McDonald's may also be true more generally. It's not about the burgers. It's about the lives behind the burgers and the limited and automatic roles we play as efficient producing and consuming agents. What is the final consequence as formal rationalism spreads from McRestaurant to McMall to McCinema to McHospital to McUniversity to . . . to what? To McChurch?

This is what seems to worry Benjamin Barber. Barber sees the rationalization process (and writes about it in *Jihad vs. McWorld*), but he is apparently more concerned with who has the power in the system (hence his misplaced concern with the infotainment telesector), not realizing that the power *is* the system. The power lies in the rationalization process itself. This is true even in the most unlikely places, such as the infotainment telesector.

Many people see increasing concentration in the print and electronic media and worry about the potential for abuse of influence. This is a legitimate concern, but it assumes that these firms want power, that they want to control what we believe, whereas I think they really want our money. What I see is increasingly fierce competition among the media giants, which drives them to ever bolder acts of rationalization. On television, for example, the reality show essentially gets audiences to produce their own shows just as McDonald's gets customers to fill their own drink cups. A true monopolist could become lazy and just show reruns or cheap game shows. It is competition and the quest for efficiency that drives them to extremes. It's not the manipulative power of the media giants that I fear, it is the possible effects of their drive to rationalize.

Thomas Friedman both recognizes the rationalization process inherent in globalization and, I think, embraces it. This accounts for Friedman's sunny but realistic attitude toward globalization. As a political reporter covering the Middle East and other troubled regions, Friedman has seen more than his share of irrational acts. I think he'd take economic rationalism over political or social irrationalism any day. He is hopeful that global capitalism will help people learn how to coordinate their actions and behave rationally—which means that they would try not to go to war, for example—even when they are not in a McDonald's. I sure hope he's right, but it is a long shot. Many people have argued that war is irrational because it is too expensive, but this doesn't seem to have stopped war. Perhaps McDonaldization—a deeper cultural process that starts with production and consumption and then eventually is absorbed into a society's DNA—will work where mere hunger for money has failed.

The Threat of McNothing

If globalization is McDonaldization, where does that leave us? As you might expect, opinions differ. George Ritzer used to hold out hope for McDonaldization, not Thomas Friedman's hope that a rationalized world will be a rational one, but hope that standardization and rationalization could produce some good things along with mountains of mediocre mass-market stuff. He seemed to be taken with his experiences at Starbucks, for example.[46]

At Starbucks, Ritzer noted in 1998, standardization and technology do more than just reduce cost and control human behavior, they also produce consistently high quality products for which customers were willing to pay a premium. "Thus, Starbucks indicates that it is possible to McDonaldize quality . . . when there are technologies that ensure high and consistent quality, and when enough patrons are willing to pay large amounts of money for the product."[47] Ritzer seemed to think that Starbucks and Ruth's Chris Steak House and a few other high-quality chains were the start of something important.

But now he's changed his mind. Ritzer's 2004 book *The Globalization of Nothing* looks at the proliferation of Starbucks in London and sees nothing to love.[48] "Such a uniform chain is one of the prime examples of nothing and its proliferation in the most visited areas of the city tend to give it the feeling of nothingness."[49] Ritzer has decided that meaningful content is difficult to globalize because it is too tied to time and place, too human, too special. To be successful, globalization has to bleach the authentic content out of products and services, make them standard, uniform, and meaningless. This, presumably, is why Nike's swoosh logo is so successful—it doesn't mean a thing.

What makes *something* different from *nothing*? You might think it is just a matter of taste—or lack of it—and I think there is something to this, but Ritzer proposes a sort of matrix of meaning to help separate content from void. Somethingness and nothingness form a continuum. Products or experiences closer to the something end of the spectrum are associated with these characteristics: unique, specific to time and place, humanized, and enchanted (capable of surprise). Nothingness, on the other hand, is characterized by its generic, timeless, placeless qualities and the tendency to be impersonal and disenchanted (rationally predictable).[50] Dinner at a friend's apartment lies toward the something end of the continuum, even if you just order in Chinese food. Dinner at the local Ruth's Chris Steak House, on the other hand, is sort of nothing, even if it is delicious. Going trout fishing is something; going shopping at the mall is nothing.

This taxonomy helps us understand how Ritzer's reaction to Starbucks might have changed, although this is only speculation. Perhaps Ritzer was taken when the first Starbucks opened in his neighborhood, and he learned to order his special type of coffee drink ("I'll have a tall skinny vanilla latte, extra foam") and became a "regular," known by the staff and recognized by other customers. Perhaps this enchantment faded away as he saw his own special experience replicated almost endlessly by other "regulars" wherever he went. Or maybe it was that seeing Starbucks in London made him associate it with Americanization, and this offended him. Or maybe he just got tired of standing in line and switched to Diet Coke; I don't really know. In any case, the coffee drinks that were so "something" in 1998 have become "nothing" today.

The Globalization of Nothing is a very interesting book because, like the best globalization stories and metaphors, it appears at a time of social upheaval and uncertainty and tells us why we are so anxious and what will come to pass in the future. We are anxious, clearly, because globalization is stripping our lives of meaning as products and relationships are rationalized down to nothing. The more globalization proceeds, the more we have and the less it means to us. Existential questions inevitably arise.

But, while I share his anxiety, I am not convinced Ritzer is right. His Starbucks turnaround bothers me a bit as does the fact that he seems to find a lot of meaning in motion pictures, which seem to me to be the ultimate embodiment of nothingness, for the most part: mass-produced, centrally controlled, identical entertainment experiences supplied indiscriminately to millions at low cost in highly controlled artificial environments by cynical media oligopolists. It's just everything that Ritzer finds empty in other circumstances. But then I'm also a bit suspicious of Ritzer's tendency to find "something" in things that he personally likes (such as chrome and glass roadside diners) while he sees only "nothing" in things that he doesn't like, such as McDonald's. I worry that Ritzer has fallen into a sort of cultural elitism, which is hard to avoid when you are evaluating the content of culture.[51]

A more serious criticism is that Ritzer distinguishes between something and nothing based upon the conditions of production. A McDonald's meal is nothing, for example, in part because it is standardized—they are all the same. But he thinks that a fine gourmet meal is something (and would be impossible to globalize) in part because of its variability—it is different each time the skilled chef makes it. But I find both sides of this division problematic.

I suspect that the customers at McDonald's are at least sometimes able to manufacture their own meaning, regardless of the rationalized environment. Standard-issue french fries can take on a life of their own when shared with grandchildren at Sunday lunch. If consumers are to be classified as part of the rationalized production process, then we must consider that they are full participants in the meaning creation business, too, and can sometimes make something out of nothing.

141

As for gourmet meals, I have eaten my share of them at wonderful restaurants. These meals were far from mass produced, but it would be a mistake to think that their pleasure comes from daily variation and inspiration.[52] In my experience, great chefs work hard to find just the right recipe and then work even harder to see that it is prepared *exactly* the same way each time.

I am suspicious of the idea that globalization is the end of culture and meaning and hopeful, even confident, that authentic content can be preserved. To his credit, George Ritzer is hopeful, too. He ends *The Globalization of Nothing* with a brief discussion of a movement that tries to use globalization against itself, to preserve the local and the authentic. This is the Slow Food movement, which is the subject of chapter 7 of this book.

But I do take seriously the rationalizing force of capitalism and globalization that is driven by capitalism, so there are limits to my optimism. I am especially mindful of the argument made many years ago by the Austrian American economist Joseph Schumpeter in his book *Capitalism, Socialism, and Democracy*.[53] Like Benjamin Barber, Schumpeter feared that capitalism would destroy democracy, but he was not worried about Jihad, McWorld, or the infotainment telesector. Rather Schumpeter was worried about the effect of rationalization on society.

Schumpeter, you see, believed that society advanced due to the efforts of bold, heroic figures. This was especially true in business, where the figures are called entrepreneurs, but the idea also holds in politics, science, and the arts. Most of us take small risks with life and mainly play it safe. But a few people take bigger risks, and some of them achieve breakthroughs that really make a difference. These risk takers, even when they fail, are the real sources of social drive and change—he called it "creative destruction"—in Schumpeter's view. Without them, the world is a pretty stagnant, uninteresting place.

The problem, Schumpeter believed, is that capitalism's drive to rationalize is really quite intense, and he thought it would eventually destroy the culture that produces entrepreneurs. Capitalism, as a dynamic force, will slowly fade into stagnant socialism, Schumpeter thought, as rational calculation replaced entrepreneurial risk taking. Thus, he said, socialism will overcome capitalism, just as Karl Marx predicted, but not through a worker revolt. Nope, the culture of calculation will swallow up capitalism from the inside out.

Schumpeter's view of politics is less well known, but he tended to see it in the same way he viewed the economy. He saw democracy as a competitive political marketplace. Like the economy, progress came through the actions of bold political entrepreneurs who took the risk of providing real leadership. And he thought that democracy, like capitalism, would be destroyed as a dynamic social force as bold political entrepreneurs were replaced by vote-calculating political managers, content to follow voters rather than leading them. Thus does democracy die, in Schumpeter's world, the victim of rationalism, not Jihad or McWorld.

* * *

Where does our study of globalization and McDonald's leave us? I don't know about you, but I feel like I have learned a great deal about McDonald's but not very much about globalization. This is the problem with using McDonald's or any single product or industry as a metaphor or image for something as complex as globalization. We quickly become caught up in the particular case and risk making false generalizations. Meanwhile, the true general globalization case, if it exists, remains unstudied for the most part.

McDonald's may in fact be an especially poor example to use in studying globalization. McDonald's seems to have a special meaning to Americans that it may or may not have to others. You can almost tell how an American feels about her country by what she has to say about McDonald's. We end up, as I have argued here, with an American view of America, not an objective analysis of globalization.

That said, studying McWorld is not entirely a waste of time. Ritzer's analysis of McDonaldization usefully highlights the rationalizing force of markets and makes us aware of the potential of cold calculation to benefit and to harm. What we need to do is to find a way to think about this process that isn't bound up in a particularly American set of values. That's what I try to do in the next chapter by looking at globalization from a different angle—through the bottom of a glass of wine.

GLOBALIZATION VERSUS *TERROIR*

Terroir. The second hardest thing about *terroir* is learning how to pronounce it. It sounds like "tehr-wahr" with the space between the syllables drawn from the back of your throat. It's a French word, if that's any help. This chapter is about the relationship between globalization and *terroir.*

Terroir is a word that is used a lot by wine people. It means *soil* in French, but in wine-talk it accounts for a good deal more. A wine is said to express *terroir* if it reflects the particular qualities of its place of origin. George Ritzer would probably say that wine with *terroir* is "something" as opposed to undistinguished generic wine that could be produced anywhere in the world, which he would dismiss, however good it might be, as "nothing."[1]

You'll know *terroir* when you taste it, I think, but defining it precisely is very hard; indeed, it is the hardest thing there is about *terroir.*[2] James E. Wilson, a geologist and wine enthusiast, wrote an entire book about the *terroir* of French wine, but still felt the need for an appendix to deal with definitional issues.[3] It's easy to see why: *terroir*, like globalization, is both simple and very complex. *Terroir*, he writes, "includes physical elements of the vineyard—the vine, subsoil, siting, drainage, and microclimate."[4] This much is clear. But there is more. "Beyond the measurable ecosystem, there is an additional dimension—the spiritual aspect that recognizes the joys, the heartbreaks, the pride, the sweat, and the frustrations of its history."[5]

Terroir is a certain idea of wine, although the idea differs from person to person. For some, it is the way that the wine reflects the specific local soils and growing conditions that shape the development of the grapes and hence the wine. For others it is this plus the specific local wine-making practices and traditions that determine the way the grapes were turned into wine (such things as grade variety selection, crush and fermentation practices, and so on). These factors especially contribute to *terroir* when they seek to draw out the particular characteristics of soil and site. Some would go on to add to *terroir* the motives and attitudes of the producers and consumers and especially their respect for traditional practices—what Wilson calls the wine's "spiritual" aspect.

Terroir is not a new idea. Adam Smith knew about *terroir*. Smith developed a taste for fine French wines and wrote knowledgeably about viticulture and the wine market in *Wealth of Nations*. "The vine is more affected by the difference of soils than any other fruit tree," he said. "For some it derives a flavour which no culture of management can equal. . . . This flavor, real or imaginary, is sometimes peculiar to the produce of a few vineyards, sometimes it extends through the greater part of a small district, and sometimes through a considerable part of a large province."[6] Wine with real *terroir*, Smith said, could sell out quickly at a high price, creating profit for the fortunate winemaker or vineyard owner.[7] But note, significantly, that the flavor of *terroir* can be "real or imaginary," a comment that suggests that even in Smith's time *terroir* was a contested concept.

Terroir is controversial; it is as controversial as globalization. Some people believe in it, but disagree about where it comes from. Are the distinctive qualities of wine created in the vineyard, at the winery, by the traditions that winegrower and winemaker embody, or all three? Philosophy, ego, and economic interests (an explosive combination) are all at stake when *terroir* is on the table. Other experts dispute the entire concept of *terroir*. They see it as a marketing tool—a way for wine producers—especially European winemakers—to differentiate and mystify an otherwise unexceptional product.[8] "On one side are 'terroirists' with a vested interest who wield the concept as a weapon on the world wine market to assert that European classics are infinitely superior and will always remain so," writes Roger Bohmrich. "On the other side, modernists reject what they perceive as bogus scientific arguments which serve to perpetuate a marketing advantage."[9]

The *Economist* reports at least one wine marketer who thinks *terroir* is simply a "SCAM, an acronym of Soil + Climate + Aspect = Mystique."[10] Indeed, if *terroir* is a wine's spirit, it is easy to see how it might be manipulated or abused—scammed, I guess. Whether it really exists or not, everyone agrees that *terroir* has value—market value. Today, as in Adam Smith's time, people are often willing to pay more, sometimes *much* more, for wines that they believe have character.

You should probably open a few bottles of wine at this point and try to taste the *terroir*, so that you make up your own mind. If you do, you'll likely discover how much globalization has come to the wine market and is transforming it. You need only look closely at your grocery store wine aisle to see that it's true. Among the hundreds of different labels that an upscale supermarket often presents you will certainly find wines from France, Germany, Italy, Spain, and Portugal—the traditional "Old World" producers. But you will also see bottles from many parts of the "New World," including the United States, Chile, and Australia. You may also find wine from Argentina, Bulgaria, New Zealand, South Africa, Greece, Slovenia, and perhaps even Canada (no, I don't mean Tundra Red and Tundra White).

And although you won't find its wines in your supermarket yet, China has quietly become a major wine-producing nation with three hundred wineries in twenty-six provinces and almost 300,000 hectares of vineyards.[11] India is also developing a significant wine industry, as is Japan. The complete global wine list, as we will see, is even longer.[12]

The McWine Hypothesis

Is globalization the enemy of *terroir*? The conventional wisdom is that global economic forces overcome, undermine, distort, and destroy the sorts of local customs, traditions, and beliefs that *terroir* embodies. If it is true generally, as we often read, that globalization is a great homogenizing force, it should be *especially* true about wine.

I want to test the hypothesis that globalization destroys *terroir*, replacing distinctive local products and practices with a mass-produced alcoholic grape product that we can call McWine. The McWine hypothesis—that globalization destroys *terroir*—encapsulates a lot of what

147

people often say about globalization in general and about consumer products like wine in particular. It is really true? No, at least not entirely. Although there are plenty of general theories about globalization, as we have seen, there are not many generalizable effects. Globalization is probably best understood through special theories that try to explain how globalization plays out in particular places and spaces. What we will find as we examine globalization and wine is this. First, parts of the McWine scenario are true—the globalization of wine displays some of the patterns and outcomes associated with "McDonaldization," for example. For the most part, however, the globalization of wine has proceeded along different lines from those found in other industries.

The effect of globalization on wine has only a little in common with its effect on fast food (McDonald's), fast breaks (professional sports), or anything else. Globalization reflects its *terroir*—it develops differently in different places and cultures. The story of globalization and wine reflects the particular characteristics of the wine industry and cannot easily be generalized. Perhaps we should be careful drawing universal conclusions from other particular cases of globalization. I'll try not to make this mistake in talking about globalization and wine.

Let's begin by constructing the McWine hypothesis—a persuasive narrative of the globalization of wine that uses a few carefully selected facts to tell a generalized story of how globalization simply destroys *terroir*. Our McWine story begins, inevitably, in the United States, at the center of the McWine world: 600 Yosemite Boulevard, Modesto, California 95354. This is the address of the global headquarters of the world's largest wine producer, the E.&J. Gallo Winery.

E.&J. Gallo is to wine as McDonald's is to fast food, so the McWine moniker fits comfortably. It is by far the largest single firm, with an estimated 30 percent of the $12 billion U.S. market for table wine.[13] A family-owned business founded by the brothers Ernest and Julio in 1933, Gallo uses its considerable economies of scale to market vast quantities of wine (seventy-five million cases in the United States alone) in ninety countries around the world.

Although Gallo produces some boutique-style single-vineyard wines under the Gallo of Sonoma label, the bulk of its production is aimed squarely at the price-conscious consumers who have never even heard of *terroir* much less tasted it. Sales of branded McWines such as Gallo, Gossamer Bay, Livingston Cellars, Carlo Rossi, Peter Vella, and Wild Vine make up the bulk of Gallo's sales. These wines are sold in single bottles, double bottles called magnums, and in even larger bottles and boxed plastic bladders (wine in a box, an efficient if unromantic package). The focus is on quantity and price. Peter Vella wines are sold in five-liter boxes, for example, while Carlo Rossi products are available in 1.5-, 3-, and 4-liter bottles. Gallo also sells large quantities of affordable wine to the restaurant trade under brand names, including Burlwood, Copperidge, Liberty Creek, and William Wycliff Vineyards. Gallo also makes "private label" wines for major U.S. retailers Wal-Mart (Alcott Ridge brand) and Albertsons (Timberwood Vineyards).

Ernest and Julio Gallo built their business according to a strict division of labor: Julio made the wines and Ernest sold them. I don't know if Ernest Gallo really appreciated the spiritual element of wine, but he did know that selling wine is not just about selling what is in the bottle. Selling wine, like selling burgers and sports shoes, is also about selling image, mystique, or *terroir*. The story is told of a sales call that Ernest Gallo made to a New York customer in the dark days of the Depression. He offered sample glasses of two red wines—one costing five cents per bottle and the other ten cents. The buyer tasted both and pronounced, "I'll take the ten-cent one." The wine in the two glasses was exactly the same.[14] Clearly, the customer wanted to buy himself an identity—the image of someone who wouldn't drink that five-cent rotgut—even if he couldn't actually taste the difference.

The insight that people do not just buy wine, they also buy an image of themselves, helps explain Gallo's decision to market its wine by establishing distinct brand names aimed at particular market segments. Why, you probably drink Gallo wine yourself! Me? Nonsense, you say. I wouldn't drink that five-cent rotgut. But many Gallo wines don't even have Gallo on the label. They have names like Rancho Zabacho, Frei Brother's Reserve, Turning Leaf Coastal Reserve, Redwood Creek, and Indigo Hills. These are wines that Gallo sells to people who don't want to think of themselves as Gallo drinkers. And they'll pay a bit more than we would for a bottle of Gallo wine just to prove it.

And this is, no doubt, the key to Gallo's success in the United States and around the world. It is also what makes many people fear for *terroir* because they consider that Gallo's success in selling carefully branded mass-market wines will drive small producers and their distinctive products from the marketplace. How can they compete, after all, with a huge business machine that churns out such vast quantities of cheap wine, using the power of the global media to push it down the throats of the world's consumers? No way. There's no way they can compete with the likes of Gallo.

It seems only a matter of time—here's the McWine hypothesis—before the world will be flooded with a lake of *terroir*-free Gallo-branded McWine packaged in convenient 5-liter plastic bladders. Soon virtually all wine will be McWine, manufactured (not crafted) to sell at low cost to a least common denominator palate—the same happily taste-free Americans who choke down endless platters of fatty Big Macs, salty french fries, and sugary colas. Globalization is death to *terroir* and the worst kind of death, too. Death by bad wine.

The Truth about McWine

The basic facts about Gallo wines that I've presented here are correct to the best of my knowledge, and yet all of the conclusions regarding the McWine hypothesis are false, especially the last conclusion that wine quality is deteriorating and globalization-Americanization is to blame. Globalization is having many effects on wine producers and consumers, but if there is one thing that wine experts agree upon it is this: the world is drinking the best quality wine it has ever had, and globalization is at least partly responsible. The McWine hypothesis is globaloney.

It is true that Gallo is the world's largest winemaker, but that does not necessarily make it the dominant player in the global wine market. As big as it is, Gallo produces less than 1 percent of all the wine sold in the world (and much less than 1 percent of the world's premium-quality wine). Gallo is not a global wine monopolist, despite its great size. This market remains fiercely if not "perfectly" competitive.

Gallo is a global firm, operating in ninety different countries, but it would be a mistake to think that its large position in the United States makes it a dominant force abroad. The global market for wine is surprisingly local, with relatively small international sales relative to total output. Most wine in the world is consumed where it was produced. With only a few (but important) exceptions, the biggest wine producers (France with 58 million hectoliters—about 7.7 billion bottles—in 2001 and Italy with 51 million hectoliters) are also the largest consumers, and they drink mainly their own wine. Only a few countries drink very much more wine than they produce: Germany, Great Britain, Russia, and (for now at least) China. And only a few countries (France, Italy, and Spain) produce a great deal more wine than is consumed on the domestic market. The global market for wine *is* important and it gets a lot of attention, but international sales are tiny compared to domestic market sales.[15]

Ernest Gallo was right: image and brands are important in selling wines, and he built a great business through branding. But the most important brands in the global wine trade today are those that raise prices and sell wine up-market, not those that dilute quality to cut price, as the McWine hypothesis suggests. One interesting exception to this rule is the recent "Two Buck Chuck" phenomenon. Wine is an agricultural product, and it is notoriously difficult to match supply and demand for farm goods. A glut of decent wine in California has allowed Trader Joe's, an upscale supermarket chain, to offer drinkable wine under the Charles Shaw label for as little as $1.99 per bottle. The wine is considerably better than the typical $2 wine, which is not extravagant praise, and has attracted customers who would otherwise spend $5 or more for a bottle of wine. This looks on the surface like the McWine scenario in action, but the dynamic is really somewhat different. McWine is cheap, but vile. In fact, it is vile *because* it is so cheap. Two Buck Chuck is cheap despite its better quality. It is an increase in quality at a lower price level that is attracting customers, not lower price itself, as in the usual "race to the bottom scenario." In effect, Two Buck Chuck has not so much lowered the price for decent wine as it has raised the relative price of better wine.[16] No wonder people buy it instead of the pricier stuff, especially if they can't taste any difference.

The McWine scenario offers us a simple way to think about the globalization of wine, but it just isn't supported by the facts. The reason is that it ignores *terroir* and its affect on the wine market. I propose that we apply the idea of *terroir* to globalization itself. If *terroir* exists (and I think it does) it means that the same grapes will yield distinctly different wine qualities depending upon local soil, climate, and winemaking culture. Globalization, I argue, is the same way. How globalization plays out in the real world (as opposed to metaphors or generalized narratives) depends upon local conditions, too. Globalization is different in the United States than in New Zealand, and it is different in the wine business than in the fast-food industry or the market for designer shoes. These different globalizations share some characteristics (just as different merlot wines will tend to have something in common), but the limit to meaningful generalization is quickly achieved; only globaloney lies beyond.

What does close examination of the global wine industry (looking beyond the McWine Hypothesis) reveal? Here are three generalizations that derive from wine's particular microclimate:

- The globalization of wine has not produced a "race to the bottom" as the McWine scenario predicts. The quality of wine has increased (and *terroir* become more important) through globalization. It isn't exactly a "race to the top" but a movement to higher ground.
- Globalization may encourage a certain degree of "homogenization" of wine, but not at the low end, as you might expect from the McWine scenario. Rather, wine experts worry that homogenizing forces are at work at the very top, where a winner-take-all market has emerged.
- It is very unlikely that huge global wine corporations will destroy small local producers the way that Wal-Mart is supposed to destroy Mom and Pop stores. Big firms do have advantages in the global wine business, especially in distribution, but small wineries have their own advantages, too. Both are likely to survive and prosper. I wonder about middle-sized firms, however. I speculate that a "missing middle" may emerge in global wine due to the particular problems that middle-sized wineries may have in responding to changing global wine conditions.

The rest of this chapter explains the reasoning behind these conclusions through a brief history of the globalization of the wine industry and a case study of one of globalization's great success stories, the New Zealand industry. We begin, logically enough, at the center of the universe of the global wine business, which is not where you might expect it to be.

How Wine Became Global

Wine has always been "global" in the sense that it has always been traded as widely as transportation costs allowed. It isn't an accident that archeologists who search ancient shipwreck sites in the Mediterranean nearly always find wine amphorae on board. The wine trade is an old one, driven by differences in taste and quality and sustained by the fact that wine was viewed as food, a necessity, not just alcohol or a luxury good.[17] Explorers and colonists took grapevines with them when they set out for the New World, expanding wine's domain from Europe to the whole world, or at least the temperate parts of it. The seeds of global wine were literally planted centuries ago.

The globalization of wine has intensified dramatically in the last thirty years. Many people point to the "Judgment of Paris" as the event that triggered the current round of global wine trade. Steven Spurrier, a British wine critic, organized a comparative tasting of top French and California wines in Paris in 1976. The blind tasting produced an astonishing result: the *Old World* judges gave the highest scores to *New World* wines. This well-publicized (and many times since reenacted) result forced a change in attitude toward New World wine, and it encouraged people like California producer Robert Mondavi to try to make wines of real quality and character, not just cheap mass-market goods.

The 1976 Paris tasting was an important milestone in the globalization of wine, because it gave credibility to New World wine, but it wasn't really the key that unlocked the global market door. For that you must go to the wine aisle in a British supermarket such as Tesco's or Sainsbury's. Until the 1970s stores like these could not sell wine; only small specialized wine shops with limited opening hours could do it. This severely limited the market for wine in Britain. A change in licensing regulations, however, put British grocery chains, with their broader distribution networks, scale economies, and longer opening hours, into the retail wine trade—and triggered the global wine avalanche.[18] The grocery chains took full advantage of this opportunity and began to search the world for wines to fill their shelves.

Grocery stores are good at selling branded products, like laundry soaps and breakfast cereal. The brand is a reputational device that assures consumers a certain level of quality, or at least it's supposed to. The idea is that you know what you are getting when you buy a name-brand commodity. It is in the brand-owner's interests to see that you are satisfied, so quality needs to be good relative to price. Brand names proved especially useful as more foreign wines began to crowd British grocery store aisles, because no one really knows what is in a bottle of wine until it is opened (especially one of unfamiliar provenance). This is true of some Old World wines, too, that are identified in complicated ways that frequently intimidate novice buyers. The supermarket chains decided to give their globally sourced wines credibility using their own brands. Tesco, Sainsbury's, and the other major chains established proprietary lines of wines imported from around the world. Their store's name on the label was its seal of quality. This strategy has been very effective: nearly 40 percent of the wine sold in British supermarkets is own-brand stock.[19] You can see the result today if you go into a British supermarket or go to www.tesco.com on the Internet.

The Tesco website provides British buyers with an expanded version of what they can find in the grocery stores: wines from producers in more than twenty-three countries, including Cyprus, Japan, Mexico, and Zimbabwe. The wines on offer include makers and labels that you would surely recognize plus an amazing range of Tesco brands such as Tesco Bulgarian Country Red (£2.55 per bottle when purchased by the case), Tesco California Zinfandel (£3.80 per bottle/case), Tesco Finest Beaujolais Villages (£5.25 per bottle/case), Tesco Finest Chablis (£7.25 per bottle/case), Tesco Finest Gigondas (£8.54), and Tesco Finest Chateauneuf Du Pape (£13.33).[20] The British supermarkets created the world's first high-volume, integrated, global wine market. They opened the floodgates, and the global wine poured forth.

You would not think that a change in British wine retailing regulation would be very important—this seems like a fairly small domestic matter—but Britain is the second-largest net importer of wine in the world (after Germany) and a country with strong historical connections not only to Old World producers like France but also to New World wine producers, especially Australia, New Zealand, South Africa, and the United States. Supermarket sales (as opposed to wine shops or restaurants) accounted for 65 percent of the British wine market in 2003, with no end in sight to their growth.[21]

Thus did Britain, which produces a little wine but buys quite a lot, become the center of the global wine universe. The distribution channels that British supermarkets carved out in the Old World and the New were soon crowded with distributors from other countries, also seeking sound wine at competitive prices. Sometimes this wine is imported in the bottle, as you might expect, but increasingly it is shipped in bulk (in giant-sized wine bladders) and bottled (or boxed) close to the final market. This practice reduces transportation costs and expands, therefore, the economic market for a country's wine. Much of China's growing thirst is slaked by Chilean wine imported in bulk, for example.

Wine's Economic *Terroir*

A rose is a rose, they say, but a rosé isn't necessarily a rosé when it comes to selecting a wine. Wine drinkers display very interesting economic behavior. Although people will tell you that they like certain types of wine (dry, sweet, oaky, fruity, and so on), in fact their economic behavior suggests that most people really buy wine by price as much as taste. Wine market segmentation based on price is important to winemakers and sellers for obvious reasons—the market segments define their economic *terroir* in the same way that their vineyard and cellar practices define their aesthetic *terroir*. This behavior is important to me for a different reason: it is the key to understanding how globalization affects the wine industry.

Wine buyers tend to divide themselves into different market segments around particular price points, which I like to think of as a staircase that connects the generic bottom of the wine market with its prestigious top. This is not new: the wine market has always been sharply segmented by price. The characteristics of the different wine market segments—who sits down to drink on which level of the staircase—vary by region or country and with such factors as income, expectations, and the prices of other food and beverage products. Because they are so important in the wine business, market segments have been studied very thoroughly.

Where do you sit on the wine staircase? The U.S. wine market contains no fewer than five main segments, ranging from cheap basic wines to very costly icon brands. Table 6.1 shows the approximate market breakdown for the United States.

Wine buyers cluster their purchases in a particular segment based upon a number of factors including income, age, lifestyle, and preference for wine versus other food and drinks. Most buyers make the bulk of their purchases in a given price category, dropping down to a lower step when necessary (tight budget or perhaps when purchasing larger quantities for a party or family gathering) and moving up a step for special occasions.

The characteristics of the wine market segments differ in a number of important ways. The most obvious difference is related to *terroir*. "Basic" wines almost by definition lack any distinctive qualities or complexity that we associate with *terroir*. They are made to provide clean and simple flavors. The three premium wine segments display increasing degrees of *terroir*, moving from blends of wine made in a regional style (Ravenswood California Zinfandel) to wines from a single region made to display that area's perceived qualities (Ravenswood Sonoma Zinfandel) to single-vineyard wines that reflect, or should reflect, very specific local qualities (Ravenswood Monte Rosso Vineyard Zinfandel). In France controlled designations such as Beaujolais (popular pre-

Table 6.1   U.S. Wine Market Segments

Category	U.S. Price	Market Share	Typical Product Identification
Basic*	Less than $5	50%	Generic wine type. Red wine, white wine. Burgundy (dry red), Chablis (dry white), Rhine (sweet white).
Popular Premium	$5.00–$7.99	34%	Wine with some indication of general character such as production region and grape varietal.
			California Zinfandel. Pinot Grigio della Venezia. Vin Rouge de Pays d'Oc.
Super-Premium	$8.00–$13.99	10%	Wine with more specific indication of character, such as specific production zone and grape varietal.
			Napa Valley Cabernet Sauvignon. Chianti Classico. Beaujolais Villages.
Ultra-Premium	$14.00–$49.99	5%	Additional indicators of character and quality such as "reserve" or specific vineyard designation, certification of regional origin or character.
			Ridge Monte Rosso Zinfandel. Robert Mondavi Stags Leap Vineyard Cabernet Sauvignon. Chianti Classico Reserva.
Icon	More than $50	1%	Luxury brand names as quality indicators.
			Opus One. Chateau Margaux. Chateau Yquem.

Note: See Michelle Tustin, "The Marketing Decade," Wine Business Monthly April 2002 (winebusiness .com/html/MonthlyArticle.cfm?AId=53988&issueId=53965 [accessed June 27, 2004] and Arend Heijbroek, Wine Is Business. Shifting Demand and Distribution: Major Drivers Reshaping the Wine Industry, Rabobank International, January 2003.

*Basic wine is sometimes further divided into two categories, Basic (less than $3) and Popular Premium ($3–$5). The $5–$7.99 category is then called simply Premium. The number and nature of the categories varies from market to market, of course, both in the United States and around the world.

mium), Beaujolais Supérieur (super-premium), and Beaujolais Villages (ultra-premium) provide similar market segmentation opportunities.

Although basic wines make up the bulk of global sales, it would be a mistake to think that this makes them the most important market segment for most producers—that's what the McWine scenario assumes, and it's just wrong. Sales volumes fall as we move up-market, but profitability tends to rise. You can make more money selling less wine, if you can charge enough for it. Lewis Perdue examined the relative profitability of wines in different market segments and reported his findings in a 1999 book called *The Wrath of Grapes*.[22] Here is what he found out.

The direct production cost of an $8 (retail) bottle of California chardonnay, Perdue reported, was $2.08, including grapes, winemaking, aging, and bottling. The total cost of the $8 bottle, including indirect expenses such as marketing and sales, administration, taxes, and interest, was $3.75. The winery (which was not identified) received $4.08 per bottle for this wine, leaving a post-tax profit of 33 cents. The difference between the $4.08 winery price and the $8 retail price went to wholesales ($1.33) and retailers ($2.59). That's where the money goes when you buy a $8 bottle of wine. (And, by the way, you can see right away why a grocery store would be interested in selling wine—their cut of the profits is large compared with the others involved.)

By comparison, an $18 (retail) chardonnay that Perdue studied had a direct cost to the winery of $4.33 per bottle (for grapes, winemaking, aging, etc.) and a total cost of $8.65 when indirect costs were included. The winery received $9.48 for each bottle, yielding a 83 cent profit. The difference between the $9.48 winery price and the $18 you pay at retail goes to marketing and sales ($2.90 per bottle) and retailers ($5.62).

The bottom line, for both winery and retailer, is that per bottle profits are much higher in the $18 ultra-premium segment than in the $8 popular premium part of the market. Although wine sales *volumes* are concentrated in the low end of the market, wine *profits* come disproportionately from the higher end. You should not be surprised, therefore, that large winemakers pursue a strategy of selling lower-priced wines to generate scale economies, especially in marketing and distribution, while focusing upon wine in the premium segments to gain higher per bottle and per case profits.

The multisegment strategy has the potential to produce more total profits than a single-segment approach. The key to understanding Gallo's success, therefore, is not to focus on its total production (which is huge, but mainly basic wine) but to appreciate its multisegment strategy and its ability to compete successfully in all but the icon segment of the market (and I would not rule out an eventual Gallo entry there). Although we tend to think of Gallo in terms of the bulk wines at the bottom end of the product line and the Gallo of Sonoma wines at the top, their real success lies in their ability to populate all of the intermediate wine market stair-steps with competitive wine brands that most buyers probably don't even vaguely associate with Gallo, such as Rancho Zabaco, Frei Brothers Reserve, Turning Leaf, Redwood Creek, MacMurray Ranch, and Indigo Hills. The strategy is multinational as well as multisegment: Gallo's product line includes Ecco Domani and Bella Sera from Italy and McWilliams Hanwood Estate and Black Swan from Australia.

The Robert Mondavi winery illustrates a slightly different approach to the multisegment strategy. Whereas Gallo began from a strong base in the basic wine category and moved progressively up-market, Mondavi started with a high-end base in Napa Valley and expanded in both directions. Table 6.2 shows Mondavi's current brand portfolio, which is both multisegment and multinational. It shows the way that the wine business is evolving.

California Woodbridge wines, Caliterra wines from Chile, and the Italian Danzante line provide Mondavi with a strong and diversified presence in the very competitive popular premium category (and allow the firm to enjoy some scale economies in distribution). You will find these wines almost everywhere. Working from this base, Mondavi has developed clearly differentiated product lines in every market segment up to and including the elite icon level. Opus One, the highest priced Mondavi wine, is a cooperative venture with Château Mouton Rothschild, one of France's elite wineries.

You might think that wineries only produce icon wines, like Opus One, to establish a reputation that will help sell bigger volumes of their regular wines. There is some truth to this, but it is important to realize how profitable icon wines can be—and how commercially dangerous it can be for a winemaker to let its position slip. This fact was driven home to me when, just as this book went to press, rumors began to circulate that Mondavi would sell off its Woodbridge mass-market business (and give up its distribution efficiencies) in order to restore the reputation of the high-profit icon brands.

Icon wines certainly cost more to produce than lesser wines (better corks, bottles, and labels; lower vineyard yields; more wine-making at-

Table 6.2   Robert Mondavi Wines 2004

Category	Brands and typical retail prices *<output of selected wineries>*
Popular Premium	Woodbridge/California ($8) *<7+ million cases produced>* Caliterra/Chile ($8) Danzante/Italy ($10)
Super-Premium	Robert Mondavi Private Selection/Central Coast ($10–$15) *<1.4 million cases>* Arboleda/Chile ($16) Kirralaa/Australia ($15) La Famiglia ($20)
Ultra-Premium	Arrowood Vineyards/Sonoma County ($20+) Byron/Santa Barbara ($20+) Robert Mondavi/Napa Valley ($20+) *<268,000 cases>* Lucente/Italy ($30) Io/Santa Barbara ($35+)
Icon	Kirralaa/Australia special designation ($60) Sëna/Chile ($80) Luce/Italy ($90) Robert Mondavi/Napa Valley special designation ($100) Opus One/Napa Valley ($200) *<30,000 cases>*

Note: Winery information from Robert Mondavi website (www.robertmondavi.com/). Retail price estimates from Pop's Wine (www.popswine.com) and Wine Spectator (www.winespectator.com) websites [accessed April 6, 2004].

tention; longer ageing; and so forth), but not disproportionately so, a fact noted by Adam Smith. And some icon wines are sold by the winery directly to select client lists, so the winery receives the retail rather than wholesale price. A $100 bottle of icon wine yields $100, whereas a $50 bottle that goes through the normal distribution network may only return $25 or less to the winery itself because of the additional marketing, distribution, and retailing costs.

The result is a much higher per bottle profit at the top of the wine pyramid. Lewis Perdue estimated that a $75 icon wine produces $41.50 profit per bottle compared, as we saw, with 83 cents for an $18 wine and 33 cents for an $8 wine.[23] A successful icon wine can be very profitable indeed, especially, as I have said, as part of a multisegment wine portfolio.

But how do you make a successful icon wine? Some people believe that great wines are made in the vineyard (natural *terrior*), and other people say it happens in the winery (superior wine-making practices), but I am quite sure that the way to produce great icon wines is to get a glowing review from Robert Parker, Jancis Robinson, or in one of the top wine-rating publications (*Wine Spectator* in the United States, *Decanter* in Britain, the *Gault Milau Guide du Vin* in France, *Gambero Rosso* in Italy, or *Winestate* in Australia). It is a bit cynical to say so, but to a certain extent the critics decide which are the successful wines in the ultra-premium and especially the icon wine segments. One reason critics are so important is that no one really knows what's in a bottle of wine until the cork is pulled—and even then you might not be sure, since some icon wines are sold young but meant to be drunk years later when they have matured. Only an expert knows what it will taste like in a dozen years. No wonder buyers rely upon expert opinions.

More than this, however, is that fact that much icon wine is purchased for reasons other than drinking: to build or complete collections or to resell as an investment. Collectors and investors understand that it is not what *they* think of the wine that is important but what *other people* think—the people they want to buy their wine. And these other people rely upon the critics, too.

Globalization's Race Up the Wine Staircase

Here is the story of how globalization has improved world wine quality, creating a race toward the top, not the bottom. The 1970s revolution in British supermarket wine sales helped to develop a global network of distribution channels that connected Britain and soon everyone else to most of the world's wine-producing and wine-drinking regions. The development of these distribution channels is important because of the mysterious nature of wine—buying wine in any quantity involves a good deal of trust (as the occasional wine adulteration scandals make clear), so relationships must be made and reputations established.[24] The British supermarket revolution got this process started at one end of the market while the Judgment of Paris did the same at the other end.

Some of the New World wine producers were found in what economists call "emerging market nations," which means that they were just opening up to international trade and investment and seeking export markets. Chile and Argentina fit neatly into this group. New Zealand and Australia also adopted outward-looking market reforms. South Africa eventually emerged from apartheid and began to seek export markets for its wine. After 1989 formerly communist countries such as Hungary, Bulgaria, and Slovenia also entered world markets. They soon discovered the political principle of quid pro quo: if you want to export wine, you must be willing to import it, too, since many of the largest wine-consuming nations are also major producers (Britain the obvious exception). Nations that want to sell wine on world markets generally find it necessary to make themselves open to wine imports as well, so while the bulk of the flows were from producers like Australia to consumers in Britain and elsewhere, a variety of smaller cross-flows between and among wine export countries also began.

Now you might expect that this rapid expansion of the global wine market would result in huge exports of low-quality plonk flooding wine shop and supermarket shelves, and certainly some very bad wines were brought to market. But globalization did not produce the bad wine. Bad wines are generally the product of closed, protected wine markets, where local or regional monopolies profit from quantity (not quality) sales. The wine is bad because it lacks competition from better products, foreign and domestic. Lazy wine monopolists or oligopolists, protected from foreign competition, have little incentive to do what is necessary to improve quality, such as reducing grape yields, replacing "quantity" grape varieties with "quality" ones, and investing in more up-to-date wine production technology. Bad wines were exported early on simply because that is what they had on hand—what they were selling at home.

In Argentina, for example, the local wine industry was protected by 100 percent tariffs, according to a study by Arthur Morris.[25] Local and regional agricultural policies encouraged "massive expansion" of the vineyard with little consideration to quality and little premium paid for better quality grapes. Wine grapes were essentially treated as just another homogeneous agricultural commodity. Not only did overall quality suffer from Argentina's closed market, but so did *terroir* since there was no incentive to produce wines that reflected distinct local or regional qualities. Indeed, all of the incentives went the opposite way. It wasn't globalization that produced bad wine in Argentina, it was the *lack* of globalization.

The opening of the world wine market exposed consumers of poor wine to examples of better wine—even and perhaps especially at the low end of the market and in the producing countries as well as the consuming ones. Consumers, who now enjoyed considerable choice in every market segment, simply avoided the poor quality stuff. Britain's supermarket chains were active participants in this movement toward quality. They could not afford to put their brand names on bottles of bad wine, even inexpensive ones, because doing so would undermine sales in other wine market segments and the value of their brand generally. The cheapest Tesco-brand wine does not have to be a fine wine, but it must be a decent wine—well-made and lacking in any consistently distasteful characteristics. Significantly, the emergence of decent wine at the low end of the market was a revolution.

The first effect of the globalization of wine was therefore to begin to drive bad wine (but not *terroir*) out of the market, especially at the bottom of the market. But that is not all. There is a great deal of inexpensive wine produced in the world, and the existence of this wine lake has brought basic wine prices down, giving winemakers around the world even more incentive to shift production up-market, into premium wines with higher potential profits. These wines must be distinctive in order to compete—they must display *terroir* appropriate to their market niche. Although basic wines remain an important market segment, I do not know of any winery that is trying to move deeper into this already flooded market. The dominant strategy today is to expand into the premium categories, to move as far up the market staircase as possible subject to the need to preserve scale economies and distribution channels.

In Argentina, Morris reports, lower tariffs made decent imported wine available, raising the bar for competition in the local market. Access to the global market staircase provided Argentine winemakers with a very strong incentive that did not exist in the closed economy to improve wines generally and especially to develop wines of greater character and distinction—wines with *terroir*. Argentine wines became not only better, but more varied and distinctive, Morris argues.[26]

Competition has made wines better overall, and the desire of winemakers to move into more profitable market segments has made wines more interesting and more varied. You can see this in the product lines that Mondavi and Gallo have developed, and you can see it on supermarket shelves and restaurant wine lists as well. No one wants to be labeled McWine.

Winemakers want to make distinctive wines, but they also need to make the differences clear to consumers. This problem has not only encouraged large producers to develop distinctive brands (the Gallo Sonoma lines, for example), but it has also created a demand among winemakers for official recognition of distinct local production zones, such as the Stag's Leap district in Napa Valley or the Red Mountain district in the Yakima Valley of Washington State. Winemakers seek to raise recognition of their best vineyards through controlled use of an official designation to differentiate their *terroir*-laden wines from others that lack such distinctive local character. The competition to differentiate and improve quality is intense.

A second effect has been the creation of multinational wineries—businesses that produce wine in several countries or regions. These international wine investments and partnerships have provided capital and technology to New World winemakers and to some Old World ones, too. Although cheaper grapes are the obvious reason a French or American firm might invest in Chilean production, there is much more to it than this. The cost of grapes, after all, is not a very significant factor in the price of a bottle of wine. Wine grapes are an agricultural product subject to the vagaries of weather, insects, and plant diseases. From a simple business standpoint, large wine firms are well advised to source products from a variety of winegrowing regions to hedge bets against natural disasters. A diversified portfolio of wines also offers some insulation from exchange rate swings and other international financial uncertainties.

Especially for European winemakers, international investment is one of the few options available for expansion. Producers in designated production zones such as Chianti Classico are heavily regulated—total vineyard acreage is strictly limited, crop yields are controlled, even the varieties of grapes are determined by law. Winemakers who wish to produce more or different wines frequently have to look outside the zone and sometimes outside their country for opportunities.

Most of all, however, international investments provide opportunities for these firms to provide an even more diversified product line and therefore to compete more successfully in many different segments of the market for wine. To be profitable, therefore, these investments must preserve and enhance the differences, not undermine the effects of *terroir*.

Can *Terroir* Survive Globalization?

The McWine Hypothesis holds that globalization produces wine that is not just cheap and bad, but all the same, uniformly lacking in character. Does globalization produce homogenization? As we have just seen, the importance of product differentiation on the wine market staircase argues against this. Wines that are the same or are seen to be so just slide down the market to a lower level. Globalization in this *terroir* actually accentuates differences because those differences have value in the marketplace. Winemakers have a strong incentive to make stylish or distinctive wine because this can command a higher price. Anyone searching for evidence against the McWine hypothesis need only go to a well-stocked grocery aisle to find a shopping cart full of counterexamples.

But two distinctly global forces *are* pushing certain segments of the wine market towards "convergence," which means dominance by a particular style of wine, a sort of homogenization. I am not *very* worried about the threats of convergence, as you will see, but still I do take the potential for problems seriously.

One trend that is often associated with the globalization of wine is the decline of wines made from indigenous grape varieties, replaced by the "international" varietals, chardonnay, cabernet sauvignon, merlot, and sauvignon blanc, that are associated with the classic wines of France. Some wine experts worry that unusual grape varieties and the local tastes, culture, and traditions associated with them will become extinct. The global markets prefer the classic French varieties, it is argued, so winegrowers who want to take advantage of export markets are essentially forced to abandon unique local wines in favor of the global standard.

Are these very special wines, often associated with a single town or district, truly endangered? Yes, I think they are. But I don't think that the villain is globalization. More often, I suspect, heritage grapes and wines disappear as cities grow and devour agricultural lands, including vineyards. Urbanization is the culprit. Local wines are more threatened by the loss of *local* lands and changing land uses than they are by *global* market forces.

If you want to understand distinctive local wines, you must look to the local markets. Small-volume local wines have always depended upon local markets for their existence. So long as local buyers are attracted to these heritage wines, they will survive and perhaps thrive, even though they aren't traded at the global market level. Pignoletto, for example, is a white grape variety indigenous to the hills around Bologna, Italy. Pignoletto wine has been produced at least since the first century C.E. (Pliny the Elder commented on it); Pignoletto today is made in both still and sparkling (*frizzante*) versions that are crisp, dry, and aromatic. You have probably never tasted even a single glass of it, however. Pignoletto is unknown to the global wine market. I have never seen a bottle outside of Italy or outside of the Bologna region, for that matter. Yet the variety is completely secure from extinction because it is much in demand in the local market. The consumers of Bologna can buy any wine they like, and they like Pignoletto—it goes well with their rich foods. The wine is very good, and the local market is capable of sustaining its production. The winegrowers have even succeeded in having an official Pignoletto DOC region established as a way of recognizing their local product and controlling its designation.

The wines that are most likely to become extinct, I believe, are those that are poorly made or made from mediocre grape varieties. They will and should lose in the increasingly competitive local wine environment. Some of the endangered grape varieties were originally treasured for their high production in the days when quantity mattered more than quality. Their economic *terroir* has disappeared and so will they. The wines that survive will be the ones that have enough distinctive qualities to keep a local market or to attract a broader one. And this will preserve the diversity of *terroir* in global wine.

But there's another threat, perhaps an even more serious one, or at least that's what some wine experts say. His name is Robert M. Parker, an American wine expert who is editor of *The Wine Advocate*, a monthly magazine, and author of many books on wine, especially French wine. Parker is thought to be the world's most influential wine writer. His wine ratings (on a 100-point scale, just like your exams at school) are loved or hated, but seldom ignored. Parker is said to have very particular preferences in wine ("American" preferences, some would say, for big and powerful wines), and people say that winemakers (especially those who make the elite icon wines) are systematically shaping their wines to conform to his palate. Is this true? Maybe.

It is hard to believe that one person could have so much power, but maybe he does. (His website, www.erobertparker.com, quotes French president Jacques Chirac as saying "Robert Parker is the most followed and influential critic for French wines in the entire world.") His wine reviews are *very* detailed and authoritative. He sure sounds like he knows what he is tasting. It is easy to see how wine drinkers might choose to be guided by Parker's ratings, especially those who are willing and able to pay a considerable amount of money for a bottle of wine. If Parker does have the power to determine how winemakers go about their craft, if his palate really rules, it is because the market for icon wines has become a global winner-take-all market.

The globalization of the wine market has affected different segments of the wine market in different ways. In the basic wine segment, competition has driven quality up and driven bad wine out as we have seen. In the various premium categories, product differentiation has increased as winemakers have tried to make more distinctive wines that can compete on the higher market stair-steps. At the icon wine level, the effect has been to focus global attention on a small number of the world's most expensive wines. Buyers in this market want the best wine (or the best of a particular sort of wine). The very best commands an enormous premium in the marketplace because its potential global demand is so vast and its supply so very limited. A single bottle of 2000 Chateau Margaux, for example, retails for more than $500. A 1997 Screaming Eagle Napa Valley Cabernet Sauvignon is $1,595 per bottle (or $19,140 per case) on the Pop's Wine Internet site.

What makes these wines worth so much?[27] It is not necessarily their taste that makes them so valuable, people say. It is more Robert Parker's taste. Some people surely purchase these wines to drink them, but many more do so to own and collect them. They want to own the very best, even if they don't always drink it. Icon wine buyers, if they are collecting or investing, cannot rely upon their own tastes alone because the market value of their wine depends upon what other people will pay for it. Winemakers respond to these forces, too. Bottom line: it is much more profitable to make a wine that will get a high Parker rating than to make an equally good wine in a different style. Top winemakers make a point to have at least one "Parker wine" in their cellars.

Do Robert Parker and the global winner-take-all wine market *really* threaten *terroir*? I understand the concern about the "Robert Parker effect," and I have even talked with winemakers who are open about their desire to exploit it. But I remain skeptical. Although I am not in a position to judge from firsthand experience, I am not convinced that Robert Parker's ratings are forcing icon wines into a single standard mold. It seems to me, from a cursory reading of *Wine Advocate*, that Parker's detailed reviews may actually promote the cultivation of a diversity of *terroir* by creating a better informed, more sophisticated set of buyers. But that's only if they read beyond the Parker number, and perhaps they do. If they don't, then the Parker problem could be serious; winner-take-all markets tend to create extreme outcomes, as we learned in the chapters on basketball and soccer, and a focus on an extreme style of wine is not out of the question.

Wouldn't it be ironic if globalization made cheap wines good, gave moderately priced wines more character, and made expensive wines all the same? That really would turn the McWine hypothesis on its head!

Globalization and Kiwi Wine

Globalization can cut both ways, and that's why I went to New Zealand, to see how the tensions of competing in global markets were playing out on the ground—in the vineyards and wine cellars. New Zealand moved from nowhere to center stage in the world of wine in just twenty-five years—a remarkable achievement.[28] Studying the globalization of the New Zealand wine industry reveals some of the typical patterns we have come to expect from globalization but also a number of factors unique to the Kiwi *terroir*.

New Zealand's recent experience with globalization has deep roots. Wine and vine came to New Zealand in the early 1800s with the first British settlers, but a commercial wine industry did not appear until the 1890s. Immigrants from the Dalmatian coast of Croatia, originally brought in as gum diggers, moved into agriculture and wine production, establishing the first commercial wineries.[29] Thus names like Babich, Yukich, Selak, Delegat, Bragato, and Nobilo figure prominently in New Zealand wine history, which is not necessarily what you would expect for a former British colony. Assid Abraham Corban founded the winery that remained the country's largest until the 1960s. Quantity was favored over quality, and the heavy-bearing Müller-Thurgau was the most-planted grape variety until the 1980s. There is no indication that the wines in the pre-globalization era were distinctive in any meaningful sense, which means that they were like the bulk wines found everywhere else in the world in those days. Some good wines were produced, of course, but the focus of the industry was on high volume, low price, with particular emphasis on sweet and fortified wines.

Two seemingly unrelated events in 1986 can be seen, in retrospect, as the birth of the modern era in New Zealand wine. The first was a price war that threatened to bankrupt the whole industry. Massive overproduction resulted in the sort of price collapse familiar to people who study agricultural markets. The situation was so bad that in 1986 the government took the drastic step of uprooting 25 percent of the nation's vineyard acreage (much of it, fortunately, the dreaded Müller-Thurgau). When these vineyards were eventually replanted, it was with classic French varieties. This was due to the second event.

Ernie Hunter is credited with bringing New Zealand wines to the world market, and I think that is exactly what he set out to do. Exporting wine to Britain and Ireland and elsewhere was a tough sell at that time, but it probably seemed like a better bet than the boom and bust domestic market in New Zealand, with its focus on low price and low quality. Hunter, a transplanted Irishman making wine in the Marlborough region, took his wines to London in 1986 and entered them in a popular competition, the *Sunday Times* Wine Club Festival. I'll bet people thought he was nuts to even try to break into the British market, but he did it. His sauvignon blanc was the hit of the show and established his brand, Hunter's; Marlborough Sauvignon Blanc; and New Zealand wines generally as something completely new in the wine universe.

Everything that I read tells me that Ernie Hunter was an enthusiastic and effective spokesman for New Zealand wines, but the key to his success, I believe, was *terroir*. Hunter really did have distinctive wines to sell—sauvignon blanc wines unlike those produced anywhere else in the world. New Zealand's *terroir*, reinforced by Hunter's salesmanship, put Kiwi wine on the global map.

I'm not a wine geek, but even I can taste the difference. French sauvignon blanc wines (Sancerre, for example) are excellent and display the true flavor of the grape (although the distinctive "cat's pee" nose that is sometimes found takes a little getting used to). California and Washington versions are often on the grassy side. They can be very good, but they are different (as they should be). Marlborough's sauvignon blancs take the wine one step beyond even the French products, however, displaying such flavors as grapefruit, melon, gooseberry, and passion fruit. The climate in the Marlborough region permits the grapes to develop and ripen more fully, giving the wines a fuller flavor profile. New Zealand winemakers who take full advantage of the *terroir* in the vineyard and in the cellar can achieve spectacular results. Many experts say, and I do not disagree, that Marlborough produces the best sauvignon blanc in the world. No wonder the British (and their supermarket chains) rushed to buy these wines. Britain's demand for Marlborough wines pulled New Zealand into the global wine supply chain and New Zealand benefited to some degree from the winner-take-all nature of the market.

New Zealand's wine industry intentionally positioned itself to export premium-class wines, an up-market strategy. New Zealand receives the highest average price of all countries that export to Great Britain—higher than Australia, Chile, or even France. New Zealand's winemakers know the market staircase very well, and their clear goal is to protect their position as a premium export brand and move up the staircase from there. The bottom end of the domestic market is filled with basic wine imports from lower-cost producers. This puts New Zealand in the interesting position of being a net exporter of wine, if imports and exports are calculated by value, but a net importer of wine by volume. It exports a small amount (by global standards) of premium-priced wines, but imports a larger quantity of low-price basic wines, mainly from Australia.

I learned a lot about globalization and wine from talking with winemakers and viticulturalists in New Zealand. I heard several key points repeated again and again in different ways by different people. The first is that the global market for wine presented both opportunities and risks. Without access to foreign markets, New Zealand's wine industry could not have developed the way it has. The domestic market for New Zealand wine has been stagnant overall in recent years and sales of domestic wine have actually declined as Australian bulk wines have taken over the basic wine segment. Premium wine producers, as a group, could not survive, much less thrive as they have, without global markets.

But there are a variety of risks associated with globalization. Jane Hunter, head of Hunter's Wines since her husband Ernie's untimely death, pointed out the problem of exchange rates. She identified the appreciation of the New Zealand dollar as Hunter's biggest short-term challenge, which is not what you'd expect. People tend to think of wine as an art or a craft, but the bottom line is that it is also a business. And international businesses are all affected by exchange rate swings. Here's my quick and dirty analysis of the situation. It all goes back to the wine market staircase effect. As the New Zealand dollar rose on foreign exchange markets, it pushed up the price of Hunter wines and other New Zealand wines (in terms of foreign currency) from, say, the super-premium category to the ultra-premium category, where there are fewer buyers and different competition, which is a problem. Hunter's could prevent this by cutting its New Zealand dollar price, but that creates other problems. It could try to cut costs, saving money in the vineyard or the cellar, but that would affect quality and *terroir*—another problem. Hunter's and the other export-oriented New Zealand producers are caught uncomfortably in the middle when exchange rates take big swings.

Winemaking has boomed in New Zealand. New Zealand's global market success produced substantial new investment in vineyards and winemaking facilities. I talked to many people who were concerned about how overproduction could affect their wine operations. I assumed at the start that they were talking about *global* overproduction—the effect new vineyards and wineries coming online in Australia, Argentina, and Chile especially. They were concerned about this, because, as Don Bird of Wishart Estate told me, anyone with 50 acres of vines is in the global market whether they like it or not (in the sense of being affected by global market conditions). But the global surplus of wine wasn't their main concern. They knew that a global wine glut would have some indirect effects on them, but they believed that New Zealand wines were a strong enough brand to overcome these forces. People who buy New Zealand wines (and pay a premium to do so) are unlikely to switch over to a generic Chilean chardonnay just because the price difference widens a bit more. That's the payoff for successful product differentiation. What they were worried about was overproduction *within* New Zealand itself.

Every winemaker I talked with had new vineyards about to enter production and knew of new wineries about to open; they were worried about a possible wine glut. It was a classic case of the fallacy of composition at work. Each individual winery could justify its own expansion plans because of the vast potential of the global wine market relative to its own small production. But what happens when all of New Zealand's wine producers expand at once?[30] It is difficult to see how New Zealand can triple its exports in the next few years—as it must do to sell all of the wine it will be able to produce—and hold onto its premium position on the wine staircase.

The winemakers fear another price war, one that would be even worse than in 1985–1986 because it might not only drive down prices but also undermine up-market New Zealand's global market niche. The problem is compounded in my view because many of the new vineyards are planted in pinot noir. New Zealand pinots can be excellent, but they do not have the same cachet in global markets as the Marlborough Sauvignon Blancs. When it comes to pinot noir, is New Zealand's *terroir* superior to Burgundy or Oregon's Willamette Valley, two places where this temperamental grape is said to sometimes fully realize its potential? This is a tough market to crack unless you have a clearly superior product, as was the case with Ernie Hunter's sauvignon blanc. I can imagine a scenario where winemakers cut the price of their prestige white wines to get distributors to take more red, ultimately devaluing their most valuable brand asset. Many people I spoke with feared a shake-out in the industry.

The way to prepare for such a crisis, I heard, is to strengthen your hold on the market position and move even farther up-market if you can—another strategy that makes sense for an individual winemaker but is difficult for everyone to do at once. Neal Ibbotson of Saint Clair Estate wanted to see more effort made to promote New Zealand's leading world market brand, the Marlborough Sauvignon Blanc, because he felt that sales of this wine, if properly promoted, could carry the rest (Saint Clair's Wairau Reserve Sauvignon Blanc was the best wine I tasted in New Zealand). But he was taking no chances. Ibbotson was focused upon improving quality at every point in the winemaking process so that Saint Clair's wines would hold their position in the marketplace.

As I have said, *terroir* is everything in the upper steps of the global wine market to which producers in New Zealand and elsewhere aspire. Neal Ibbotson wants to strengthen the image of Marlborough Sauvignon Blanc to this end. David Barmsley wanted to go further. He is a winegrower in the Raparua district of Marlborough, just up the road from Hunter's. He would like to see a special Raparua designation created, so that the quality of his grapes and the wines made from them would be officially recognized. This is the logic behind the movement, which I see in every wine-growing country and region, to create recognized production zones and sub-zones to differentiate wines from their generic cousins. Such designations would be especially useful during a wine glut because they might help a winemaker maintain price and brand position in a falling market. Certainly a producer without a special feature (geographic designation, high Parker rating, etc.) will be hard pressed to survive if a price war breaks out.

New Zealand does yet not officially recognize production zone designations, however, so whereas some winemakers in Sonoma County, California, can use the "Dry Creek" designation to indicate their particular claim to *terroir*, the best that New Zealand producers can do is to use a relatively geographical designation such as Hawke's Bay or Marlborough. *Terroir* is very valuable, however, so a number of winemakers in Hawke's Bay have essentially created their own special designation in the form of a private brand name. They have formed the Gimblett Gravels Winegrowing District association and copyrighted a logo for the controlled use of winemakers in the district. Soil in the 500-hectare region is particularly stony and unproductive (and was destined to be a gravel quarry before its wine growing potential was discovered), just the kind of terrain that often produces outstanding wines in France (the Graves or gravel region), Italy (Grave del Friuli), and elsewhere.

I talked with Steve Smith, who spearheaded the Gimblett Gravels movement. Smith impressed me as having a clear understanding of vineyard, winery, and marketplace. He now runs the Craggy Range winery, a NZ$60 million (about US$40 million) destination winery in Hawke's Bay. Craggy Range owns vineyards in several of New Zealand's key wine-growing regions, which allow it to make a range of single-vineyard super-premium, ultra-premium, and icon-class wines. It's a world-class operation if I ever saw one.

Smith is a firm believer in *terroir*, and he is counting on a global market for his elegant wines (especially in the United States) to make the big investment pay its way. He doesn't think in terms of globalization versus *terroir*, however, because he sees them as related and mutually reinforcing. Smith told me he thinks of the market as drinks versus wine. You can be in the drinks business, he said, or the wine trade. Both are global markets, but different ones. The drinks business is a commodity business. To be successful in the wine trade, however, you have to accentuate *terroir*. Globalization reinforces *terroir*, he suggested, by making it more valuable.

In the end, my trip to New Zealand was most useful in preventing me from walking away with a smug attitude about globalization and wine. From the wine drinker side of the table it is easy to see globalization as an unambiguously beneficial process: there are more choices and better wine at each market step. Pretty nice. But globalization is always more complex than it seems on the surface. New Zealand's winemakers have benefited greatly from the global market position that Ernie Hunter and others helped establish. But keeping that position will be difficult in the face of growing domestic and foreign competition and changing global financial trends. Globalization has been good for New Zealand wines, but it hasn't been all good all the time. The story is unique to wine and unique to New Zealand. I guess what I am saying is that globalization has *terroir*.

Bigger and Smaller

Let me conclude this chapter by returning to the McWine hypothesis: globalization produces big corporations that flood the world with tasteless, Big Mac–wines. I hope I've convinced you that globalization has made wines better rather than worse. But what about the future of small wineries versus big corporations?

The giants of the wine industry—the top five are Gallo, Constellation Brands, The Wine Group, Beringer Blass, and Mondavi—account for only a small fraction of total world wine sales (probably less than 5 percent, although it is difficult to say exactly because privately held Gallo doesn't publish production statistics). So it would be easy to say big firms pose no threat to smaller winemakers. But that's not true. Big corporations have some clear advantages in the global wine market, and the big are likely to get bigger, especially by acquiring smaller wineries. Gallo, for example, has recently purchased Mirassou and Louis M. Martini, two historic California winemakers—the first time it has acquired wine brands rather than developing its own. (As this book went to press, Constellation Brands announced that it would purchase all of Robert Mondavi's operations for an estimated $1.03 billion.)

It is natural to assume (the McWine hypothesis again) that the advantage that big wine businesses have over smaller ones is in marketing, but selling wine isn't exactly like selling french fries or basketball shoes. There isn't a true mass market, more like a collection of micro-markets, and different strategies are needed in each market segment. Big firms have some advantages, but they are not necessarily decisive ones—and they can have disadvantages, too, such as Gallo's reputation for making cheap wines. Their *real* advantage is in distribution—the ability to get their wines on store shelves and restaurant lists—which is the current global wine bottleneck. Wine distribution is an incredibly complex and fragmented process, especially in the United States. Big sellers have the resources to develop efficient distribution systems—big pipes through which they can pump all of the brands in their portfolios.

Does this mean that the Gallos of the world will buy up all the small wineries? No, I don't think so, because small wineries don't need big pipes to pump their output into global markets—a fact that Craggy Range's Steve Smith taught me. A winery that makes five thousand cases a year needs to find a way to sell those five thousand cases at a good price. A distribution system that creates a demand for fifty thousand cases is a problem, not a solution. Sometimes small really is beautiful: small wineries may be better off exploiting the advantages of small scale—selling their wines directly to customer lists or through well-developed relationships with specialized wine merchants and high-end restaurants. None of the makers of ultra-premium or icon wines that I have talked with have any interest in being on a supermarket shelf.

That's not how they want to position their brands. And they couldn't make enough wine to fill the big distribution channel in any case. Small wineries don't need the economies of a huge pipeline and they have offsetting advantages of their own. Some of them *will* be snapped up by the industry giants, but only because of the prestige they can lend to the company's brand portfolio.

Small wineries (and those with superstar reputations, even if they are not so small) are safe, for the most part, protected by their *terroir*. But I don't think this is true of the hundreds of medium-sized wineries, the ones that are too big to ignore the global markets and too small to have established an efficient way to compete in them. Many of them will be acquired by a wine giant, as were Louis M. Martini (Gallo), Ravenswood (Constellation Brands), Sterling Vineyards (Diageo), R. H. Phillips (Vincor), Clos du Bois (Allied Domecq), and Chateau Souverain (Beringer Blass).

These wineries will be absorbed, but not homogenized. Their wines will get better and become if anything even more distinctive (Robert Parker's taste aside). Because that's how globalization works in the world of wine.[31]

* * *

How does globalization affect people, culture, and traditions at the grassroots level? I confront this question in the next chapter by looking at two especially interesting case studies. One looks at the globalization of rags—*your rags*. The other considers the significance of a global consumption cult that has as its symbol an Italian snail. On to chapter 7 and "Grassroots Globaloney."

GRASSROOTS GLOBALONEY

What does globalization look like to the people who don't live in Mc-World, who are too poor to buy a Big Mac, who live in the countries that cannot even attract a McDonald's in the first place? How does it change their lives down at the grassroots level? Does it give them hope and opportunity or does it simply crush them?

These very complicated and important questions tend to produce very simple and confident answers, which is a symptom of globaloney. The debate over grassroots globalization tends to follow strict ideological lines. One side argues that globalization is an unstoppable force for good while the other sees it as the great destroyer of indigenous culture and society, a force that must be opposed. Both sides support their claims with statistics and anecdotes that hide as much as they reveal.

Does globalization help or hurt the poor? Statistics on the world distribution of income are notoriously difficult to analyze and interpret—you can basically find data to support whatever conclusion you like. The closer you look, the more confusing it becomes. You get different answers, for example, depending upon whether you focus upon inequality between countries (taking the nation-state as the unit of mea-

175

sure) or individual inequality, including income gaps within as well as between nations. China, which is a special case of globalization through market socialism, is another problem. What happens to inequality within China is almost as important to the global statistics as what happens everywhere else combined. I'm afraid that statistics provide evidence for everyone and comfort for no one, at least not for me. Per capita gross domestic product is in any case a very limited measure of the human condition.

It is no help that each side supplements its statistics with personal narratives and vignettes. These stories give globalization a human face that the statistics lack, which is why they are persuasive, but such stories tell only part of the story. You can string together stories to be as optimistic or pessimistic as you please.[1] These accounts of globalization are interesting, as stories of real people usually are, and they can be persuasive, but they are still globaloney—grassroots globaloney.

Globalization at the grass roots is muddy and messy and doesn't fit neatly into any ideologically defined box. The purpose of this chapter is to muddy up the waters so that, paradoxically, it might be a bit easier to see what's actually happening at the grass roots in all its rich detail. Here are two examples that illustrate what I mean.

The Global Wardrobe

Everyone knows that clothing and apparel is a global industry. The sight of a foreign label is no longer a novelty to clothes-buyers of the world. Indeed, our closets have become a sort of United Nations of wearable goods. No matter who you are or where you are in the world as you read this paragraph, the chances are very good that if you are wearing clothes at all, you are wearing at least one imported article of attire. For the record, here is my personal fashion manifest of the clothes I am wearing as I write this paragraph: fleece vest (USA), cotton sport shirt (Bangladesh), cotton pants (China), leather belt (Argentina), leather shoes (Brazil). My eyeglasses were made in Italy. There is nothing even slightly unusual about this multinational outfit. Your clothes probably have an equally diverse provenance. Do you know where your clothes come from? If you don't, now would be a good time to look.

Our clothing travels so far and has such a complicated path on its way to our wardrobes that it accumulates a certain personal history—a transnational biography, in the words of Karen Tranberg Hansen, an anthropology professor at Northwestern University.[2] The biography of a silk blouse, for example, begins where the silkworms were raised and the silk harvested through the production of the fabric, the design and production of the blouse, its passage through the commodity chain to a store where someone buys it for herself or as a gift. The biography does not end there, but continues as the garment is worn and thus attends meetings, goes to weddings, and so forth.

Although each biography is different, there are perhaps some generalizations that can be made. Like the wine trade, the market for clothing is highly structured and segmented, and this serves to differentiate the biographies. Designer clothing, for example, is more likely to have European stamps on its passport—France or Italy, for example—and to have felt the touch of handwork, not just machines, at some point along the way. True designer original garments are mainly born in Paris, Milan, or New York—but mainly Paris. Their biographies intersect repeatedly because of the particular customs and rituals of the social class they adorn (couture more commonly appears at the opera gala than a Wal-Mart grand opening, for example).

The biography of a cotton sport shirt or blouse of the sort you see in a Lands' End catalogue is much different. These are the real global travelers of the textile world—they seem to come from everywhere and go everywhere, although this is not literally true. My own closet, which is unexceptional in this respect, includes sport shirts with these original ports of call: Bangladesh, Cambodia, Peru, Malawi, Egypt, Malaysia, United Arab Emirates, Pakistan, United States, and the Philippines among others. There is no central provenance—no Paris or Milan—for sport shirts and the like. But this may soon change, however, because the Multi-Fibre Arrangement is due to expire in 2005.

Between 1974 and 2005 world trade in textiles and clothing was governed by the Multi-Fibre Arrangement (MFA). Under the MFA, textile and clothing exporting countries had to agree to limit their foreign sales to specific quantities (export quotas). Textile producers in, say, Korea could not collectively export more than the agreed national quota. The quotas were negotiated on an individual country basis and so were grossly unequal and inefficient. Some countries were able to hold out for large quotas while others had to settle for tiny ones.

The purpose of the MFA was to regulate trade in textiles and clothing and thus to contain somewhat the rabid protectionism of textile workers and factory owners in Europe, the United States, and other rich countries. I think the idea was that trade agreements in general would be easier if textile protectionism could be isolated this way just as agricultural subsidies effectively took the farm lobby out of the debate. Minus these two strong political interests, the movement toward free trade made good progress for many years.[3]

What happened if a country wanted to exceed its export quota? Well, it could always produce above the quota limit and sell the excess under the table, in the international black market. Some of the suspiciously cheap clothing being hawked by street merchants may bear black market biographies. The one *legal* way around the limit was to build a factory in a country that had room to spare under its quota, which is exactly what happened. Textile producers, especially those in East Asia, fanned out across the globe in search of unused export quotas. They built factories abroad because they could not export more clothes from their existing factories. You could say that these factories (and your multinational collection of "made in xxx" labels) were built by the MFA.

Between 1974 and 2005, therefore, the biography of most common clothing items was determined less by the tension between function and fashion than the conflict between politics and economics. Politics—the desire to regulate textile trade to control political pressures—had the effect of scattering the seeds of the textile industry quite widely. When the MFA is completely phased out in 2005, these export quotas are supposed to disappear. No one is quite sure what will happen, and it may take many years to observe the final results. Perhaps old-fashioned protectionism in the United States and elsewhere will kick in and prevent any radical rearrangement of textile origins. Perhaps, as some of my friends complain only half in jest, everything will simply be made in China—that's the trend they see wherever they look. More likely a new balance of politics, economics, and technology will emerge. Whatever happens, your sport shirt's biography will tell the story.

Now it's time to complete the story. Clothes do have biographies, or at least we can think of them that way, and these biographies are increasingly transnational or global in both the supply chains that bring these items to us and the patterns of travel and migration that carry them along as we wear them. This much is correct. Here's the missing part: we assume that the global biography of our slacks and shirts ends with us. We see clothes and the clothing trade as a process that reaches its peak, or perhaps just its conclusion, when it reaches us. Sometimes I admit this is true. An old shirt is worn out; it gets tossed in the trash, its remaining biography brutally short: dumpster, garbage truck, landfill, oblivion. Frequently, however, a new global journey begins. Your discarded clothing enters the grassroots side of globalization—the global market for secondhand apparel.

The Biography of a Blouse

Worn clothing is an important first-world commodity export. According to the U.S. Department of Commerce, which actively promotes this trade, the United States exported more than 350 million kilograms (about 385,000 tons) of used clothing in 2003. Total U.S. earnings were almost $240 million or about 30 cents per pound.[4] When you see big containers coming off a ship and going onto trucks or railroad cars on their way to Costco or Wal-Mart, remember this: they come into the United States full of new products and go back stuffed full of your old clothes, or at least many of them do. Other major exporters of worn clothing are Germany, Great Britain, the Netherlands, and South Korea. The United States is number one in the used clothing trade, but there is a lot of competition.

This trade goes by many names. You can call it worn clothing or used clothing or secondhand clothing. The term *recycled clothing* is often used in the trade, and I don't see anything wrong with it, because it emphasizes the fact that the clothes are reused and not wasted. I sometimes call it the "rag trade" but I do not mean it in a derogatory way. It isn't that the clothes are rags (although some—the worst quality ones—become rags), but because this is a slang term for the clothing trade generally that inevitably comes to mind when you see a thousand-pound bale of mixed clothing.

Who buys our worn clothing? The people who are otherwise mostly left out of globalization—those in sub-Saharan Africa—are the largest market for used U.S. clothing (although in many cases the clothing's biography includes an intermediate stop in Canada, India, or Pakistan for sorting, rebundling, and transshipment). Other important markets include Eastern Europe, Central and South America, and South and Southeast Asia.

Worn U.S. clothes are number one globally, in quantity terms, but they are not the most desired in all markets. European clothing discards are preferred in some markets because of their higher quality. Exports from Japan and Korea are more popular than U.S. goods in Southeast Asia, however, because similarities in body sizes mean better fit. I saw used clothing for sale when I lived in Bologna, Italy. Bologna is a rich city that considers itself a fashion center, but about once a month an open-air used-clothing annex would appear next to the usual Saturday market, and people would come out to pick through the piles of merchandise. I don't know where these clothes came from and I didn't think to ask, but some of the men's coats had an unmistakable Austrian cut. My favorite find (although I didn't buy it) was a marching band uniform from an Oklahoma high school. What an interesting biography that outfit must have had!

People in rich countries refer to the garments by many different names. "Thrift store merchandise" is common American usage, and thrift stores and charity shops are important outlets. In Britain you'd call them "jumble sale clothing." There is nothing even vaguely international about these names because the goods, although often produced abroad, are seen as "domestic" goods. In third world countries, however, the real provenance of used clothes is hard to ignore, so slang terms for them have evolved to help explain their passage from abroad. In Haiti, for example, worn clothing imports were once called *Kennedys* because of an association with aid shipments of used clothing during the Kennedy administration. In eastern Zaire the term *Vietnams* was sometimes used because of the urban myth that the bundles contained the personal effects of soldiers killed in the Vietnam War. In Ghana the name is "dead white men's clothes." When rich white men die, the reasoning goes, their closets are purged and sent to Ghana. There is some truth to this, as we will see.

In Zambia, the term *salaula* applies, which means to pick or to choose in the Bemba language.[5] I especially like this term because, whereas the other names offer explanations for how foreigners' clothing came into the local market, *salaula* emphasizes its appeal to the buyers: choice. Used clothing, although not always cheap, is less expensive than new apparel and often better quality than home-produced goods. It gives customers an opportunity to choose, to be buyers, and to exercise consumer sovereignty in a world where such economic freedoms are often proscribed by poverty.

How do millions of pounds of worn clothing get from here (the first world) to there (everywhere else, but especially Africa)? Here's a real case—an authentic biography—as reported in *The Guardian* to help you see how the dots connect. Michael Durham traced the 10,000-mile journey of a £50 rayon woman's blouse (made in USA, as it happens) from Leicester, England, where it parted company with its original owner, to the Zambian market where a high school teacher bought it for 10,000 *kwachas* (Zambia currency units) or about £1.50.[6]

The blouse, which was bought on a whim and never actually worn, was dropped off at a charity collection bin at a Tesco parking lot along with a pile of other unwanted items from the back of the closet. A lot of worn clothing passes through charity collection bins. Sometimes these bins are owned and operated by a named charity (Goodwill Industries, Salvation Army, etc.), but this particular one was actually run by a commercial firm, Ragtex UK, which paid the associated charity, an organization for cerebral palsy patients called Scope, for the right to use its name. Scope did benefit from the donation to some extent, but did not actually handle the goods, which were trucked directly to a Ragtex sorting facility nearby. There is nothing unusual about this relationship between Scope and Ragtex except perhaps that Scope received a fixed £100 per bin payment from Ragtex for use of their name; in other cases I am familiar with the donation is made on a per pound basis instead. Sometimes, I understand, the donation bins have no charitable connection whatsoever and exist purely for the receipt of clothing for resale. Donors may suppose that *all* such bins benefit a charity, but this is apparently not the case.

Once at the Ragtex warehouse, the blouse and all the other donated clothing and household items began a complex sorting process. A conveyer belt carried the clothing past workers who picked out items for different market segments. Designer or "vintage" clothing is often sorted into a special bin for resale at local specialty shops. For the most part, however, the clothes are sorted by gender (male, female), age (children's versus adults), type (underwear, jeans, blouses), weight (tropical, which excludes heavy items like coats, and mixed), and quality (items with obvious holes or stains sorted apart from newer-looking goods). Unwearables are sorted as "mixed rags" which have value, although obviously less than wearable attire. Mixed rags become industrial rags, used in foreign factories.

The sorting and bundling of clothes is an important process. Recyclers like Ragtex must be keenly aware of what types and sizes of clothing are popular in different foreign markets. The rag trade is a competitive one, and poorly sorted bales are guaranteed to lose customers. No buyer wants to open a bale and find it filled with unsellable items—too big, too small, too heavy, too light, too worn. *Salaula* means choice, and in this competitive market even beggars can be choosers, in the literal sense, so sorting must be carefully done.

I visited a recycler in Fife, Washington, because I wanted to see for myself how the sorting room operated.[7] But the Savers Company warehouse where I went no longer operated a sorting line for clothing. Sorting is a very labor-intensive process, as you can imagine, and they could not compete with foreign operations. So Savers now ships 1,000-pound bales of unsorted clothes to foreign operatives who sort, rebundle, and resell. I did see sorting lines for other products, however, such as housewares and shoes. Savers even sorts the tons of used books it receives each year, selling many of them through the Amazon.com system.

Savers operates a chain of thrift stores in the United States and Canada that are associated with local charities. Donations are received directly at the stores, and the charities receive a per pound payment without having to handle the goods. Items that aren't sold at the thrift shops are trucked to a regional sorting facility like the one I visited, where they enter the global market.

The blouse that we are following was in good shape and quickly found its place in a shrink-wrapped 45-kg bale of similar items inside a 40-foot shipping container aboard a merchant ship bound for Africa. Two months later it arrived at the port of Beira, Mozambique, where it was loaded onto a waiting truck and sent on its way to Zambia. The blouse passed through several hands before the school teacher bought it. Typically one merchant purchases the container full of baled clothing, buying perhaps one container per month. The individual bales are then sold individually to smaller merchants, who may sell the goods themselves in market stalls or sort them and repackage for sale to traveling sellers.

The container of blouses and other items we are following was purchased by a merchant named Khalid, according to Durham's account, who resold this particular bale to a trader named Mary, who operates a stall in the Kapata open-air market. Mary paid 950,000 *kwachas* (about £150) for the 45-kg bale—an unusually high price that indicates the high expected quality of the goods. Priscilla Msimuko, the schoolteacher, bought the blouse from Mary for 10,000 *kwachas* (£1.50) or the equivalent of a day's pay. I can't help trying to calculate profitability—how many rayon and polyester blouses do you suppose there are in a 45-kg bale? At least a couple of hundred, I'd guess, maybe more. At £1.50 each you'd only need to sell about half of them to come out ahead. Even if most of them sold for less than the initial 10,000 *kwachas* offering price, and some do not sell at all, this could be a fairly profitable business in the context of what opportunities Zambia may offer to someone with limited capital.

This story—donor to charity to sorter to middleman to market stall to buyer—is the common thread that binds the forgotten biographies of our discarded clothes. The story is repeated endlessly with only a few variations. George Packer traced "the long chain of charity and commerce [that] binds the world's richest and poorest people in accidental intimacy" in an article he wrote for the *New York Times Magazine* in 2002. (The article was titled, "How Susie Bayer's T-shirt Ended Up on Yusuf Mama's Back.")[8] The garment in question in this U.S. case study was a thoroughly used and slightly stained gray T-shirt with "University of Pennsylvania" emblazoned in red and black across the front. The shirt was a tax-deductible donation to a local charity thrift shop that could not possibly find buyers for all the old T-shirts it receives. It, along with other unmarketable goods, is sold for 3 cents a pound to a textile recycler, Trans-Americas Trading Company. Packer reports that as much as 80 percent of the 2.5 billion pounds that Americans donate to charity each year end up in the recycling system, at Savers or Trans-America or any of the hundreds of other firms in the business.

Incredibly, even a beat-up T-shirt has an international market, but it is near the bottom of the food chain: tucked into one of the 540 "mixed Africa A and B grade" bales in a container bound for Uganda. Like the British blouse, the University of Pennsylvania T-shirt passed through several hands, and it is interesting to see where the money went. The wholesaler who bought the container paid about 13 cents per shirt, including the freight costs, according to Packer, and sold them off to smaller traders for about 19 cents per shirt. (No one trades individual shirts at this stage, however, so the price is only illustrative; all of the business is done by the bale.) The bales are then sorted once again and repackaged for smaller traders, who paid the equivalent of about 60 cents per shirt. These traders take their goods to rural village markets, looking for a buyer until one is eventually found. The T-shirt changed hands for the equivalent of $1.20 and started a new chapter in its biography.

I would like be present when one of those bales is opened in a African village market. The bales are very tightly compressed back at the warehouse because container freight is charged by volume, not weight. You pay the same for a light container as a heavy one, as I understand it, so each bale is jammed with merchandise. Merchandise just gushes out when you cut the cord. Jeff McMullin, who explained Savers operations to me, said that a good deal of care is given so that the best merchandise is right at the top when the bale is opened; that way the buyer can see that there is value and retail customers have an incentive to dive in for the choicest goods. A bale of shoes, for example, always contains at least two pairs with brand names such as Nike or Reebok, and these are packed so that they are the first thing the customer sees when the bale is opened. This isn't done to try to disguise the product mix or misrepresent the contents. It is just that every bale inevitably contains mainly a mass of items that will ultimately pay back the bale's cost, a few things that will be hard or impossible to sell, and a couple of high-demand articles that spell real profit. No one wants to have to search around hoping to find those profit-makers, so the recyclers know to put them right on top.

There are three questions that I get asked again and again when I talk to people about the recycled clothing trade. The first is, do they clean and press the clothes before they ship them to Africa? The answer is that, as I understand it, the clothes go into the containers in the same state of clean or dirty as when they were put into the donation bins. So I hope you wash those old clothes before you give them to charity. The same is true when they arrive at Africa or a similar market, except that some merchants will pick out the very best items to wash and iron and sell for a higher price, perhaps even marketing them privately to people who do not want to be seen shopping in the market for used clothes.

Does it ever happen that the person who has made a particular new shirt in a third world factory, say, ends up buying back the same item on the used clothing market? Does the global apparel trade ever circle back on itself like that? This is the second most-asked question, and my answer is that it is theoretically possible, but not very likely. The politics and economics of the Multi-Fibre Arrangement determine where clothes are made. A completely different system of political protectionism and economic necessity determines where they go on the used clothing market. Almost none of the new clothing found in first world stores comes from sub-Saharan Africa (Malawi is one notable exception), but much of the used product ends up there. It's possible, therefore, but not likely that a shirt could come full circle.

The final question is how do these people feel about wearing rags? And the answer is that they do not seem to view them as rags (and, objectively, most of the goods we give to charity are not really rags). Rags are what they might have to wear if they could not buy used clothes. Karen Tranberg Hansen, the anthropologist who has done the best research in this field, reports that recycled clothes in Zambia are considered "new" if they come from a newly opened bale, and so have not been picked over or worn previously by anyone in Zambia, for example. This is why the opening of a *salaula* bale of clothing is an important event—it is the opportunity to have first pick from a grab bag of "new" clothes.

Manufacturing Globaloney

What should we think about the global trade in secondhand clothing? One thing that struck me when I first started learning about it is how important it has been, in an indirect way, in the development of globalization theory. You can hardly read a book about globalization, either pro or con, without coming across a vignette involving a T-shirt. Here's the scenario. Traveling in remote China or Africa, I unexpectedly come upon a local resident wearing a Michael Jordan T-shirt or something similar. This experience inspires a "globalization moment"; I come to understand just how deeply globalization or Americanization has penetrated the world. I suddenly realize that people in this remote locale are seeking out the same symbols of consumer society that I seek—that they are being corrupted by the same forces of media, multinationals, and overconsumption as I am. The T-shirt says it all. That's how globalization works.

Having studied the rag trade, however, we know that there is a less dramatic but much more likely explanation for that red number 23 Chicago Bulls T-shirt: it was right on top when the *salaula* bale popped open in the village market. With so many of these shirts discarded every day as American closets are cleaned out, it really isn't a miracle that people like Thomas Friedman see one or two of them in Africa or Nepal, rather it is a wonder that they don't find them *everywhere*! Oh, I guess they do. I wonder how many globalization theories have been concocted from mistaken interpretations of America's secondhand clothing exports?

What is the *correct* interpretation? How *should* we think about the used clothing trade? It seems to me that what you think of it depends a lot on whether you look at it closely and whether you accept it for what it is. The superficial facts can very easily be molded to fit standard globalization rhetoric. The details, however, tell a story all their own. It is a classic case of details versus grand design, which is one of the hallmarks of globaloney.

Although there are people who paint too rosy a picture of how the rag trade benefits the poor who participate it in—who make more than they should of the "win-win" situation—by far the biggest offenders are those who oppose the secondhand clothing trade, seeing in it only a further manifestation of an exploitive and empty McWorld. Let me go through some of the typical charges made in the antiglobalization literature and compare them to a more detailed and nuanced view of the facts.

- The secondhand clothing trade is typical of the inequality built into the capitalist world system. Third world people wear the third-rate rags that the rich of the world cast off. The poor dress in rags so the rich can wear fine clothes.

Who says that secondhand clothes are rags? Who gives meaning to the clothes that people wear? I begin with this statement because it raises an important intellectual question: do people have to accept the meanings that other people assign to their actions and acquisitions—or are they able to manufacture their own meanings and significance? Are the buyers sovereign, capable of forming their own opinions, or are they mere stooges assigned to play a silent part in a grand global drama? I am disappointed that some globalization critics have so little respect for the ability of people, even poor people with little education, to create meaning and significance from their own world.

One of the main conclusions of Karen Tranberg Hansen's thorough study of *salaula* in Zambia is that the people (about 80 percent of Zambia's population wear secondhand clothing) have taken full control of the meaning of these goods and have created a completely original culture from them. It isn't that they have refused to accept foreign meanings, I think, it is simply that they made their own. It probably never occurred to them that they could not do this. *Salaula*, Hansen notes, has become the opposite of rags. "Because rags are a metaphor for lack of access, salaula stands for opportunity, choice, and new chances."[9]

- It is immoral to charge third world people for these old clothes. They should be given to them for free.

I wonder how many would be given away, given the high cost of transportation and distribution, if they had to be given for free? The cost of the charity would discourage the practice, I think. Or the clothing then would get dumped in the port city and never make its way to the villages where it may be needed most. But, honestly, I think most of these clothes would go into the landfill instead of going abroad, adding to the environmental problems of the exporting countries. I also doubt that the distribution system would be as widespread and efficient if there were no money to be made.

I'm also a bit concerned about the economic and psychological effects of free goods. Economically, free clothes tend to crowd out clothes that do cost something, so there would be serious problems for the merchants who do sell clothes (unless they bribed some corrupt official to get access to the best items in each bale). Psychologically, people treat free goods differently from those things they have to pay for. This could start a cycle of waste and dependency. Maybe it is best that buyers pay for what they get and pay for the cost of getting it there, too.

- But making money is the problem, isn't it? The rag trade is just another way for the rich countries to exploit the poor.

That's not the answer I got when I did the math. Secondhand clothing is a profitable business, I am not denying that, but it seems to me that most of the profit ends up in the developing countries. Think back to the figures that George Packer cited in the *New York Times* article. The U.S. recycler received 13 cents a pound for its bales. Out of this it had to pay shipping costs (perhaps $10,000 per container), sorting costs (very labor intensive), local trucking and handling costs, and make a donation to the sponsoring charity. If these firms make large profits, it must be because they move huge volumes.[10] The difference between the 13-cent cost and the $1.20 final selling price goes to pay expenses and provide incomes to indigenous merchants and traders.

That $1.20 price is relatively high, compared with third world income, but what do you suppose other products cost? Clothing made in inefficient local factories usually costs more. Homemade clothes are expensive, too, in the time they require, and may not have the same good quality as secondhand apparel. Actually, I think it is amazing that these goods are so cheap. The prices I read about in the African markets are about the same as I see in local thrift shops, which measure transportation costs in miles not oceans. It is really amazing that clothing can travel so far so cheaply and get in the hands of people who want it.

But citizens of the third world aren't the only ones who wear used clothes. Plenty of first world people do, too, as indicated by the existence of thrift shops, jumble sales, and secondhand stores in Japan, Europe, and the United States. Sometimes globalization critics make it sound like everyone in rich countries wears fine new clothing and everyone in poor countries goes around in rags. In fact, however, secondhand is everywhere. Who did not receive some hand-me-down clothes while growing up? Hand-me-downs are secondhand clothes recycled within a family, and they are an accepted fact of life even in rich countries. As families have grown smaller and more fragmented, I guess, some intrafamily recycling has been replaced by interfamily sales, through garage sales and so forth, and by indirect and anonymous recycling through charitable donations. Market relations have replaced family relations insofar as clothes are concerned.

Interestingly, one of the reasons that used European clothes are often preferred over American items in foreign markets may be because Americans now tend to give away clothes rather than hand them down. Clothes you hand down need to be well made and well taken care of because you personally know the recipient. Clothes you wear for a while and then give away do not—you don't feel the same connection to the new user.

- That's another problem. Doesn't this whole system just encourage global capitalism and consumerism?

I don't think having or not having a secondhand clothes market has very much to do with global capitalism. If you took away the worn clothes market third world residents would simply have fewer options. Maybe that's the problem: I tend to think that options are a good thing—that's probably my consumerism talking—and more options are better, all else being equal. If I weren't already driven by consumerist values, I might not think this way. But there you have it; I am a victim of my culture.[11] Nonetheless, it does seem that the rag trade offers people in third world countries a good opportunity to earn an income if they sell used clothes, provided they can establish the necessary relationships and earn a good reputation, and an economic way of using their incomes to purchase what they need.

I find it interesting that the global secondhand clothing trade is seen by some as exploitive and disempowering. Microfinance, on the other hand, is viewed in just the opposite light. Micro-loans are small $10 to $50 loans made to small-scale merchants who use these funds to buy materials that they work in some way and resell. Borrowers pay back the loan, earn some income, and are able to perhaps borrow more next time. Micro-loans are seen as empowering, giving people at the grass roots income, opportunity, and independence. One of the shibboleths of the antiglobalization movement is that macrofinance (World Bank, Citicorp, etc.) is bad, but microfinance (the Grameen Bank in Bangladesh is the most famous example) is very good. But what do you think people do with their micro-loans? In Africa, at least, they sometimes use them to buy a small bale of used clothes, which they resell.[12] It seems to me that microfinance and the rag trade are not so much different as they are two sides of the same informal economic coin.

- Huge imports of used clothes, dumped by first world economies, put indigenous textile and clothing companies out of business. This is just another example of how the neoliberal policies of the World Bank destroy third world economies and trap them in a vicious cycle of dependency by making it impossible for them to repay international loans.

These issues are raised in a documentary film called *T-Shirt Travels*, which was recently aired on PBS,[13] the U.S. public television network. I wasn't able to see it because my local station cancelled network programming in favor of an earnest fund-raising campaign. (They need the money, they say, so they can afford to telecast controversial and informative documentaries—like *T-Shirt Travels*.)

Although the World Bank isn't on the list of the top ten things I think of when I look at a bale of used clothes, there certainly is a connection. It is true, on one hand, that the market-oriented, open-economy policies that the World Bank, International Monetary Fund, and World Trade Organization (WTO) favor are useful to the second-hand clothing trade. But the issue isn't a simple one (globalization issues seldom are). "When it comes to salaula, the Zambian government is caught in a balancing act of mediating between its different constituencies," Hansen writes, "the overseers of the IMF/World Bank-sponsored structural adjustment program, who insist on obtaining conditions to encourage a 'free' market; local garment and textile manufacturers, who argue for import regulation to protect their ailing industry; and three-fourths of the population, who have seen both their formal job prospects and purchasing power erode over the years of the third republic. It is hardly surprising that the government's stance has been equivocal."[14] The conflict is not so much between Zambia and the World Bank as between the interests associated with the Zambia textile factories, which want to keep secondhand clothing out, and the people who buy worn clothes, who mainly want to let it in. This is a problem of intersecting domestic political interests at least as much (and probably more) than it is a story of global economic governance.

It is true that Zambia's textile industry declined (disappeared, really) at the same time that secondhand clothes imports increased, but correlation is not causation in this case. "It is easy, but too facile," Karen Tranberg Hansen writes, "to blame salaula for the dismal performance of Zambia's clothing and textile manufacturing industries."[15] She blames macroeconomic mismanagement; a combination of national economic policies that produced high inflation, making all domestic industries less competitive; and problems specific to the clothing sector: "High import dependence, high capital intensity, inappropriate technology, poor management, and lack of skilled labor, especially in textile-printing technology . . . resulted in gross underutilization of capacity."[16] It is no wonder that Zambians found imported products, even used ones, a better choice.

- Yes, but they still lost the jobs, didn't they. How will Zambians survive if they continue to lose good jobs, like those in the textile mills?

I'm surprised to find out that textile mill jobs are good ones. I usually hear textile factories described as sweatshops—the kind of jobs that no one wants. I guess that when the World Bank promotes these jobs they are bad, but when its policies discourage them they are somehow transformed into good jobs.

In any case, the rag trade creates jobs, too, just like microfinance does. Think of all the people who make a living selling and sorting worn clothing. It is difficult to count up the number of jobs that the rag trade creates because they are widely dispersed, whereas factory jobs are geographically concentrated, but I know they're there. I'd like to say that these jobs are better ones and that they are free from corruption, poor working conditions, and so on, but I don't think that is always true. Textile factory jobs and market selling jobs are different. It is maybe more secure to work in the factory, but the conditions are worse. Being a merchant entrepreneur is risky but offers a better upside. Better or worse? It isn't so easy to say.

- The bottom line is that the rag trade is just another example of how McWorld works. And who does McWorld benefit? The power elites in the infotainment telesector—the ones who create the logos that sell the products that poor African peasants line up to buy.

The bottom line is nothing like this at all. I hope it is clear that the global trade in secondhand clothes has little to do with McWorld or any of the other simplified images of globalization that you find in the press. The rag trade is what it is—it has its own unique shape, feel, and biography—and should not be treated as some pliable raw material that can be molded and pressed to fit into a standard shape or form. It is not an example of some powerful global metaphor at work but rather a classic case of how different institutions and practices evolve over time to try to deal with the problems of material existence in an interconnected world.

Secondhand clothes teach us that while globalization may sometimes exploit the poor of the world, at least occasionally it offers them opportunities, too. Or, more exactly, they are able to make opportunities out of it—to manufacture a piece of globalization that *benefits* them. This is a theme that I think bears closer examination, which is why we turn next to a grassroots movement that aims to use globalization to fight globalization's effects.

Grassroots Power: The Slow Food Movement

"I remember when in 1986 Carlo Petrini organized a protest against the building of a McDonald's at the Spanish Steps in Rome," writes Alice Waters in the foreword to *Slow Food: The Case for Taste*. "The protesters, whom Carlo armed with bowls of *penne*, defiantly and deliciously stated their case against the global standardization of the world's food. With this symbolic act, Carlo inspired a following and sparked the Slow Food movement. Three years later, delegates from fifteen countries came together in Paris to pledge to preserve the diversity of the world's foods."[17]

The Slow Food movement is a global organization that aims to resist globalization and, in fact, to use the means of globalization to preserve and protect some of the very elements of local culture that global markets threaten to overwhelm. It is an ambitious movement, to say the least. There are about 77,000 Slow Food members in 48 countries organized into 700 local chapters or *convivia*. By far the highest concentration of Slow Food members is in Italy: 40,000 members in 360 chapters. I have been a Slow Food member since 2003. One of my students was doing research on the movement and I became interested (or, as José Bové would say, it "provoked me"). The movement is growing rapidly, especially in the United States.

The title—Slow Food—is not a translation of an Italian phrase (I think it would be *cibo lento*). The movement is called Slow Food—

English words—in all countries and all languages. (Its official logo is a drawing of a snail—*slow* food, get it?) It is impossible to misinterpret the meaning: Slow Food opposes Fast Food on its own terms (and in its own language). No one is surprised to learn, therefore, that the defining moment for the Slow Food movement was a protest at a McDonald's in Rome. It fits the picture perfectly.

But the origins of the Slow Food movement are actually much different—the image of Slow Food versus McWorld is a little bit of baloney, really, manufactured to be especially easy to digest. Slow Food is more complex than this, which is why I find it so interesting. "Many people see Slow Food as the direct antagonist of fast food, especially McDonald's," says Carlo Petrini, the movement's founder and president. "This view would be true if it were not so reductive, and if we had ever mounted a campaign against the king of hamburger chains."[18] Protests, like Bové's attack on the Golden Arches or the anti-WTO Battle in Seattle, are not Slow Food's style. "Our choice is to focus our energies on saving things that are headed for extinction instead of hounding the new ones we dislike."[19] Like *salaula*, Slow Food is about choice.

Indeed, Slow Food is not really opposed to either McDonald's in particular or to fast food in general—there are many traditional street foods that are fast and good, Petrini says; who would want to give them up?[20] The picture of Carlo Petrini confronting Big Mac with a bowl of *penne rigate* is a false image of the Slow Food movement, really, but a very useful one because it defines the movement in a way that is obvious and familiar, especially to Americans. This is useful when your real agenda is both more subtle and more ambitious.

The *terroir* of the Slow Food movement is rooted in the 1970s and a group of young leftist students in the Northern Italian city of Bra.[21] Petrini's account makes Bra sound like a smelly factory town in terminal decline, but one where the people had not yet completely lost their sense of connection to the earth. Petrini and his friends were members of ARCI (*Associazione Ricreativa Culturale Italiana*)—generally described as a left-wing cultural and recreation association[22]—and from this base they formed the Free and Praiseworthy Association of the Friends of Barolo. (Barolo is the great red wine produced in the Piedmont of Italy, where Bra is located.) The group's interest was food and culture and its desire was to learn more about these things and to compare their own culinary heritage with that in other regions of Italy.[23]

There is a lot to compare if you travel Italy north to south, and you are unlikely to see only the differences in pasta shape, especially if you come from the industrial north and are already a bit on the pinkish side of the political spectrum. "[I]f you paid attention to material culture and thought about people's working lives and everyday routines, and the basic enjoyment of earthly goods," Petrini writes, "you began to see the enormous potential of Italy's agricultural and regional heritage in term of both its traditions and its economic potential."[24] The group formed Arcigola; *Arci*, from ARCI, the social club (but also to suggest "arch" as in highest authority), and *gola* meaning appetite (many of the founding members worked on a culinary magazine called *La Gola)*.

Manifesto dello Slow Food

Slowly, the dots were being connected, from politics to food to culture to economics and then, as we will see, back to politics again. "The first people to call themselves 'arcigolosi' or 'archeaters,'" Petrini writes, "were an offshoot of that sector of the 1970s political militancy that coalesced around the daily *il manifesto*."[25] Arcigola's first official publication, as near as I can tell, was a food and wine supplement to *il manifesto* titled *Gambero Rosso* or "red prawn." I've been told that the color of the prawn is a political rather than culinary statement and I don't doubt that it is true. The November 3, 1987, issue of *Gambero Rosso* featured the *Manifesto dello Slow Food*—the Slow Food manifesto. With publication of this statement of principles in the food section of a left-wing newspaper, the Slow Food movement was really born.

There are three things that you need to know about the Slow Food movement. First, it really is an antiglobalization movement, although it makes every effort to avoid the "G-word." The Slow Food manifesto instead refers to the "Fast Life," of which fast food is just one aspect. "We are enslaved by speed and have all succumbed to the same insidious virus: *Fast Life*, which disrupts our habits, pervades the privacy of our homes and forces us to eat *Fast Foods*," it reads in part. "In the name of productivity, *Fast Life* has changed our way of being and threatens our environment and our landscapes. So *Slow Food* is now the only truly progressive answer."[26] The movement is about food, but not *just* about food.

The Slow Food movement is true to its *terroir*—its international organization today reflects its roots in the ARCI social club. This is to say that Slow Food is many things, not one single thing. It is, at the grassroots level, still very much a federation of social clubs. The local chapters host social events that are for the most part relevant to the organization's stated goals. But it is not a burden to attend the meetings, at least in my experience. The *gola* or appetite is well served.

If the Fast Life is about the global, then the Slow Life must celebrate the local. Slow Food events promote local foods, local cooks, local growers and makers, local ingredients, and traditional methods. To a certain extent, the Slow Food movement serves as a marketing organization for these local products and producers, adding an economic interest to the mix. Many members and convivium leaders own restaurants or specialty food shops, write newspaper columns, or are active in the food/wine/hospitality industry. Their participation in the Slow Food movement is personally rewarding, I am sure, and not entirely inconsistent with their economic interests.

Slow Food also promotes what we might call gastronomic tourism, which stems from the founders' early desire to compare their own culinary heritage with that of other regions of Italy. Slow Food has thus always encouraged members to travel, taste, and discuss—to spread the movement's message globally. The focus, of course, is on local foods, producers, ingredients, and recipes. The goal of Slow Food tourism is to have an authentic or "typical" experience.[27] The organization's grandest and most recent effort in this regard is called Slow Food Planet, an emerging world atlas of eating.[28] If you are going to Beijing, for example, and you want to know where to stay and what to eat, drink, and buy, Slow Food Planet will tell you.[29] Slow Food members have thus far posted guides for such destinations as Genoa, Turin, Budapest, Graz, London, New York, Sydney, Reykjavik, and Walla Walla, among others. Gastronomic tourism supports the movement's principles, its social mission, and the economic interests of many of its members.

The Slow Food movement is opposed to the industrialization of food, which means that it supports small farms, biodiversity, and efforts to resist mono-cropping. It opposes the introduction of genetically modified products into the food chain. This gives Slow Food a political agenda to balance or reinforce its economic and social aspects. The movement has opened an office in Brussels now, the better to lobby European Union officials on these issues.

Finally, the Slow Food movement organizes all of these elements around a program of education, not confrontation. The program is very comprehensive, beginning with the Days of Taste (Semaine du Goût) for schoolchildren and climaxing with the University of the Science of Gastronomy (Università di Scienzia di Gastronomiche) which opened in 2004. The Days of Taste are intended to introduce an element of gastronomic education into the typical school curriculum. The point is not to create pint-sized gourmets, although this may happen, but rather to stress the idea that we should give as much attention to what goes into our bodies as to what goes into our heads. Students are educated about food quality, with some emphasis on the classic Slow Food qualities of local, natural, and authentic.

The university is an attempt to take Slow Food education to a higher level, to facilitate research and education about food, taste, food science, and food culture at the highest level. Students take two-year and three-year degrees on two Northern Italy campuses (near Cuneo and Parma). In addition to classrooms and research facilities, the university offers a noteworthy wine library and really good restaurants.

The Ark of Taste (Arca del Gusta) is another aspect of Slow Food education. The Ark is a symbolic vessel meant to contain the Slow World's endangered species. Raising a product to the Ark of Taste, such as the tiny (the size of a 50-cent piece) Olympia oysters of Puget Sound, is a way of saying that this is a food with *terroir*—a history and connection to a particular people and place. It is an excuse to publicize the product and to raise public awareness about its existence and possible extinction. It is a way of educating people about food one product—oyster, cheese, mushroom, or berry—at a time.

The Presidia (I Presídi) goes one step beyond the Ark of Taste. In military terminology, the *presidia* are the defense battalion, a sort of homeland security force. Slow Food recognizes that endangered food products cannot simply be put into museums like pottery shards. They will disappear unless they must have sufficient "economic impact" to be preserved in living form by the market.[30] The Presidia is the active defense against such extinction. It funds projects to help producers of Ark foods gain an economic foothold and expand local markets. A study of the Presidia's programs in Italy by economists at Bocconi University concluded that the economic impact was significant in increasing production and establishing markets for several local products. Although funding to bring together producers, establish quality standards, and so forth can be useful, the power of the Presidia is not limited to its financial impact. When a product is raised to the Presidium, all aspects of the Slow Food network are brought to bear on it. "The study showed how a Slow Food Presidium acts as a cultural matrix, bringing together territory and product, typicality and quality, in which the term 'environment' finds its clearest expression as the 'context of life in the local community'—and new recognition in the local market," according to the report.[31]

The heritage turkey project is an example of the Presidia's potential in the United States. I think everyone knows that the modern Thanksgiving turkey bears little resemblance in appearance or taste to the American wild turkey, which Benjamin Franklin famously championed as the national symbol. The big-breasted factory bird is pretty much everything that Slow Food opposes in food, but how can heritage species of turkeys be preserved in the face of market forces? The answer so far has been to use the Slow Food movement to educate members and others about heritage turkeys and to create a wider market for these products, especially at the Thanksgiving holiday. These old-fashioned turkeys can cost as much as $80 each (versus $10–$12 for the industrial product), and it is hard to see how they could generate a sustainable "economic impact" without Slow Food's help. With it, however, they just might survive.

The Presidia uses economic means to achieve political ends. The goal of these programs is not simply to keep some local cheeses in production, but to contribute ultimately to larger social and political changes. This point is clearly made in an article called "Slow Food and Lula," in the July 2003 issue of *Slow*, the magazine that Slow Food members receive. Paolo Di Croce described a visit he made to Brazil along with several other nongovernmental organization representatives, to meet with members of President Lula's new government. "Slow Food counts for little in Brazil," he writes. "A handful of members and a few Convivium leaders."[32] But the Brazilian officials were both knowledgeable about Slow Food and enthusiastic to gain its support for a "Zero Hunger" program.

The Lula government wanted to use Slow Food's ideas—and its global influence—to help shift Brazilian agricultural policy away from export-driven mass production toward a more diverse system that would support smaller producers and, by producing more for local markets, help eliminate hunger among the poor. Slow Food and the Brazilian government signed an agreement calling for Slow Food to use the Presidia to identify, support, and draw global attention to Brazil's program in general and to specific local products in particular. Slow Food's credibility—and its ability to focus worldwide attention and resources—made it a useful tool for Lula's government as it sought to enact radical reforms in Brazil's agricultural policy.

"This is a historical agreement for Slow Food," Di Croce writes.

On the one hand it puts a great deal of responsibility on our shoulders, obliging us to guarantee support to a huge, complex, far-away country in the middle of a delicate political period pregnant with great expectations for the most diverse and poorest social strata. On the other hand, it reiterates our desire to share the positive experience of the Italian Presidia with the rest of the world . . . as examples of sustainable quality farming capable of responding to the demands of the most varied types of land.[33]

At the very top of the Slow Food pyramid is the Slow Food Award for Defense of Biodiversity (I Premio). These awards recognize individuals and small organizations for their contributions to the global mission of Slow Food. The 2003 awards ceremony in Naples recognized a number of important contributions, including that of Kuul Darjaa, a rancher who lives in the Republic of Tuva, a remote place in Southern Siberia near the border with Mongolia.[34] Kuul Darjaa's achievement was to organize a breeding program to restore and preserve native Tuva breeds of livestock and their distinctive contribution to the global gene pool. The Association Tefy Saina in Madagascar also received an award for its work with rice farmers. It developed a system of natural rice production that achieved high yields with traditional rice strains without resort to the environmentally damaging slash-and-burn techniques traditionally used.[35]

True to its agreement with President Lula to use its influence to support and recognize Brazilian efforts, Slow Food presented a special award to the Kapéy Association—The Union of Krahô Villages.[36] The Krahô are one of 215 indigenous peoples living in Brazil. The award recognizes their efforts to recover and reintroduce a native variety of maize called *pohumpé*. The revival of this crop has helped preserve Krahô culture and practices, according to the award citation, and suggests a practical approach to preserving biodiversity.

I have not attended a Salone del Gusto (Hall of Taste) but I hope to do so eventually. The first meeting in 1996 was like a grand food and wine fair, but with a Slow Food focus on taste, *terroir*, education, and of course socializing. The meetings drew a lot of attention, which is what happens when you bring together excellent food and wine along with people who want to eat and drink, talk, debate, and—oh, yes—change the world. The 2002 meeting attracted 140,000 participants and became an opportunity for what Carlo Petrini calls "cultural marketing."[37] The Salone are now a global forum for education, promotion, and political activism—an opportunity to focus worldwide attention on critical issues in a way that is much different than blowing up a hamburger store.

This brings me to the next important thing that you must understand about the Slow Food movement. It uses the means and media of globalization to undermine and oppose the substance, culture, and ideology of globalization, aka the Fast Life. Carlo Petrini seems to understand that a philosophy of *terroir* is more robust and sustainable if there is a market for it. The Slow Food movement builds its market in several ways, mainly at the local chapter level (I'll talk about this more in a moment). The Slow Food website (www.slowfood.com for the American movement, the global site is www.slowfood.it) certainly displays global ambitions. But it is Slow Food's command of the media that I find most impressive.

The first real publication of the Slow Food movement was a newspaper food supplement called *Il Gambero Rosso*. This modest initial effort has evolved into one of the world's great food and wine periodicals, and, although it is not officially part of the Slow Food movement, it certainly gives comfort to those who are. The October 2003 Italian edition of *Gambero Rosso* ran to more than 350 pages overall—a hefty size for a monthly magazine—and was heavy with advertisements. (A smaller version of *Gambero Rosso* is also published in English.) As in any food magazine there are recipes and articles about chefs and their restaurants. *Gambero Rosso*, however, pays special attention to regional foods and artisanal producers. *Terroir* has pride of place in *Gambero Rosso* just as it does at Slow Food.

The first Slow Book was published in 1987. It was called *Vini d'Italia* and was a guide to the best wines in Italy. Now a joint publication of *Gambero Rosso* and Slow Food Editore, *Vini d'Italia* is updated annually. It is the bible of Italian wines and wine tourism. My copy is a dog-eared 1999 English version.[38] It runs almost 650 pages and lists 10,120 wines from 1,536 winemakers. Each producer of a quality wine receives a brief written evaluation, and the individual wines are rated, with three glasses (*tre bicchiere*) the top award. Getting *tre bicchiere* from *Vini d'Italia* is like being blessed with a 90 + rating from Robert Parker—the ultimate seal of quality.

My favorite Slow Food publications are the *Osterie d'Italia* guidebooks.[39] These books promote gastronomic tourism in Italy by scouring the country, even the smallest villages, for small restaurants, cafes, wine bars, and restaurants that serve authentic "typical" regional dishes. In Pesaro on the Adriatic coast, for example, *Osterie d'Italia* sends you down a tiny walkway to Antica Osteria la Guercia where Roman-era frescos of winemaking (and drinking) can still be seen on the walls. This is not a Big Deal place but the home of *piatti della tradizione pesarese*—traditional dishes including a crisp and flaky griddle bread and a savory clam and bean soup.

What I like about the guidebooks and the other Slow Food publications is that they make money and they sell the message. Economically, they promote the interests of the Slow Food Editore and the restaurants, bakeries, cafes, cheese shops, wineries, and artisanal producers who get mentioned. They serve an economic function, and a social one, too, I suppose, and they serve a political function as well. They draw a world of attention and resources (both scarce in today's world) and focus them on a few matters of serious concern. Slow Food is like the rag trade in that it shows us how the grass roots do not just survive globalization or resist it, but shape it and give it substance and meaning.

On the Road with Slow Food

I am cautiously optimistic about the Slow Food movement's ability to reshape globalization from the ground up. My recent experiences in Italy, the birthplace of Slow Food, contribute to my feelings. I was in Italy to give a lecture about globaloney and I decided to use the opportunity to learn firsthand about the movement and its influence. Here's what I found.

I was fortunate to be in Bologna for the meeting of the local Slow Food chapter where a traditional local product, *mortadella classica*, was raised to the Presidia. About seventy-five of us sat at two long tables at the historic Cantina Bentivoglio on via Mascarella near the University of Bologna to do what Slow Fooders everywhere do: eat, drink, and talk. *Mortadella classica* is the real deal: it has nothing whatsoever to do with your vacuum-packed grocery store baloney. Here's how it is described in its Presidia entry:

> The Presidum's mortadella classica is made from pork from heavyweight Italian pigs and preservatives (only a bare minimum), and flavored with salt, black pepper grains, ground white pepper, mace, coriander, and crushed garlic. It is then cooked in stone ovens at a central temperature of 75-77C. The casing is made strictly of pigs' bladders. When sliced, the meat is not red and pinkish like the industrial variety, but pale brown with much more complex aromas.[40]

Bologna is a city of great food and the everyday ordinary mortadella that you buy in the market there, at the Tamborini delicatessen, for example, is a beautiful product of great delicacy and complexity. But the *mortadella classica* we were served that night really was a thing apart, a stunning revelation not just to me but to the Bolognese there as well. I am sure that the event (along with other programs planned by the Presidia) will help create a wider market for and appreciation of the work of Salumificio Pasquini & Brusiani, the local mortadella maker.

The wines we drank with the mortadella were provided by Azienda Agricola Tizzano, a distinguished local producer. I think the Tizzano wines, including both still and *frizzante* versions of the Pignoletto I mentioned in the last chapter, are very good and would be well received anywhere in the world. But its market is decidedly local, and I think the Slow Food event was a good opportunity for the winery to showcase its products alongside such outstanding food. The problem with making really good wine in the Colli Bolognesi (the Bologna Hills geographic designation), one of my tablemates explained, is that Tuscany with its global reputation for great wines is right next door. Who is going to pay top dollar for a Bolognese wine (especially a Pignoletto variety that you've never heard of) when you can buy a famous Tuscan wine that is rated in all of the magazines? So Tizzano's market must be local if they are to have a market at all. In any case, I learned, producers like Tizzano could not supply a larger demand for their wine if one were to appear. Everything that affects the quantity of production, the proprietor Gabriele Forni explained, acreage, crop yield, and so forth, is strictly regulated by the rules of the DOC. Tizzano cannot make *more* wine because of these regulations, or even very much *different* wine, so they try to make better wine and to make a better market for the wine in the local region. Slow Food, I concluded, could be very useful in this regard.

As good as the wine and mortadella were, the star of the evening was a local dentist, Dottor Romano Foschi, who had set about to make the classic Bolognese pork products using absolutely no additives or preservatives of any kind whatsoever. He was willing to go far beyond tradition in search of natural flavors and processes. The results were simply magnificent—the purest expression of pork that you can imagine. But it was almost impossible to buy these meats. Production was very limited, prices correspondingly high, and distribution direct from the maker only. In a way, Dr. Foschi's incredibly delicious products were almost too pure for Slow Food, his methods too extreme and his production too tiny to be consistent with Slow Food's market methods.

The Bologna dinner was encouraging. It showed me why Slow Food could be so effective on its native soil. The event served social, economic, and educational purposes very well and the political agenda, while present, was subtly in the background.

A dinner in Norcia did less to feed my optimism. Norcia is a tiny walled city high in the mountains of southeast Umbria. It is famous for its lentils, truffles, prosciutto, and wild boar and as the birthplace of Saint Benedict. Norcia is a Slow Food city if I have ever seen one, but not a Slow City—part of the network of towns, mainly in Italy, that have made an official commitment to the Slow Food movement's principles. Indeed, Norcia did not even have a Slow Food chapter, and so none of its distinctive local products were recognized in the Ark or Presidia. Perhaps they were not as endangered as the products found just across the border in Le Marche (where Slow Food influence is stronger). Seated at long tables with local business and political leaders, we feasted on course after course of local specialties and tried to start a conversation about Slow Food. It was a wasted effort, however. Norcia wasn't for Slow Food or against it, as near as I could tell, it was just sort of oblivious to the movement. Clearly the globalization of the Slow Food movement is as uneven as every other kind of globalization I have ever studied.

I was disappointed to discover that Slow Food was not on everyone's mind in Italy. I figured that Norcia, one of Italy's great food cities, would also be a great Slow Food city, but the movement didn't seem to have any impact there. The most common response in Norcia and elsewhere in Italy, even among "foodies," when I would bring up Slow Food was a shrug of the shoulders. Slow Food? Yes. So what about it? Maybe this is a particularly Italian response to a particularly Italian organization with particular political and geographic roots. Everything in Italy is political, I have learned, and regional, too. Slow Food sits in the left-north (left politically, north geographically) in this cultural geography and many of the people I talked to were maybe left-south or center-right-north.

I didn't find the broad grassroots support for Slow Food in Italy that I expected. But maybe a grassroots globalization movement, even one as ambitious as Slow Food, doesn't really have to infiltrate the grass roots. In fact, ironically, maybe it is most effective, from the political standpoint, when it is a grassroots movement of influential urban elites, like the people around the table in Bologna. Grassroots elites? Maybe I drank too much wine.

Another dinner in Umbria forced me to consider a dark side of the Slow Food movement that I had not previously noticed. We were staying near Deruta at an *agritourismo*, which is a sort of farmhouse bed and breakfast. The farm seemed to typify the Slow Food ideal. Not only was the prosciutto made from one of the farm pigs, for example, we even knew the pig's name, Timmy. What about the Slow Food movement, I asked? Our host shook his head. Very bad, he said. It can ruin everything. When Slow Food identifies an artisanal product, like a cheese or a salami, he explained, then suddenly everyone has to have it precisely because it has been given the Slow Food stamp. It must be the best. So they all rush in to buy this great thing, the supplier of which of course cannot possibly meet this new demand. The producers try, but in doing so they cut corners or make compromises and end up destroying the very qualities that they set out to preserve. That's what my Umbrian host saw in the Slow Food movement.

This was a very different, almost cynical view of Slow Food's effects, but I knew what he was talking about. He was describing how a winner-take-all market works (as we first learned in chapter 3). Once people or products are ranked, the way *Gambero Rosso* ranks wine and restaurants, then why settle for second best (even if it is almost as good)? The market for the finest or most authentic and wholesome products is not large in absolute terms, but it is huge compared to the ability of artisans to satisfy it once Slow Food or someone else turns on its spotlight. The flip side of the Presidia, then, is that the "economic impact" that can save a local product from extinction under one set of circumstances may instead bury it.

Another internal contradiction in the Slow Food strategy made the news as I was finishing the first draft of this chapter. Slow Food, of course, tries to think global and act local. So consumers are encouraged to purchase local products from local makers and growers. But some Slow Food projects, like the heritage turkey initiative, can only succeed if the market for critical products expands well beyond the local area. So sometimes, Slow Food says, you ought to buy products from far away, when they are "merit" goods. This contradiction—buy local except when you shouldn't—showed up on the op-ed page of the *New York Times*. "Shoppers at farmers markets in cities around the country might feel virtuous because they're filling their baskets with eggs and chard and apples offered by farmers within driving distance," wrote Patrick Martins, director of Slow Food U.S.A.

> But markets and community supported agriculture programs, wonderful as they are, can't by themselves save American agriculture. To do that, we have to look beyond the "eat local" slogans at the farmers markets in New York, San Francisco and Chicago and think of how to give American consumers across the country access to regional products that might disappear unless they are raised in much larger numbers. In some cases the answer is to think locally—but to ship nationally.

Global trade and mass communication tend to erase cultural and biological diversity, but as the writer Michael Pollan argues, we can turn them into powerful tools for rescuing this diversity.[41] Clearly, navigating this global–local geography is a tricky task.

Manufacturing Globalization

The rag trade is an example of grassroots globalization, where people have been able to resist globalization or to shape it to suit their values and needs. Slow Food goes further, plotting to use global forces like the media and politics to create a different species of globalization entirely. These two examples don't prove that globalization is good for the world's grassroots cultures—it is impossible to do that with one or two or ten case studies—but they should make you doubt that globalization is *always* bad at the bottom. It ought to make you wonder if some of the arguments about a race to the bottom and scorched grass roots aren't just more globaloney.

I do believe that ordinary people have more control over their lives than is commonly acknowledged in the globalization literature. In the old days, I guess, we might have leaned upon nations and nationality to define life's parameters and establish identity. If, as I keep reading, globalization is tearing down national walls, then it might be logical to conclude that we are unprotected from global forces and can only be overwhelmed by them. But maybe, just maybe, we have the ability to manufacture our own identifies. Perhaps, as nation-states become less important as defining institutions, food and clothes (and sports teams and the like) have become more important.[42] This could account for the unexpected attention that they get from globalization commentators.

*   *   *

The paradox, clearly apparent in both of this chapter's case studies, is that we create globalization even as we use it to manufacture our own identities. The image that we create of globalization is thus our own image. No, that's too strong. That gives us too much responsibility for globalization (and globaloney). But it is the idea that I want you to hold in your mind as you turn the page to begin the next chapter.

GLOBALIZATION AND THE FRENCH EXCEPTION

No book about globaloney would be complete without a chapter on the French and their attitude toward globalization, Americanization, and market forces generally. The French have a certain idea of globalization—and globaloney—that demands our attention.

Why do the French hate globalization so? José Bové became a national hero when, provoked by the existence of a McDonald's restaurant, he destroyed it. What is it about globalization—or about the French—that has created and nurtured such deep and sometimes violent animosity? I have developed a theory of French antiglobalist sentiment. It is a very good theory—an excellent one by the admittedly pitiful standards of the globalization literature. It has everything a good globalization theory should have, including elephants! It is, appropriately, 100 percent globaloney. That is, it is a big theory based on vivid images, a compelling narrative, and little in the way of evidence. It is dramatic and convincing—and highly problematic. But I think it contains a good deal of truth nonetheless.

My plan in this final chapter is to present my theory of French globalist exceptionalism and then, as I have tried to do with the theories of others, to expose its flaws and undermine it as best I can by appealing to facts, not images, metaphors, and selective observation. Against all odds, I believe, this tortured and seemingly self-destructive process is not entirely a waste of time. It produces in the end a number of clear claims and findings that tie together the various themes developed in the first seven chapters and in this one about the French, too. It is an exercise in globaloney that sums up what I have learned about the subject and, I hope, gives you something to walk away with.

An Apology to the People and Nation of France

This chapter is going to use the French reaction to globalization to make some broader points about how and why globaloney is produced and consumed. I will therefore necessarily and intentionally begin by distorting French attitudes and actions. I need to do this to make my point, but I acknowledge that it is unfair, so I want to apologize in advance—just as those who have similarly manipulated Michael Jordan, McDonald's, Starbucks, Coca Cola, and Mickey Mouse probably should have apologized to their victims. Nothing personal. It's just business.

An apology to France and the French is especially appropriate, however, because in some respects they are my heroes. Although I am going to accuse them of blatant antiglobalist globaloney, I have to say that they lead the world in their resistance to globaloney of the other kind. This book, *Globaloney*, has relentlessly criticized antiglobalization rhetoric, but my earlier book, *Selling Globalization*, concentrated on the opposite side of the debate. *Selling Globalization* argued that globalization was vastly oversold. Certain political, economic, and intellectual interests promote globalization, I argued, as a way to advance their own agendas, which often as not have little connection with globalization at all. My harshest criticisms was aimed at the *hyper-globalists*—a term coined by the French—who promote globalization as an irresistible force that no state and no person can stop or control. Your only choice is to accommodate it (and accept the business-friendly policies it requires) or be left out and doomed to backwardness.

Manfred B. Steger's 2001 book *Globalism: The New Market Ideology* advanced this argument much further.[1] Steger argued that the *hyper-globalists* have been able to dominate the globalization debate, and advance their political and economic agendas, not because the facts are on their side but rather because they have been able to establish ideological hegemony. They have sold an idea of globalization (globalism) that, once accepted, requires submission to the policies and practices that are associated with it. The triumph of globalization, which is so often proclaimed, is really, according to Steger, the triumph of the ideology of the globalists.

Globalism, Steger argued, has five main points.[2] It claims that (1) globalization is a natural economic process of market expansion, implicitly privileging economic factors over political and social ones. It is (2) irresistible and irreversible. No one (3) is in charge of globalization. It is an impersonal natural force that is not associated with any particular class, group or interests. Globalization therefore (4) benefits everyone. Furthermore, it promotes democracy (5) by shifting power away from elites. Steger argued effectively that each of these points is false but, taken together, they form a very powerful rhetoric and effective political tool. Globalism paints an image of a world where accepting globalization (and whatever policies and interests are attached to it) promises great benefit while rejecting these interests is futile, corrupt, and ultimately self-destructive.

The truth, as Steger obviously understands and as *Globaloney* hopes to make even clearer, is that globalization reflects its *terroir* (to use another French term). The grand universalisms that globalism proclaims create a vivid but unrealistic image—a sort of false global universalism. Globalization is more complicated than this. Globalization is political and cultural, not just economic (claim 1). It has been both resisted and reversed in previous historical eras (2). There are elites with strong interests tied to globalization (3) who will seek to promote and adapt it for their own uses. It does not necessarily benefit everyone (4) nor is it an especially democratic process (5).

Here is where the French exception comes in. Globalism swept the world in the 1990s, or nearly so. No one seemed immune to its outrageous claims except the French. They just weren't buying it. "What is the market?" asked French prime minister Édouard Balladur.[3] "It is the law of the jungle, the law of nature. And what is civilization? It is the struggle against nature."[4] Civilization is France's mission in the world (at least according to the French). Succumbing to globalism and the law of the jungle was never an option.

French intellectuals wrote books condemning globalization, such as *Firing Back: Against the Tyranny of the Market 2* and *The Economic Horror.*[5] French farmers brought Paris to her knees by clogging the roads with agricultural equipment whenever the idea was raised that they adapt to global market forces. The Académie Française constantly monitored French language use to keep foreign words out and maintain linguistic purity and independence. The French culture ministry performed a similar function more generally, working to preserve and advance French films and music in resistance to the global assault of foreign (mainly English-language, often American) alternatives.

The defining institution for France is not the market or even the church—it is the state. Even in the heady globalization frenzy of the 1990s, the French state showed itself to be up to the task not just of resisting global forces, but of advancing the interests of France and of civilization, especially through its influence on European Union policies. The single currency, the euro, is in many ways a French invention designed to allow France and Europe to resist the force of American monetary hegemony. The proposal for a European Union constitution is also a French initiative (former French president Valéry Giscard d'Estaing was the draft document's chief architect) intended to put a distinctly French stamp upon the state, globalization, and governance, at least so far as Europe is concerned. Even the European Union's famous "banana" trade war with the United States, fought over European trade preferences for Caribbean-grown bananas, was rooted in French principles—the need to resist the law of the market jungle.

Globalism, as Manfred Steger defines it, is globaloney, pure and simple and the French are to be congratulated for resisting it with such energy. But they went too far. Resisting globalist ideology is one thing (it is a French thing—*très* cool, *très* smart, *très* French). Violence directed against innocent hamburgers, and the intensity of the French reaction in general, is another. Mere resistance to globalization does not justify the actions of someone like Astérix look-alike José Bové, who became a hero for destroying a McDonald's that provoked him by its very existence.[6]

No, the French see the same images and hear the same narratives as you and me, and they seem to resist them, which is good. But it's not necessarily because they see through the rhetorical curtains that fool the rest of us. Their response is as much emotional as intellectual, and it is based upon a particularly French understanding of globalization.

Aida versus *Aida!*

If you want to understand why the French react so strongly to globalization you must go to the theater—twice. First go to the opera house and see Giuseppe Verdi's great work, *Aida*, which was first performed in 1871. Then go to the playhouse, or wherever touring Broadway musicals are performed in your town, and see the Walt Disney production of *Aida: The Musical* (which I'll call *Aida!* with an exclamation point to differentiate it from Verdi's *Aida*), which has first performed in 1999. Everyone thinks *Aida* is a story about elephants and pyramids (because it is set in ancient Egypt), but it is really a story about globalization and the nature of the relationships that it creates and sustains. The difference between *Aida* and *Aida!* explains why the French so emotionally oppose globalization today. *Aida* is globalization *à la français*—as the French understand it. *Aida!* is globalization as it is or seems to be—a nightmare!

Verdi's *Aida* was written during the age of Victorian globalization late in the nineteenth century. As you may know, the Victorian globalization was by some measures even more complete than globalization today. Products, people, and money moved around the world with great fluidity—less regulated, on the whole, than they are today. The political organization of globalization was much different, however. Globalization was state-based and Europe-centered. It was overtly imperialistic in form, built on explicit colonial empires (Africa and Asia) and economic dependencies (Central and South America) that amounted to the same things. Verdi's opera *Aida* was created as a commentary on imperial globalization. Here's how the story unfolds.

Aida is a story about a love triangle: an Egyptian soldier Radames is torn between his own Princess Amneris and an enslaved Ethiopian princess, Aida. Although the play is set in Egypt, complete with elephants, it is easy to see that the Egyptians are really Europeans (Romans, probably, since Verdi was Italian). That Aida is Ethiopian gives it away—Ethiopia was an Italian colony. The musical love triangle is really about the tension between imperial center (Princess Amneris) and colonial periphery (Aida), with the dual conquering/civilizing spirit of Europe (Radames) caught in the middle. Verdi's European audience was comfortable in its imperial opera society. It is no accident that so many colonial capitals featured ornate opera houses—just part of the civilizing mission. But the Europeans were also sympathetic to the demand for colonial independence that is the flip side of conquest and civilization. They could relate very well to the tensions Radames felt.

Verdi's use of symbolism in this opera is *very* powerful: noble Aida, who represents the conquered nations, is made a *slave*, not just a subject or servant. At the end of the first act priests actually consecrate the imperial sword that enslaved her. Forced to choose, Radames takes Aida the Ethiopian over Princess Amneris—a fatal mistake. The lovers are found out, captured, and sealed together in a tomb, there to die. The story ends in death and a prayer for peace. The tension between empire and colony is left unresolved, which is also a fitting commentary on Verdi's times, which left unresolved so many such themes.

Walt Disney's *Aida!* is a story about globalization today.[7] Although it is tempting to say that it is an American view of globalization, because Disney is an American company and this is an American production, the facts undermine this conclusion. *Aida the Musical* ("suggested by the opera," the program says) features music by British rocker Elton John, lyrics by Tim Rice (of *Jesus Christ Superstar*, *Evita*, and other global musicals), and book by David Henry Hwang of *M. Butterfly* and *Golden Child* and Linda Woolverton of *Lion King* and *Beauty and the Beast*. This is a multinational, multicultural, overtly commercial operation. Maybe that *does* make it distinctly American, I suppose, but you can also argue that it is more of a global than a national product.

The Elton John musical is set in Egypt, just like Verdi's opera, but by the dress of the players we know that it is really London or New York (or even Paris, I suppose). The Egyptians are waging a war of conquest against Nubia, not Ethiopia, which is a significant change. Instead of colonial revolt against the center, we have white aggression against the black periphery. North versus South, White versus Black. Very clear: wealth and power-seeking capitalists versus exploited indigenous natives. The context is thus transformed from Victorian imperial globalization to contemporary capitalist globalization. The Elton John musical makes the new context especially clear by transforming Princess Amneris, literally, into a material girl. She celebrates conspicuous consumption, even singing a song about the glory of wearing beautiful clothes (although later she shows us that she knows it is only a sad facade).

Here are three significant points to consider in comparing the *Aida/ Aida!* productions. First, both involve North–South conflict. But Ethiopia initiates the violence in Verdi's version—a colonial revolt—while the capitalist center is the exploitive aggressor in the *Aida!* Disney play. The force of conquest has shifted from politics to economics, from empire to multinational corporation, from state to market, from France to the United States.

Second, both stories feature a revealing act of generosity by Radames toward his conquered foes to show us that he appreciates the moral dilemma of his (and our) position. Some of the Ethiopians get *freedom* in Verdi's opera—a significant gift in the imperial context because, of course, it stresses the power of the state and the reality of enslavement. The act is generous in the Disney musical, too, but the gift is much different: Radames gives some of the Nubians his worldly possessions (his worn or recycled material goods) rather than their freedom—a rather cynical statement about globalization today in my opinion and one that stresses its materialist rather than humanist values.

Finally, the endings differ in significant ways. Verdi's opera, as already noted, ends somberly with prayer and a call for peace. It is a sad ending, one dominated by the weight of fate and the hope that it can be overcome by human heart and mind. Radames and Aida die in the Disney version, too, but I think it is actually presented as a happy ending tailored to a feel-good society. The lovers reappear post-death, apparently reborn, at a high-end exhibition of ancient Egyptian artifacts—the kind of blockbuster museum show or gallery opening you might see in London or New York (or Paris). The tension between capitalism and indigenous culture is easily reconciled by the Disney folks: capitalism triumphs, but indigenous culture lives on—in museums, movie theaters, the Broadway stage, and on pay-per-view television. We, the audience, don't need to pray that the contradictions will be reconciled—we have resolved them ourselves by the act of buying our $75 tickets. Redemption has a market price in *Aida!* globalization.

Prospero and Caliban

What do *Aida* and *Aida!* have to do with the French reaction to globalization? My argument is that the French, like many people around the world, see globalization as imperialism in a new suit of clothes. This much is unexceptional. What makes France an exceptional case is the particular nature of their *own* imperial experience. French imperialism was *total* imperialism. Conquest was total: economic and political domination was not enough. French imperialism insinuated itself into every crack and crevice of colonial society: language, culture, education, food, music, literature, everything. And the relationship between imperial center and colonial satellite was not that of equals or even relative unequals. It was about civilization versus savage nature, exactly as Balladur said about globalization today. And the job of civilization does not end with money and power—it extends seamlessly to the very roots of social culture, to the seeds of savage nature. That is how France understands imperialism and therefore globalization. *Aida*.

You do not have to take my word for this. You can ask the people who were subject to French total imperialism. They have much to say, and they say it well—in the good standard French they were forced to learn as children—because their intellectuals and leaders were all educated in elite French *écoles* and came to understand their colonial condition as seen through imperial French eyes.

Total imperialism could be seen, heard, tasted, and felt in every corner of the French empire. Take clothing, for example. The citizens of France's colonies were pressured to dress like the French as well as talk and eat like them. "The way people clothe themselves," writes the Martinique-born francophone intellectual Frantz Fanon in *A Dying Colonialism*, "together with the traditions of dress and finery that custom implies, constituted the most distinctive form of a society's uniqueness, that is to say the one that is the most immediately perceptible."[8] (I am what I wear and how I dress, sings material girl Princess Amneris in Disney's *Aida!*—capturing the idea exactly). French imperialism's single-minded drive to establish European patterns of dress and to suppress other styles, including especially the scarves worn by Muslim women in Algeria, surely had many effects on their colonial subjects. Did it civilize them? I'm not sure. But perhaps an unintended consequence was to create a market for secondhand European-style clothing in unlikely parts of the world. I wonder just how much of the global trade in worn and recycled American and European clothing owes its existence to tastes created a hundred years ago by French total imperialism?

From what I have said, French imperialism sounds rather ghastly. If antiglobalists view commercial advertisements for Nike shoes and Air Jordan T-shirts as aggressive actions of cultural oppression, I cannot imagine what they would think of French total imperialism, which explicitly sought to transform indigenous societies into caricatures of France in the name of civilization, to "transform the sociocultural complexion of the whole area by a massive indoctrination in all things French."[9]

But it was done with good intent. The special mission of France, according to French intellectual tradition, is to civilize the world, to overcome savage nature. O. Mannoni described the relationship as *Prospero and Caliban* in his book on the psychology of French colonization in Madagascar, drawing upon two famous characters from Shakespeare's play *The Tempest*.[10] Propsero is "civilized"—drawn to books, possessing mystical powers to influence people and control nature. Prospero is French, I think, although in *The Tempest* Shakespeare made him Italian. He is certainly civilized. Caliban is a brute—an ignorant *savage* (a term first used by Europeans to describe the indigenous peoples of newly discovered lands). He is a slave: he has traded his freedom for Prospero's fine language (a trade imposed by the French on their own colonial subjects). Caliban is not really civilized by this process, I suppose, as he might be in a French version of the play, but at least he is not simply exploited without a compensating benefit, as "savages" sometimes are.

These, then, are the key elements of my theory of French globalization. France's view of globalization is deeply rooted in its own imperial experience (the *Aida* experience), which continues even today in some respects through France's special relationships with many of its former colonies.[11] French leaders find it difficult even to think of globalization in other than imperial terms. In *France in an Age of Globalization*, for example, former French foreign minister Hubert Védrine says that "America today is much more than the British Empire and closer to what the Roman Empire was compared to the rest of the world in that era. . . . American globalism—the 'World Company' to use the expression of a spoof on French television—dominates everything everywhere. Not in a harsh, repressive military form, but in people's heads."[12] You can see the French attitude. Empires. Domination. Everything. Everywhere. Clearly this is hyperbole, but according to my theory it reflects the way that the French would organize globalization if they were in charge of it. It would be total globalization that seeks to alter fundamentally all aspects of politics, economy, and society, recasting them in the mold of the imperial center. That's what they expect, so that's what they see. Everything. Everywhere.

That such a globalization would be controlled (and not the result of decentralized market processes) goes without saying. The French idea of globalization is state-centered and controlled—it is *intentional* globalization, nothing accidental about it. No wonder that French-inspired antiglobalists are always looking to see who is running globalization. (Multinational corporations? Media moguls? Who?) It goes without saying that *someone* must be pulling the strings. Individualist, market-based globalization makes the French nervous. It "has its merits," Védrine writes, "but it leads to the fragmentation of collective structures. The United States is very much at home in this sort of world. I don't think France is ready to submit to this type of globalization without seriously examining it first."[13] The idea that one must *submit* to individualism says a lot in itself.

And, finally, globalization, like imperialism, is a relationship between Prospero and Caliban, between the civilized master and the savage slave. If this is true, you can see why globalization would enrage the French. You can see why a Frenchman might feel provoked, even by an innocent hamburger restaurant. The French see all around them the evidence of globalization, but not *their* globalization—not civilizing, state-centered, French globalization. Look around: foreign clothes, foreign music, foreign literature, foreign films. It must seem to the French that they are the victims of someone else's total globalization. Even their language is under constant assault, especially from the Internet where English is the lingua franca.

And the invasion is not just on the surface; it has spread deep into the heart of France like some particularly virulent form of cancer, infecting even France's blood, its wine. The great French wines like Chateau Margaux and Chateau Latour still sit comfortably at the top of the global wine market staircase, but this may have as much to do with Robert Parker's influence (an American!) as French wine tradition. The superiority of French vine and wine is no longer unquestioned. Indeed, France's reputation in this new era of globalization has sunk so low as to permit direct insult.

The *Financial Times* reports that David Levine, a London hotelier and restaurateur, has built his own winery in the Loire Valley, importing buildings and equipment literally lock, stock, and barrel from—gasp!—Australia. "Local builders had no idea how to build a modern winery," Levin says. His white wines feature "New World winemaking techniques—modern hygiene standards, stainless-steel tanks, temperature-controlled fermentation" and so on. They reject French winemaking traditions. The new wine is intentionally sold as a simple varietal (sauvignon blanc) not under the local designation (Touraine Appellation d'Origine Controlée). The regional designation "is no longer a guarantee of quality," according to the winemaker, Thierry Merlet, a Frenchman trained in Oregon and South Australia. "What matters is the soil, the winemaking and the marketing. What drives us is what we can sell. If the customer wants to drink Sauvignon Blanc, then that's what we should put on the label."[14] Thus are a thousand years of French wine tradition replaced in one stroke by the savage law of the market jungle. You can see how insulting this would be to the French.

What is most maddening about this situation, from the French point of view, is the way that the Prospero–Caliban relationship has been reversed, as this wine example makes clear. It isn't wise, civilized Prospero, with his books and fine wine, who is directing the action of the play. No, it is a savage Caliban who watches television situation comedies, slurps down liters of Coca Cola, and lives by the law of supply and demand. *This* globalization is simply crazy—the culture of the *idiots* is being imposed upon the island of civilization.

And who is the Caliban? The French idea of globalization is not faceless and impersonal. (This is one reason why they have succeeded in resisting the idea of pro-market globalism.) French globalization is intentional and directed; someone has to pull the strings. The French have even coined a term—*dirigiste*—to describe a directed system of central command and control. Who is in charge of globalization? It should be Prospero/France, of course, but now instead it is Caliban/America. Savage, uncultured America, the original Caliban, now plays Prospero, as Mickey Mouse did in the sorcerer's apprentice segment of *Fantasia*, and with the same disastrous result. Worse, perhaps America probably thinks that *it* is Prospero and that France and the rest of the world are uncultured Calibans. Oh my. That is more provoking still! No wonder France is upset.

Once the idea has entered your mind that the United States has assumed the imperial role and assigned to France the position of savage colonial, as I argue it has penetrated the minds of the French intellectuals, then your eyes and ears constantly seek out and find evidence that reinforces it. This is the principle behind Adam Smith's "Newtonian" rhetoric—provide an argument that lets people connect the dots for themselves and they will accept your conclusions without question. People like connecting the dots—it gives them a feeling of satisfaction to do this.

You will find plenty of evidence to support this outrageous idea, once you have it planted firmly in your mind. You will see crude American culture and products and influence everywhere and each observation will make you utter, "Caliban, Caliban"—if you are inclined to that sort of thing. McDonald's will figure prominently in your nightmares, of course. There are only a few McDonald's in France compared with the thousands of French (and Italian and Chinese) restaurants, but the Golden Arches will stand out in your mind because of their branded imagery. A similar number of unbranded souvlaki stands or sushi bars would not even be noticed both because of their unbranded visual diversity and because they represent dots that your theory cannot conveniently connect. They, and all other evidence that might contradict the theory, become invisible.

You will hear acres of English (or American) language, too, especially on television and the Internet. And each one of these un-French phrases will have the same effect, reinforcing the idea of American global imperialism. You will feel like you are submerged in American influence, drowning in it, as this exchange between Hubert Védrine and Dominique Moïse illustrates.

> Moïse: Is globalization the same thing as Americanization? Why does the United States seem to be like a fish in water in this new global world?
>
> Védrine: "Like a fish in water" is exactly the right expression. The United States is a very big fish that swims easily and rules supreme in the waters of globalization. . . . Americans get great benefits from this for a large number of reasons: because of their economic size; because globalization takes place in their language; because it is organized along neoliberal economic principles; because they impose their legal, accounting, and technical practices; and because they're advocates of individuals. They also benefit because they possess what the writer and philosopher René Girard has called the "mental power" to inspire the dreams and desires of others, thanks to their mastery of global images through film and television and because, for the same reasons, large numbers of students from other countries come to the United States to finish their studies.[15]

This exchange really captures everything that I think is true about the French attitude toward globalization and Americanization. "Rules supreme" recalls imperialism. "Mental power" reinforces the image of Prospero. And the list of items that are "imposed" rather than chosen or adopted reminds me of France's own total approach to colonial domination.

I am not the first one to see a link between globalization/Americanization and French imperialism. Here is how Pierre Bourdieu, a leading French antiglobalization intellectual, diagnoses the situation in *Firing Back: Against the Tyranny of the Market 2.*

> This word [globalization] embodies the most accomplished form of the *imperialism of the universal*, which consists, in universalizing for a soci-

ety, its own particularity by tacitly instituting it as a universal yardstick (as French society did for a long time when, as the supposed historical incarnation of human rights and of the legacy of the French Revolution, it was posited—especially by the Marxist tradition—as the model of all possible revolutions).[16]

Former French foreign minister Hubert Védrine also notes America's universalizing tendency. "The foremost characteristic of the United States, which explains its foreign policy, is that it has regarded itself ever since its birth as a chosen nation, charged with the task of enlightening the rest of the world."[17] "What is immediately striking about this pronouncement, the obvious fact that jumps right out," writes Jean-François Revel, "is how perfectly it applies to France herself. Even the American quotations that Védrine produces in support of his thesis nearly all have their literal equivalents in the clichés of French political and cultural narcissism."[18] France reacts so strongly to America and Americanization, these comments suggest, not because it is so foreign to the French but because its total imperialism is so familiar to them.

I understand how the French respond to globalization and why it makes them crazy, and I admire them for it, but I cannot bring myself to approve of it. This is because I am American and my sense of globalization is probably rooted in an idea of American imperialism. For Americans, globalization is about choice; it is about the French and the rest choosing to look like Americans or to use American language, if that's what they want to do. They can even wear Michael Jordan T-shirts if they want to. There is no central command, no *dirigiste* control. Everyone constructs an identity out of the various goods and bads that are on offer today, and globalization is the mongrel condition that results.[19] This is how we Americans rationalize our empire. We can't be blamed for it, we say, they did it to themselves the same way we have done it to ourselves. We are, at worst, only accidental imperialists.[20]

When the French backlash takes the form of ritual destruction of a hamburger store, I am dismayed, but I understand. Dismay turns to grief when a young woman is killed in the process, as happened in an antiglobalization bombing of a McDonald's store in Brittany in 2000.[21] I am more discouraged yet when antiglobalization seems to take the form of a *dirigiste* movement to resurrect total imperialism by, for example, forcing little Muslim schoolgirls to give up their modest headscarves.[22] This reminds me too much of what Frantz Fanon wrote about French policies in Algeria in *A Dying Colonialism*.[23] If anything is worse than total globalization American-style, it is total imperialism French-style.

The Theory Critiqued

Having proposed a globaloney-style theory of French antiglobalism, I must now subject it to critique. There is much to criticize both in style and substance. Although my theory is very grand and rooted in history, it is skimpy when it comes to supporting evidence. For the most part, it relies upon metaphors (French globalization is *Aida*, the French reaction to globalization is Caliban) to advance the argument rather than cold hard facts. The rhetoric is persuasive, I think (I am proud of my little theory), and it contains more than a grain of truth, but let's look at it more closely to see just how convinced we should be by it.

Aida and *Aida!* (the Verdi opera and Disney musical) form the first image. The critical reader may wonder just what a nineteenth-century Italian opera and a twentieth-century Broadway musical have to do with France and its reaction to globalization. And I admit that this is somewhat problematic (translation: there is a hole in the argument big enough to ride an elephant through). It is the same problem that we have with hamburgers—what do they really tell us about the globalization of anything other than hamburgers or maybe french fries? Something, but not very much. Rationalization (the key to McDonald's success) is related to globalization, but they are not the same things. The same relationship holds for *Aida* and the French view of globalization.

I asserted that Verdi's opera tells us how the French think of globalization and the Disney musical is what they see happening to the world today—and I really do think this is true. But it is incorrect to insert the French here—they are not especially relevant to this conclusion. It is natural that each musical work should reflect its own time and the particular concerns of that time. *Aida* tells us what cultural elites were worried about a hundred years ago when they thought about global problems. *Aida!* reflects contemporary concerns. Both works must make some valid connections with their audiences or they would not be performed. Taken together, they probably reveal a good deal about how popular culture and social concerns have evolved over more than a century. Inevitably, they reveal something about France, too, but not France in particular. Probably, and this is point that I will return to later, what we see in *Aida* and *Aida!*, what we find interesting or shocking, reveals more about ourselves than about globalization.

The case is only a little better if we look closely at Prospero and Caliban. Stealing a page from Frantz Fanon's analysis of life under French rule, I used these characters from Shakespeare to suggest a particularly French attitude toward the relationship between imperial center and colonial satellite. Certainly Prospero seems to have some of the qualities some people might associate with the French—arrogance and humanism, for example. We might identify with Prospero, but not empathize for him. The portrait of Caliban is brutal and sympathetic by contrast. The image is powerful and the link to French colonialism, through Fanon's analysis, is authentic, but it would be a mistake to say, as I do, that French attitudes then or now are so stark and simple. Shakespeare's play *The Tempest* is an English work, not a French one, and the image of Caliban is probably rooted in English experience more than French.

But how do we know that Caliban symbolizes colonial domination at all? "To ask such a question may seem perversely naïve," writes literature professor Meredith Anne Skura, "but the play is notoriously slippery." She notes that

> There have been, for example, any number of interpretations of Caliban, including not only contemporary post-colonial versions in which Caliban is a Virginian Indian but also others where Caliban is played as a black slave. . . . Most recently one teacher has suggested that *The Tempest* is a good play to teach in junior colleges because students can identify with Caliban.[24]

"Interpretation is made even more problematic here," she continues, "because . . . we have no *external* evidence that seventeenth-century audiences thought the play referred to the New World."[25] As best scholars can tell, Elizabethan audiences took Caliban at face value—a universal symbol of ignorance, not a pointed and particular reference to Virginian Indians in particular or colonial peoples in general. Try as they might, scholars have been unable to make Prospero and Caliban match up to any narrative of actual colonial experience. It doesn't matter, however, for the link sticks—the power of Newtonian logic. "So long as there is a core of resemblance, the differences are irrelevant," Skura writes, stressing the irony of the situation.[26] Fuzzy logic and weak evidence may be unusual in the field of literary analysis, provoking Skura's commentary, but those of us who work with globaloney run into them all the time.

Moving beyond rhetoric, my theory is globaloney because it is so simple—it claims that a complicated condition (French attitudes toward globalization) can fully be understood in terms of a single factor (French imperial experience). Not many interesting human conditions can be traced to a single root. There are usually many factors that apply. For example, Philip H. Gordon and Sophie Meunier cite five major reasons for French antiglobalist sentiment in their excellent book *The French Challenge: Adapting to Globalization.*[27]

First, globalization challenges the central role of the state in French life "because of the degree to which it requires abandoning state control over the economy—and thereby over society."[28] By challenging the state, globalization alters the fundamental structure of French domestic relations; no wonder they are suspicious of it. Second, it threatens French culture—and not for the first time. "This is, of course, an old theme," Gordon and Meunier write, "going all the way back to the interwar period, when French writers first started to criticize U.S. mass culture, conformity, and emphasis on material wealth."[29] Third, globalization challenges the idea of France. "Whereas the French republic was based, in theory, on rationality—the enlightened state engaged in the improvement of the collective destiny of the French people," according to Gordon and Meunier, "globalization is inevitably a messy and disorderly process that interferes with the state's ability to play that role."[30]

The fourth way that globalization challenges France is by undermining its influence in international diplomatic circles. French was once considered "the language of diplomacy," and France has certainly claimed a privileged position in international relations. Globalization, Gordon and Meunier argue, shifts negotiations to a new field where the United States occupies the commanding heights. France's self-proclaimed special mission to civilize international affairs is one victim of this movement—a deeply felt loss of French influence.

Finally, say Gordon and Meunier, the French oppose globalization because they are so comfortable without it. France is a beautiful country, with rich urban cultures, strong rural traditions, good food, and good wine. What do the French (or at least the French elites) have to gain from globalization? Nothing! What do the French (or at least the French elites) have to lose? The obvious answer is everything, but that is too harsh. Globalization has its price, so something will be sacrificed, but who knows what it will be. The fact is that the French do not know what they might lose and this *uncertainty* allows them to imagine that they could lose everything. Their anxiety is understandable and not a uniquely French phenomenon.

These five factors provide a deeper explanation for French attitudes toward globalization than does my simple theory, but even they only scratch the surface. Antiglobalization reflects its *terroir* just as globalization does, in my opinion, and there are within France many social, political, and economic "microclimates" that produce distinctive attitudes and concerns. France is, after all, a nation with 246 different cheeses.[31] Why should it have fewer opinions about globalization?

In fact, the biggest problem with my theory of French antiglobalism is that it asserts that France is *against* globalization. A closer look at the facts might suggest that France is both comfortable with globalization and has successfully adapted to it.

When you ask the French if they favor globalization, they express understandable reservations and, sometimes, downright opposition, often associating it with Americanization. I think many Americans are suspicious of globalization, too, especially now that it is often associated with the "outsourcing" of jobs abroad. But if instead you present the French people with the products of globalization, they seem to take to them without much hesitation, just like people in other countries. Take McDonald's for example. Although the McDonald's stories that get the most attention feature antiglobalization protests, perhaps the biggest story is this: McDonald's is more popular in France than in any other country in Europe.[32] The French like it in part because McDonald's has adapted its menu to French tastes (local cheeses are often featured, for example) and in part because of its American image. Don't be shocked: if Americans enjoy French wine bars and Italian coffee bars, why shouldn't a French family go to McDonald's for a simulated "American experience"? McDonald's cannot compete with France's great cuisine, but is that its purpose? "I can love good food," says Vanesse Decler, a customer at a Parisian Golden Arches store, "and I can also love McDonald's." Clearly she knows the difference.[33] *Vive la différence.*

The French intellectual Jean-François Revel questions whether anti-Americanism really exists in France (and elsewhere) in the way it is often portrayed. Anti-Americanism, he writes, "is less a popular prejudice than a *parti pris* of the political, cultural and religious elites."[34] America and globalization are useful scapegoats and straw men for elites on the political left and elites on the political right. If Americanization/globalization did not exist, someone would have to invent them in order to be able to oppose them (and to sell the policies of opposition).

Are the French really "closet globalists" who outwardly oppose globalization but inwardly embrace it? Yes, I think so. France, like the United States, believes that it has a "universal message" to offer the world.[35] It is difficult to square such global ambitions with narrow, parochial attitudes and actions. France has struggled with this contradiction and chosen to embrace globalization, in my view. The die was cast more than two decades ago.

The Socialist François Mitterrand was elected president of the French Republic in 1981—at the very moment when Margaret Thatcher and Ronald Reagan were leading their countries toward free-market individualism—the ideology of globalism. Mitterrand set out to lead France in the opposite direction, nationalizing industries, not privatizing them, and reasserting the role of the state. "The Mitterrand experiment, in other words, was an early rejection of the logic that would later be called globalization," according to Gordon and Meunier.[36] The results were economically devastating, however, because France, even then, was too much tied to the world economy to pull itself back into an inward-looking *dirigiste* regime. Economic crisis came in 1983. Mitterrand installed a new policy team in 1984 and began to embrace globalization in practice while continuing to question and oppose it as a theory.

Although all of the talk is of France's resistance to globalization, the real story, according to Gordon and Meunier, is how successfully France has adapted to it. It is still taboo to talk about this, I suppose, because the myth of France's resistance to globalization is important to its national identity, but the changes are a fact of life. The mystery of France's closet globalization is partly tied up in the European Union. Europeanization (with France in the lead at least part of the time) is also globalization in many respects. Gordon and Meunier call it "globalization by stealth."[37] "While it would be an exaggeration to suggest that France has completely abandoned *dirigisme* and that the legacy of the state-led approach has disappeared . . . the country's economic landscape has changed," they write. "In a country known for its deep, ideological divisions, the differences between Left and Right on the economy since the Mitterrand U-turn (in practice if not in rhetoric) have been minimal. . . . [E]conomic management since 1983 has been driven more than anything by the need to adapt the French economy to the requirements of the European and global markets."[38]

Gordon and Meunier suggest that France in globalization is a fish in water, particularly in comparison with some other countries that have not made so determined and successful a commitment to evolve. You could say that France has embraced globalization since 1983 and, even more, it has successfully sought to shape globalization, to give it a particularly French style, through its influence upon the ever-expanding European Union. Why isn't this fact more generally appreciated? Probably because French antiglobalist rhetoric is so forceful. The rhetoric creates an image of France that is easy to understand and that emphasizes one or two memorable images and events. It is, I guess, a particular kind of globaloney: franco-baloney. The facts of French globalization are complicated and more difficult to appreciate because they require patient, detailed analysis. In a world that seems increasingly to be defined by Attention Deficit Disorder (ADD), rhetoric nearly always trumps details.

If you want to find examples of French opposition to globalization you will find them; just look for José Bové or for the latest ruling about a new word from the Académie Française. But if you want to find evidence that France is getting along swimmingly, you have only to look around. French globalization is everywhere.

French globalization is especially apparent in markets for luxury and designer products, like great champagne and couture fashions. The great names of French commercial culture dominate these markets at home and abroad. Great transnational firms have been constructed around them, extending France's global reach. This is true even in the wine business. Cloudy Bay, a prominent winery in New Zealand, for example, is owned by the French global conglomerate LVMH (Louis Vuitton Moët Hennessey). LVMH owns wineries in France, Spain, Australia, New Zealand, Argentina, Brazil, and the United States. Its other businesses (perfume, liquor, jewelry, watches, newspapers, and retail stores) are equally global in scope. If globalization did not already exist, LVMH would have had to invent it in order to spread French style and taste.

The French embrace of globalization is not limited to luxury goods; it reaches down to the grass roots. The second-largest mass-market retailer in the world is a French firm called Carrefour.[39] Carrefour employs more than 420,000 workers in its 10,000 stores in 29 countries. About half of its sales are in France, where it is the clear market leader, but its reach is nearly global: Europe (Belgium, Switzerland, Romania, Czech Republic, Slovakia, Spain, Greece, Italy, Poland, Portugal, Turkey), the Americas (Argentina, Brazil, Columbia, Mexico), and Asia (China, Indonesia, Japan, Korea, Malaysia, Singapore, Thailand, and Taiwan). On March 17, 2004, Carrefour opened its fifth huge superstore in Beijing (the forty-fourth in China).[40] The major hole in its global strategy: the United States, home of Wal-Mart.

Wal-Mart, the U.S. store giant, is bigger than Carrefour, but less global. Wal-Mart employs over a million people in 3,200 stores in the United States, 643 in Mexico, 236 in Canada, 267 in Great Britain, and about 300 in six other countries (Puerto Rico, Argentina, Brazil, China, South Korea, Germany, and Great Britain).[41] Wal-Mart has much greater sales than Carrefour because of its key position within the world's largest market, the United States. I find it interesting that each company has thus far avoided entering its global rival's home market, although this may change as Wal-Mart moves to develop a more truly global market strategy.[42] (One news report suggests that Wal-Mart will effect a global strategy in the most obvious way—buying Carrefour![43])

Wal-Mart is bigger than Carrefour in part because most of its stores are vast superstores, including especially the cavernous Sam's Club warehouse stores. Carrefour invented the superstore—it calls them *hyper-markets*—and operates more than seven hundred of them around the world, including the forty-four in China. But most of its outlets are smaller, ordinary supermarkets, discount stores, and tiny convenience stores (plus special stores that provide products to restaurants and food-service operations). Carrefour's embrace of global retail markets is thus both wider than Wal-Mart's and deeper, reaching further into the villages and neighborhoods, encompassing all income classes—no wonder Wal-Mart would want to buy the company rather than compete with it. Carrefour is the world's retailer, if such a thing can be said to exist, and a particularly French expression of globalization.

Of course no argument about globalization is complete without a discussion of food. If France is such a global creature, you must be thinking, where is the French McDonald's? Why don't I see French food in every strip mall? How can you say that France has embraced globalization if it hasn't spread its cuisine to the far corners of earth?

The answer to this challenge is that France has already done so— indeed, did so decades ago—but on particularly French terms. Don't look for corporate or franchised fast-food chains, however. The French patronize these sorts of restaurants, but they are really American creations. (There is one international fast-food chain with a French name—Pret A Manger sells baguette sandwiches and some other

French-style fast foods—but it is actually a British firm and most of its menu items reflect this fact.[44]) Globalization reflects its *terroir*; French globalization has to take its own distinctly French form.

French culinary globalization is less visible than the American version because it lacks a brand name and a coordinated global advertising strategy, but its influence upon global food is if anything much more total, more complete. Independent French restaurants, bistros, cafes, and bakeries cover the globe far more thoroughly than any American corporate concern could or would. One legacy of French imperialism is that good French food can be found in places, such as Central Africa, that contemporary globalization has not yet touched. You can get a good fresh croissant and decent café au lait in places around the world where the only Big Macs you will see are on satellite TV broadcasts of NBA playoff games.

There are certainly more French restaurants and food establishments outside of France than there are McDonald's, Burger King, Kentucky Fried Chicken, and Wendy's stores outside of the United States. I am tempted to declare France the true King of Culinary Globalization, but I don't think it is true. Certainly French influence is stronger than America's, but I would not be surprised to find that Italian food is almost equally ubiquitous or that Chinese food is the most global of all. American food, despite all the hype, probably rates no better than fourth or fifth (depending upon where Indian food falls in the rankings).

Here is my bottom line on France and globalization. If we judge by rhetoric, France is against globalization. If, however, we make our call based upon some of the factors that are most often cited in the globalization literature—high-end branded goods, restaurant food, and mass-market retailing—we find that France is a creature of globalization more than you might otherwise suppose.[45] My theory of why France hates globalization is globaloney for several reasons, the most important of which is this: France has in fact embraced globalization, although it is a nervous embrace. I understand the feeling—it's that *Aida* embrace, isn't it? We Americans embrace globalization in the same way. The French exception to globalization is not exceptional at all.

Lessons Learned

What should we think about globalization? If you have followed me this far you should be realizing that it seems to be very difficult to make any generalizations about globalization without committing an act of globaloney. Indeed, most of what we think we know about globalization seems to be tainted with at least a trace of globaloney. Why? Each chapter of this book has suggested a reason.

Globaloney is useful, we learn in chapter 1, especially in politics. Henry A. Wallace and Clare Boothe Luce taught us how globaloney can be used to sell a political agenda that may have little or nothing to do with globalization. I am reminded of this fact daily. Why just yesterday my county government decided to build a "world-class" golf course on some vacant land near the bay. One of the reasons was because the golf course would attract global CEOs who would fly in on their private jets to play golf, see the wonderful golf course, and decide to invest millions or billions of dollars on business expansion here. That's globaloney of the most basic sort, comparable to Wallace's open skies plan, but it sells the idea of a publicly funded golf course better than the obvious reason: we want it so that we (and our friends) can play golf on it. The real argument is a legitimate one—there are thousands of municipal golf courses in the United States that were built for the recreational use of local taxpayers—but the globalization argument sells better.[46]

Globaloney is easy, according to chapter 2. Although I don't really "blame it all on Adam Smith," I think I do show how the rhetoric of globaloney works. Newtonian rhetoric is as effective now as it was then. And it is satisfying, too. People like to connect the dots and to feel like they understand how the world works based upon a sketchy theory. This is especially true in times like these, when the world seems to be changing rapidly on many intersecting planes. Anxiety is understandably high. The images and arguments of globaloney provide simple answers that give comfort in turbulent times.

Michael Jordan's case shows us just how easy it is to use globalization to create heroes and, especially, villains. Because globalization is such a complex process, it is always necessary to leave things out. You can tell almost any story you want simply by carefully selecting your facts. If you want to say that the globalization of basketball is based upon Michael Jordan, Nike, and the media push of the "infotainment telesector," well, you can do that very effectively. But if you probe a bit deeper into the history of globalization and the influence of "international players," you get a somewhat different answer. The Michael Jordan story is not completely false, but it doesn't tell the whole truth either.

I learned how easy it is to edit the facts to fit a particular story line when the PBS series *Commanding Heights* was first broadcast a few years ago. This six-hour documentary was based upon a book of the same name by Daniel Yergin and told the story of globalization in a particular way. I was teaching a class on globalization at the time and my students were reading Thomas Friedman's *The Lexus and the Olive Tree*. Friedman tells the story a bit differently than Yergin's video does. To make a long story short, I didn't have time to show all six hours of the video, but I wanted my students to see both sides of the debate, so I used a pair of VCRs to splice together two different condensed versions of the PBS series: one faithful to Yergin's message and another that told the story Friedman's way. All I had to do was *leave out* the right scenes and I could tell the story *any* way. If I can do this with a couple of VCRs, imagine what globaloney I could produce with just a few more resources.

I try to tell the whole truth in the chapter on soccer globalization, although that obviously is impossible in the constraints of a book chapter. What I find is that no single story, image, or theory can explain all of the complicated effects I found. Significantly, globalization affects basketball and soccer in some ways that are similar and many ways that are different. Generalizations about globalization are as dangerous as a David Beckham corner kick. This chapter also reveals the bias that Americans introduce when they study globalization. Instead of seeing globalization, they see only America. That's why basketball, not soccer, defines globalization for U.S.-based sports fans.

No book about globalization is complete without a discussion of McDonald's, but I am not sure why. I think McDonald's figures in so many accounts of globalization because the authors are Americans who instinctively look for American icons as they travel abroad. You cannot miss the Golden Arches, so they build their theories around them. But McDonald's isn't a very good example of globalization, Americanization, or anything else, really. Like Michael Jordan, McDonald's is most important as an exception to the rule. If you really wanted to understand the globalization of food, I argue, you ought to look at Chinese food. In any case, the success of McDonald's is due to rationalization not globalization, as George Ritzer has pointed out.

No one has really tried to tell the story of globalization in terms of wine. When you see wine around the world, you think of wine, not globalization. But you do see wine almost everywhere, so perhaps someone should. If you think of globalization this way, you get some interestingly different answers. Globalization can be a race to the top, not the bottom. Globalization can strengthen local cultures and traditions as well as undermine them. Globalization reflects its *terroir*—it has different effects in different places. The story of globalization and wine should not be generalized to other products and industries except to say that each case is different. You've got to sweat those devilish details if you want to really understand what is going on. My "General Theory of Globalization" is that a general theory is impossible. Globalization links together diverse economic, political, and cultural nodes, which react and inter-react in a myriad of ways. The lack of a Grand Theory is unfortunate—it complicates things—but we should not be ashamed to admit it. Physics lacks a General Unified Theory of Everything, as they call it, but it hasn't stopped physicists from doing useful work.

The conventional wisdom is that globalization destroys local culture—it crushes the grass roots. Perhaps this is so, but I am suspicious of universal generalizations. The global trade in worn clothes—*salaula*—and the Slow Food movement suggest to me that at least sometimes it is possible for the grass roots to stand up to globalization, to create meaning from it, and even to use globalization against itself as a way of sustaining local identity. Given all this, is it even possible for a book like this to have a conclusion—a single memorable bottom line? Well, here it is.

The Promised Conclusion

My conclusion is that globalization is like the Mirror of Erised in J. K. Rowling's *Harry Potter and the Sorcerer's Stone*.[47] Most mirrors reflect their viewer's image, accurately for the most part if always reversed. In Rowling's book, however, the Mirror of Erised has a special property; it reflects the viewer's deepest hopes and fears. When you gaze into the Mirror of Erised, you see what you want to see and what you fear to see, not what's really there.

It is easy to see why globalization should work this way. Globalization is devilishly complicated. It has too many data points for anyone's mind to process correctly. No wonder our eyes seek out familiar patterns. When we look at globalization, therefore, we tend to focus upon those parts that reflect what we want to see or what we fear to see. Then we tend to connect these details to form grand theories or universal generalizations. We do this for the most part because it is such a satisfying thing to do—Adam Smith was right about this, as about much else.

The image that is reflected in the Mirror is mainly our own because each of us selects the details that are most important to us and with which we are most familiar.

This property of globalization, alas, makes it especially prone to manipulation. Hopes and fears are great motivators. Worse, we tend to accept them as valid motivators rather uncritically because they are our own.

I want to be clear about one thing: I am not saying that globalization doesn't exist, that it is only an image in our mind's eye. No, globalization is real enough all right. You can see it at work when you study particular cases, then it's clear enough. It's only when you try to back up and see the whole thing that the globaloney kicks in.

We should not really be surprised that globalization works this way. Globalization is a big thing, a transformative process that produces much anxiety even among those it is most likely to benefit. If you want to find parallels to globalization in history, you need to look for equally significant transformations, such as the Renaissance in Europe or the Industrial Revolution in England. The Mirror of Erised metaphor turns out to work for these transformative events, too. Because these events are fixed firmly in the past, you would think that we would know for sure just how they turned out, but that's not the case. Historians have repeatedly revised their theories, seeing first one image in the Mirror and then another. Why?

David Cannadine, the distinguished British historian, has noted that each historical revision has not so much reflected new *facts* as changing *contemporary conditions*—the changing hopes and fears of the observers.[48] When historians studied the Industrial Revolution in its immediate aftermath, for example, they focused upon social conditions and class relations because those were the particular problems of their own time. The contemporary problem changed in the 1920s and 1930s, Cannadine writes, and so did interpretations of the Industrial Revolution. War and economic cycles came to the fore and social conditions retreated into the background, so these problems dominated theories of the Industrial Revolution. During the 1950s and 1960s, when economic growth was a more immediate concern, historians reinterpreted the history of the Industrial Revolution in this light. As growth slowed in the 1970s and 1980s, according to Cannadine, new interpretations of the Industrial Revolution emerged, stressing its gradual rather than revolutionary nature.

And during the technology boom of the 1990s, I have observed, the story of the Industrial Revolution was retold yet again, this time focusing on "disruptive technologies" like the railroads and the opportunities and problems they created. It's funny, but not surprising I guess, that wherever we look we see our own contemporary anxieties.

Cannadine's conclusion about the Industrial Revolution is that no person and no era can really understand it. "[T]he dominant interpretation which prevails (albeit not completely) in any given generation is never more than a partial view of that very complex process," he writes. "In that it draws attention to some important aspect of the subject, it is never going to be wholly 'wrong'; but in that it gives disproportionate emphasis to a limited number of considerations, it is not likely to be wholly 'right', either."[49]

Cannadine is right, I am convinced, about both the Industrial Revolution and other complicated transformations, including globalization. Any broad generalization or universal conclusion is bound to be wrong, even if there is a germ of truth at its center. What, then, can we safely say about globalization? Here are my conclusions.

- Anyone who says that globalization is all bad or all good is all wrong. Globalization cuts too many different ways to be all this, that, or the other thing.
- Globalization is real, but it is difficult to observe objectively. I think this is especially true of Americans, but that's probably just because I am an American myself.
- Never trust a metaphor. Metaphors and images are not facts, nor are they substitutes for facts. They are rhetorical devices used to manipulate facts so that they seem to line up in convenient ways.
- That said, give some thought to my Mirror of Erised metaphor and ask yourself how much your beliefs about globalization reflect your own personal hopes and fears. While you are getting personal, consider that. . .
- Personal anecdotes are facts, but not very trustworthy ones. The facts that an anecdote contains are always filtered and screened as part of the telling. They are always limited by the experiences of the teller and can easily be manipulated. It is a shame that they are so persuasive, when skillfully told. It is not an accident that I have drawn frequently upon personal anecdotes to make some of my points in this book. Sometimes you've got to fight fire with fire.
- The truth is in the details, because knowing the details is the only

way to know for sure how globalization affects a particular situation. But the devil is in the details, too, because the facts about globalization are messy, complicated, and constantly changing.

It is probably impossible to avoid reading globaloney and even writing or speaking globaloney yourself. Globalization and globaloney are joined at the hip. But it may be possible to learn to recognize globaloney and to avoid *believing* it. Having read this book, I hope you have become a more critical consumer of globalization stories. I hope that the next time you encounter a bogus argument about globalization, you will pause and say, "Globaloney. Why that's nothing but globaloney." That's the first step on your road to clear thinking about globalization.

What Is at Stake

"[T]he ideas of economists and political philosophers, both when they are right and when they are wrong, are more powerful than is commonly understood," wrote John Maynard Keynes in *The General Theory of Employment, Interest, and Money.* "Indeed the world is ruled by little else. Practical men, who believe themselves to be quite exempt from any intellectual influences, are usually the slaves of some defunct economist."[50] Keynes believed in the power of ideas—good ones and bad ones—to direct our actions and so to shape our world.

So do I, which is why I have written this book. Globalization, it is said, is an idea whose time has come, a powerful transformative force. What we believe about globalization affects how we react to it and, therefore, how it evolves. If our ideas are wrong—if we are the "slaves" of globaloney—our actions will be wrong, too. So we must be critical consumers of ideas.

It is easy to believe that globalization is Americanization that is driven by giant media corporations. Sometimes, in some particular places, this is certainly true. To say that it destroys "real" culture and replaces it with consumer culture is certainly true, to a certain extent, but not universally true. To think that globalization is always and everywhere good for the rich, bad for the poor, and a worldwide race to the bottom is wrong—just as wrong as the opposing globalist dogma that it benefits everyone everywhere.

Globaloney theories are useful—they distract practical women and men from the real issues. This makes them dangerous. To make a general theory of globalization is almost certainly a mistake. Not because it is unfair to media moguls, hamburger corporations, and international banks, although it might be, but because it lets the real villains off the hook, the business people, politicians, and intellectuals who use globalization as a way to advance their own particular interests. José Bové famously destroyed that McDonald's store, for example, to oppose the injustice of globalization. Thinking globalization to be foreign, he attacked the wrong enemy. All the real villains in his little drama—if they are villains—were much closer to home. Bové became a celebrity, but the real forces of French globalization, which are distinctly French, were certainly undeterred. Indeed, they might have been grateful!

When it comes to globalization, it seems like the devil is everywhere. The devil is in the details of how globalization actually plays out on the ground and, as I have shown, those details are quite varied.

The devil is in the grand design, too, in the theories that condition the way we think about globalization and react to it and so how it evolves. The theories we study in this book prove to be more rhetorical than real—poor guides to practical people seeking answers. But the theories are so appealing, so satisfying, that they distract us from the facts and so blind us to the real consequences of our actions. That's why we need to be especially careful to be sure that what we believe about globalization is real and not just globaloney.

NOTES

Introduction

1. I have always believed that Mark Twain coined the phrase "the devil's in the details," but I cannot find a direct quote. Mark Twain did say that the difference between the almost-right word and the right word is like the difference between the lightning bug and—lightning! And, in *The Mysterious Stranger*, the presence of the devil is indicated by the fact that all the details are error-free at a typesetter's shop. So I think it is fair to associate Twain with this phrase.

2. See Henry Nash Smith, *Mark Twain's Fable of Progress: Political and Economic Ideas in* A Connecticut Yankee. (New Brunswick, N.J.: Rutgers University Press, 1964).

3. James H. Mittelman, *The Globalization Syndrome: Transformation and Resistance* (Princeton, N.J.: Princeton University Press, 2000).

4. Michael Veseth, *Selling Globalization: The Myth of the Global Economy* (Boulder, Colo.: Rienner, 1998).

5. Benjamin R. Barber, *Jihad vs. McWorld: Terrorism's Challenge to Democracy* (New York: Ballantine, 2001) and Walter LaFeber, *Michael Jordan and the New Global Capitalism* (New York: Norton, 2002).

6. Thomas L. Friedman, *The Lexus and the Olive Tree: Understanding Globalization* (updated edition) (New York: Anchor Books, 2000).

7. Say "tehr—WAHR."

Chapter 1   The Globaloney Syndrome

1. *Congressional Record* 89:1, 761.

2. Karen Lowry Miller, "Globaloney: The New Buzzword," *Newsweek Issues 2003* (Winter 2002/2003): 52–58.

3. Henry A. Wallace, *The Century of the Common Man* (New York: Reynal & Hitchcock, 1943).

4. Wallace, *The Century*, 7.

5. Wallace, *The Century*, 8. Apart perhaps from isolation, these are charges that citizens of less-developed countries might level at the United States today.

6. Wallace, *The Century*, 58.

7. Wallace, *The Century*, 58.

8. Wallace, *The Century*, 65–66.

9. Wallace, *The Century*, 68.

10. Wallace, *The Century*, 61.

11. Wallace, *The Century*, 60.

12. Wallace, *The Century*, 68.

13. Wallace, *The Century*, 42.

14. *Congressional Record* 89:1, 759.

15. *Congressional Record* 89:1, 760.

16. *Congressional Record* 89:1, 761.

17. *Congressional Record* 89:1, 763.

18. *Congressional Record* 89:1, 761.

19. *Congressional Record* 89:1, 762.

20. *Congressional Record* 89:1, 762.

21. *Congressional Record* 89:1, 761.

22. *Congressional Record* 89:1, 763.

23. The idea for calling globaloney a "syndrome" was suggested by the title of James H. Mittelman's fine book, *The Globalization Syndrome: Transformation and Resistance* (Princeton, N.J.: Princeton University Press, 2000).

24. Michael Veseth, *Selling Globalization: The Myth of the Global Economy* (Boulder, Colo.: Rienner, 1998).

25. Harold James, *The End of Globalization: Lessons from the Great Depression* (Cambridge, Mass.: Harvard University Press, 2001).

26. Michael Veseth, ed. *The* New York Times *Twentieth Century in Review: The Rise of the Global Economy* (Chicago: Fitzroy Dearborn, 2002).

27. Jo-Anne Pemberton, *Global Metaphors: Modernity and the Quest for One World* (London: Pluto Press, 2001).

28. Pemberton, *Global Metaphors*, 109.

29. Pemberton, *Global Metaphors*, 185.

30. Pemberton, *Global Metaphors*, 170–71.

31. Thomas L. Friedman, *The Lexus and the Olive Tree: Understanding Globalization* (New York: Anchor, 2000).

32. Norman Angell, *The Great Illusion: A Study of the Relation of Military Power in Nations to Their Economic and Social Advantage* (London: Putnam, 1911). Michael Mandelbaum, *The Ideas That Conquered the World: Peace, Democracy, and Free Markets in the Twenty-First Century* (New York: Public Affairs, 2002).

33. Friedman, *The Lexus and the Olive Tree*, 250.

34. Friedman doesn't present them as laws, of course, but that's how they are often (mis)understood.

35. BBC News Online, "Profile: Jean-Marie Le Pen," news.bbc.co.uk/1/hi/world/europe/1943193.stm [accessed June 7, 2004].

36. Data are from the United Nations Report, *International Migration 2002* www.un.org/esa/population/publications/ittmig2002/2002ITTMIGTEXT22-11.pdf [accessed June 7, 2004].

37. H. Ross Perot with Pat Choate, *Save Your Job, Save Our Country: Why NAFTA Must Be Stopped—NOW!* (New York: Hyperion, 1993).

38. See José Bové and Françoise Dufour, *The World Is Not for Sale: Farmers against Junk Food*, translated by Anna de Casparis (New York: Verso, 2001).

39. William Greider, *One World, Ready or Not: The Manic Logic of Global Capitalism* (New York: Simon & Schuster, 1997).

40. Greider, *One World, Ready or Not*, 11.

41. Jarrod Weiner, "Globalisation: The Political Function of Ambiguity," in *About Globalisation: Views on the Trajectory of 'Mondialisation*, edited by Bart Deschutter and Johan Pas (Brussels: VUB Press, 2003), 22.

42. Greider, *One World, Ready or Not*, 337.

43. Wendell L. Wilkie, *One World* (New York: Simon & Schuster, 1943). Wilkie was the 1940 Republican candidate for U.S. president.

44. Wilkie, *One World*, 2.

45. Manfred B. Steger does a particularly good job of puncturing the hyper-globalization myths in *Globalism: The New Market Ideology* (Lanham, Md.: Rowman & Littlefield, 2002).

46. Daniel Yergin and Joséph Stanislaw, *The Commanding Heights: The Battle for the Global Economy* (New York: Touchstone, 2002).

Chapter 2   Blame It All on Adam Smith

1. William Greider, *One World, Ready or Not: The Manic Logic of Global Capitalism* (New York: Simon & Schuster, 1997).

2. This quote and the next one are my own fabrications, of course, meant to capture a particular style of rhetoric. I don't mean to suggest that Greider or Ohmae actually wrote these *particular* phrases.

3. Kenichi Ohmae, *The Borderless World: Power and Strategy in the Interlinked Economy* (New York: HarperBusiness, 1990).

4. Adam Smith, *An Inquiry into the Nature and Causes of the Wealth of Nations* (New York: Modern Library, 1937), 3. Original publication year: 1776.

5. Smith, *Wealth of Nations*, 4.

6. Smith, *Wealth of Nations*, 4–5.

7. Smith, *Wealth of Nations*, 5.

8. Smith, *Wealth of Nations*, 5.

9. Smith, *Wealth of Nations*, 5.

10. Smith, *Wealth of Nations*, 11.

11. Smith, *Wealth of Nations*, 17.

12. Ian Simpson Ross, *The Life of Adam Smith* (New York: Oxford University Press, 1995), 88–94. Interestingly, Ross is a professor of English (not economics) at the University of British Columbia.

13. Wodrow's notes quoted in Ross, *Life of Adam Smith*, 91.

14. Vivienne Brown, *Adam Smith's Discourse* (London: Routledge, 1994), 10–18.

15. Wodrow's notes on Smith's lectures, quoted in Ross, *Life of Adam Smith*, 93.

16. Friedrich List, *The National System of Political Economy*, translated by Sampson S. Lloyd (London: Longmans, Green and Co., 1904). Original publication year: 1841.

17. List's biography is found in "A Brief Memoir of the Author" in *National System*, xxix–xxxviii.

18. List, *National System*, 102.

19. List, *National System*, 102.

20. List, *National System*, 103.

21. List, *National System*, 103.

22. William Greider, *One World, Ready or Not: The Manic Logic of Global Capitalism* (New York: Simon & Schuster, 1997).

23. Greider, *One World, Ready or Not*, p. 12.

24. Greider, *One World, Ready or Not*, 12

25. If you want to follow up on this idea, I recommend that you begin by reading Oz Shy, *The Economics of Network Industries* (Cambridge: Cambridge University Press, 2001).

26. Thomas Frank, *One Market under God: Extreme Capitalism, Market Populism, and the End of Economic Democracy* (New York: Doubleday, 2000).

27. William Greider, *The Soul of Capitalism: Opening Paths to a Moral Economy* (New York: Simon & Schuster, 2003).

28. Greider, *Soul of Capitalism*, 7.

29. Greider, *Soul of Capitalism*, 7.

30. Motherhood is the unused symbol.

31. Greider, *Soul of Capitalism*, 300.

32. Paul Krugman, *The Great Unraveling: Losing Our Way in the New Century* (New York: Norton, 2003).

Chapter 3   Michael Jordan and NBA Global Fever

1. There were also several pro-globalization faces present. The meetings probably would have failed even without the violent protesters outside the meeting halls because of disagreements among the "faces" inside, all of whom

favored expansion of global trade, but differed with respect to the rules of the game. The emergence of a potent developing-country "reform" face was a significant factor in the meetings' collapse.

2. Anarchist Action Collective, quoted on tompaine.com: www.tompaine.com/feature2.cfm/ID/2589 [accessed June 8, 2004].

3. This is what Manfred Steger calls "globalism." See Manfred B. Steger, *Globalism: The New Market Ideology* (Lanham, Md.: Rowman & Littlefield, 2002).

4. Walter LaFeber, *Michael Jordan and the New Global Capitalism* (New York: Norton, 1999). The "new and expanded" edition is copyright 2002.

5. LaFeber, *Michael Jordan*, 27.

6. Not Mao? How strange.

7. LaFeber, *Michael Jordan*, 28.

8. George Ritzer, *The Globalization of Nothing* (Thousand Oaks, Calif.: Pine Forge Press, 2004). Ritzer's McDonaldization thesis is discussed in chapter 5.

9. LaFeber, *Michael Jordan*, 139.

10. LaFeber, *Michael Jordan*, 143.

11. Quoted from pp. 7–8 of Nike's fiscal 2003 SEC Form 10-K filing as found on Nike's investor relations website, www.nike.com/nikebiz/invest/reports/ar_03/10-K_FINAL.PDF [accessed January 5, 2004].

12. LaFeber's book is also powerful because it does make many valid particular points about particular situations. It is only his tendency to generalize from these particulars that I find problematic.

13. LaFeber, *Michael Jordan*, 156–57.

14. Alexander Wolff, *Big Game, Small World: A Basketball Adventure* (New York: Warner, 2002). Many of the facts in this section are taken from this book.

15. Wolff, *Big Game, Small World*, 7.

16. They took volleyball, too, after it was invented at the YMCA Training School in 1895 by William Morgan.

17. I have heard it said, but I cannot verify it, that basketball still plays an important role today in the work of Mormon missionaries, that basketball is the official sport of the Mormon Church, and that the church is the largest sponsor of organized basketball in the world. I repeat these uncertain claims here just to suggest that the idea of a link between Christian missionary work and basketball is still important.

18. Glocalization is the process by which global phenomena are adopted in local communities and endowed with local meanings and significance.

19. Wolff, *Big Game, Small World*, 239.

20. "Catch the Fever" was the theme of a recent NBA advertising campaign.

21. The game was played on Monday, January 5, 2004, in Denver. All five San Antonio starters might have been internationals if Ginobili had been

healthy (he did not play). One other game was played that night with internationals making up half of the starting lineups. Two or three internationals answered the opening buzzer in several games. No game was played entirely with U.S. players.

22. For an excellent discussion of team loyalty in American professional sports, see Andrei S. Markovits and Steven L. Hellerman, *Offside: Soccer & American Exceptionalism* (Princeton, N.J.: Princeton University Press, 2001), 52–98.

23. www.nba.com/players/international_player_directory.html [accessed January 5, 2004].

24. www.ymca.int/ymcas_country/national_profile/Argentina.htm [accessed January 6, 2004].

25. Facts about Ginobili are taken from Larry Rohter, "Argentina in the Grip of Manu Mania," *New York Times*, June 4, 2003, C19.

26. These facts and many others in this section are taken from "Home and Away" by Peter Hessler, *New Yorker* (December 1, 2003), 65–75. This is the best profile of Yao Ming that I have read. Hessler is a sports journalist who actually speaks Chinese and was therefore able to interview Yao and his Chinese colleagues directly.

27. Hessler, "Home and Away," 66.

28. As many as fourteen million Chinese have viewed televised NBA games according to Hessler, "Home and Away," 72.

29. Hessler, "Home and Away," 70.

30. I do not have room here to go into all of the ways that local cultures have shaped the meaning of basketball around the world. See Wolff, *Big Game, Small World*, for a more detailed analysis.

31. These figures are taken from a NBA fan website: www.hoopshype.com/salaries.htm [accessed on January 7, 2004].

32. The article is dated May 22, 2003, and was found at sportsillustrated.cnn.com/basketball/news/2003/05/21/lebron_upperdeck_ap/ [accessed January 7, 2004].

33. Thomas L. Friedman, *The Lexus and the Olive Tree* (New York: Anchor Books, 2000). See chapter 14, "Winners Take All," 306–24.

34. Friedman, *The Lexus and the Olive Tree*, 318.

35. Robert H. Frank and Philip J. Cook, *The Winner-Take-All Society* (New York: Free Press, 1995).

Chapter 4   The Beautiful Game and the American Exception

1. I will use the terms *soccer* and *football* interchangeably, with a preference for *soccer* to avoid confusion, since I do also talk about American football in this chapter. Both terms refer to the game known as "association football."

2. Sid Lowe, "The Circus Starts Here," *World Soccer* (August 2003), 5.

3. Gavin Hamilton, "United Ready to Splash Beckham Cash," *World Soccer* (August 2003), 10.

4. The film's website is www2.foxsearchlight.com/benditlikebeckham/ [accessed June 8, 2004].

5. *Metrosexual* was one of the buzzwords of 2003. To be metrosexual means to be a heterosexual male who is interested in fashion, design, jewelry, cosmetics, and so forth. David Beckham's name is often used in the explanation of *metrosexual*.

6. The home countries of these players follow: Zinedine Zidane and Thierry Henry, France; Ronaldo and Roberto Carlos, Brazil; Pavel Nedved, the Czech Republic, and Ruud Van Nestelrooy, the Netherlands. Beckham (England) is an excellent player. I am not arguing that he is anything other than highly skilled. But it can be argued, successfully I think, that his relative value as a commercial product exceeds his relative value as a player on the field.

7. Fédération Internationale de Football Association.

8. Lowe, "The Circus Starts Here," 5.

9. Eduardo Galeano, *Football in Sun and Shadow*, translated by Mark Fried (London: Fourth Estate, 1997), 21. A most excellent and interesting reference on the history of soccer is Bill Murray, *Football: A History of the World Game* (Aldershot, UK: Scolar Press, 1994).

10. Galeano, *Football in Sun and Shadow*, 21.

11. This was in England early in the Christian era, according to Soccer 101 at www.soccernova.com/html/soccer_101/world_history.htm [accessed June 8, 2004].

12. Galeano, *Football in Sun and Shadow*, 22.

13. www.soccernova.com/html/soccer_101/world_history.htm [accessed June 8, 2004].

14. Andrei S. Markovits and Steven L. Hellerman, *Offside: Soccer & American Exceptionalism* (Princeton, N.J.: Princeton University Press, 2001), 13.

15. See www.soccernova.com/html/soccer_101/world_history.htm [accessed June 8, 2004] for a chronology of world football history.

16. Murray, *Football*, 214–15. Soccer became popular in India but not because anyone was forced to play it. Murray reports that it spread the usual way: British soldiers played it for their own recreation and pretty soon Indians were playing, too.

17. Alex Bellos, *Futbol: Soccer, the Brazilian Way* (New York: Bloomsbury, 2002), 27.

18. V. I. Lenin. *Imperialism: The Highest Stage of Capitalism* (New York: International Publishers, 1939).

19. Galeano, *Football in Sun and Shadow*, 31.

20. The term *soccer* is derived from a reference to the adjective *association* in association football—a connection that is more obvious to the eyes than the ears.

21. Galeano, *Football in Sun and Shadow*, 54.

22. Gideon Rachman, "Passion, Pride and Profit," *Economist* special section (June 1, 2002), 4.

23. Rachman, "Passion, Pride and Profit," 4.

24. There is much to say about how the business of soccer evolved in the second half of the twentieth century, but I don't have room to do the story justice. So I am leaving out many dots here and not connecting all of the rest. For a complete analysis see Stephen Dobson and John Goddard, *The Economics of Football* (Cambridge: Cambridge University Press, 2001).

25. All figures from "World Soccer Rich List," *World Soccer* (July 2003), 18–25.

26. Real Madrid is in the top Spanish football league. Manchester United and Chelsea are in the English Premier League. AC Milan and Juventus (of Turin) are in the Italian Serie A. Bayern Munich is in the German Bundesleague.

27. Union des Associations Européennes de Football (UEFA)

28. Rachman, "Passion, Pride and Profit," 4.

29. Zidane won the award for the third time in 2003; Ronaldo won for the third time in 2002; Figo won in 2001.

30. As of 2004 it is too soon to know if Abramovich's strategy has worked. He was able to purchase football talent at bargain prices, relatively speaking, because of the financial problems of teams generally. Chelsea has done very well in the Premier League competition, but so have Arsenal and Manchester United, and it is unclear how many super-squads can survive at the top.

31. Rachman, "Passion, Pride and Profit," 4.

32. Rachman, "Passion, Pride and Profit," 4.

33. Rachman, "Passion, Pride and Profit," 7.

34. This data comes from a detailed press release, dated July 30, 2003, for *The Deloitte & Touche Annual Review of Football Finance.* www.footballfinance .co.uk/publications/arff2003release.pdf [accessed June 8, 2004].

35. See Immanuel Wallerstein, *The Capitalist World Economy* (Cambridge: Cambridge University Press, 1979).

36. All data in these tables is from fifaworldcup.com [accessed January 20, 2004]. Information on transfers is from www.footballtransfers.info [accessed January 20, 2004].

37. Jack Bell, "Soccer Report," *New York Times*, January 20, 2004, C16.

38. Alex Bellos, *Futbol*, 10.

39. Eric Weil, "Carry On Selling," *World Soccer* (September 2003), 26.

40. For a deeper study I recommend Richard Giulianotti, *Football: A Sociology of the Global Game* (Cambridge: Polity Press, 2000).

41. Quoted in Rachman, "Passion, Pride and Profit," 6. Significantly, Valdano does not characterize the Argentine style.

42. Giulianotti makes this point.

43. This account is based on Murray, *Football*, 134–37.

44. Murray, *Football*, 136.

45. See Giulianotti, *Football* for a very readable introduction to this literature.

46. Tim Parks, *A Season with Verona* (New York: Arcade, 2002).

47. One of the racist issues involves "monkey grunts" that the fans use to insult opposing players, particularly black players. This practice certainly seems racist to me, but my impression from reading Parks's book is that his fellow *ultras* simply tried to pick the most insulting possible response to each opposing player—and "monkey grunts" seemed to work against black players. When they were accused of racism, one reaction was to chant "monkey grunts" against opposing white players, too. They saw themselves as harsh and aggressive fans, extremists, but not racists.

48. Derek Hammond, "Class War!" *FourFourTwo* (January 2004), 83–86.

49. Which, I think, makes this a globalization effect.

50. Giulianotti, *Football*, 18.

51. Giulianotti, *Football*, 19.

52. See the film's website at www.finelinefeatures.com/sites/cup/ [accessed June 8, 2004].

53. David White, "Choice between Demands of Club and Country Puts Africa's Soccer Stars in a Dilemma," *Financial Times*, January 24/25, 2004, 3.

54. Eric Weil, "Buenos Aires: Busyness as Usual," *World Soccer* (June 2003), 22.

55. Franklin Foer has recently argued that the American exception goes beyond indifference to resentment of soccer. Foer, a political journalist, claims that the American reaction to soccer mirrors the social divisions created by globalization. I don't agree with this conclusion, but I still find Foer's book very interesting in other respects. See Franklin Foer, *How Soccer Explains the World: An (Unlikely) Theory of Globalization* (New York: HarperCollins, 2004).

56. Markovits and Hellerman, *Offside*. Answers three, four, and five in this section are based upon the analysis presented in this book.

57. Joe McGinnis, *The Miracle of Castel di Sangro: A Tale of Passion and Folly in the Heart of Italy* (New York: Little, Brown, 1999).

Chapter 5   Globalization as McWorld

1. Karl Marx and Friedrich Engels, *The Communist Manifesto: A Modern Edition* (London: Verso, 1998), 39.

2. Marx and Engels, *Communist Manifesto*, 39.

3. Marx and Engels, *Communist Manifesto*, 40.

4. Taken from Vernon's obituary in the *New York Times* (August 28, 1999), reprinted in Michael Veseth, *The New York Times 20th Century in Review: The Rise of the Global Economy* (Chicago: Fitzroy Dearborn, 2002), 15–16.

5. Facts about the first McDonald's restaurants are taken from John F. Love, *McDonald's: Behind the Arches* (New York: Bantam, 1995), 9–29.

6. Love, *McDonald's*, 15.

7. Love, *McDonald's*, 19.

8. This is the Big Mac Index or purchasing power parity. See www .economist.com/markets/Bigmac/Index.cfm

9. Thomas L. Friedman, *The Lexus and the Olive Tree: Understanding Globalization* (New York: Anchor Books, 2000), 486.

10. McDonald's online shareholder information at www.shareholder.com/ mcd/Charts.cfm [accessed February 10, 2004].

11. Stefano Polacchi, "Ristoranti d'Italia Unitevi!" *Gambero Rosso* 135 (April 2003), 48–51. You need to do more than just sell pizza to make this list of Italian restaurants abroad.

12. If you want to know what Tomaso's book might say about globalization and Americanization, read Beppe Severgnini, *Ciao America! An Italian Discovers the U.S.*, translated by Giles Watson (New York: Broadway Books, 2002).

13. David Y. H. Wu and Sidney C. H. Cheung, eds., *The Globalization of Chinese Food* (Honolulu: University of Hawaii Press, 2002).

14. The other Friedmans know better—they are more likely to assume that their native cuisines can only be prepared properly at home.

15. Saritha Rai, "Tastes of India in U.S. Wrappers," *New York Times*, April 29, 2003, W1, 7. The menu in Muslim regions of India includes chicken but not, obviously, pork.

16. Rai, "Tastes of India," W7.

17. Tyler Cowen, *Creative Destruction: How Globalization Is Changing the World's Cultures* (Princeton, N.J.: Princeton University Press, 2002).

18. Available online at www.theatlantic.com/politics/foreign/barberf.htm

19. Benjamin R. Barber, *Jihad vs. McWorld: Terrorism's Challenge to Democracy* (New York: Ballantine, 2002).

20. Regardless, anyone seeking specific insights into the Islamic response to globalization will find few insights here. That's not what Barber wants to talk about.

21. The index listing for McDonald's reads like this: McDonald's, 7, 23, 78, 99, 128, 132, 297, in France, 12; in Japan, 18; and local culture, 12, 155, 182; in Russia, 198, 249.

22. Barber, *Jihad vs. McWorld*, 23.

23. Barber, *Jihad vs. McWorld*, 129.

24. Barber, *Jihad vs. McWorld*, 12.

25. Barber, *Jihad vs. McWorld*, 155.

26. Barber, *Jihad vs. McWorld*, 78.

27. Barber, *Jihad vs. McWorld*, 7. Barber uses a quote from George Steiner to complete his thought here.

28. Barber, *Jihad vs. McWorld*, 99.

29. OK, so maybe Barber has a point.

30. I make an exception to this generalization, however, for the first McDonald's in Russia. Launched as a partnership between McDonald's of Canada and the Moscow government, it was a creature of the Cold War—more about politics, at least initially, than economics. The Moscow McDonald's *was* a Trojan horse.

31. Sidney W. Mintz, "Swallowing Modernity," in *Golden Arches East: McDonald's in East Asia*, edited by James L. Watson (Stanford, Calif.: Stanford University Press, 1997), 189.

32. "Management Brief: Johannesburgers and Fries," *Economist* (September 27, 1999), 75–76.

33. For example, Matt Haig, *Brand Failures* (London: Kogan Page, Ltd., 2003). There are many others of this genre.

34. James L. Watson, ed., *Golden Arches East: McDonald's in East Asia* (Stanford, Calif.: Stanford University Press, 1997).

35. James L. Watson, "Transnationalism, Localization, and Fast Foods in East Asia," in *Golden Arches East*, 6.

36. Watson, "Transnationalism," 7.

37. Watson, "Transnationalism," 7.

38. Watson, "Transnationalism," 9.

39. David M. Cuttler, Edward L. Glaeser, and Jesse M. Shapiro, "Why Have Americans Become More Obese?" *NBER Working Paper* w9446. (Cambridge, Mass.: National Bureau of Economic Research, January 2003).

40. The study also suggests that obesity is due less to increased amounts consumed at each meal (the "super size" effect) and more to an increased number of meals consumed, which may be related to convenient access. The study's findings may be especially applicable to fast foods, but they apply to foods generally.

41. George Ritzer, *The McDonaldization of Society* (Thousand Oaks, Calif.: Pine Forge Press, 1993, 2000).

42. Ritzer, *The McDonaldization of Society*, 23.

43. Just as *Jihad vs. McWorld* is not, Barber says, about Islam.

44. Ritzer, *The McDonaldization of Society*, 15–16.

45. This upside of dehumanization was the subject of a cartoon, which featured two dogs seated at a computer. "On the internet," one dog tells the other, "no one knows you're a dog."

46. George Ritzer, *The McDonaldization Thesis: Explorations and Extensions* (Thousand Oaks, Calif.: Sage, 1998), 178.

47. Ritzer, *The McDonaldization Thesis*, 178.

48. George Ritzer, *The Globalization of Nothing* (Thousand Oaks, Calif.: Pine Forge Press, 2004).

49. Ritzer, *The Globalization of Nothing*, 165.

50. Ritzer, *The Globalization of Nothing*, 20.

51. I'm not alone in this. See Martin Parker, "Nostalgia and Mass Culture: McDonaldization and Cultural Elitism," in *McDonaldization Revisited: Critical Essays on Consumer Culture*, edited by Mark Alfino, John S. Caupto, and Robin Wynyard (Westport, Conn.: Praeger, 1998), 1–18.

52. Except perhaps on the Japanese television show, *Iron Chef.*

53. Joseph A. Schumpeter, *Capitalism, Socialism, and Democracy*, 2nd ed. (New York: Harper and Brothers, 1942, 1947).

Chapter 6 Globalization versus *Terroir*

1. George Ritzer, *The Globalization of Nothing* (Thousand Oaks, Calif.: Pine Forge Press, 2004).

2. See, for example, Roger Bohmrich, "Terroir: Competing Perspectives on the Roles of Soil, Climate and People." *Journal of Wine Research* 7:1 (April 1996): 33–37. Bohmrich's bibliography gives a feeling for the international dimension of the debate. His own pragmatic definition of *terroir* is that it is a relation or interaction (of known or unknown type) among natural factors that has the potential to produce a specific character in an agricultural product such as wine (or cheese such as Parmesano-Reggiano, I suppose).

3. James E. Wilson, *Terroir: The Role of Geography, Climate, and Culture in the Making of French Wines* (Berkeley: University of California Press, 1998).

4. Wilson, *Terroir*, 55.

5. Wilson, *Terroir*, 55.

6. Adam Smith, *An Inquiry into the Nature and Causes of The Wealth of Nations* (New York: Modern Library, 1937), 155–56.

7. Smith's discussion of wine comes in the chapter "Of the Rent of Land." He argued that much of the price of a fine wine constituted rent because the best wines commanded high prices due to their scarcity more than the cost of production.

8. No one really knows what is in a bottle, for example, until the cork is pulled (or the screw-cap opened). Wines are made in different styles and can vary from year to year depending upon weather conditions, winemaker decisions, and other factors. Wine corks can distort wine flavors, too, so bottles from the same case may not taste the same. And individual tastes are notoriously varied and variable. It is very hard to know if you will like what's in that bottle unless you open it.

9. Bohmrich, "Terroir," 42.

10. Gideon Rachman, "The Globe in a Glass," *Economist* survey (December 16, 1999), www.economist.com/displaystory.cfm?story_id = 268095 [accessed June 3, 2004].

11. Tom Stevenson, *Wine Report 2004* (New York: DK Publishing, 2003),

292. In terms of area under viticulture, China ranked number eight in the world at the time this report was published.

12. Wine has been globalized, but it is not truly "global." Geography and climate prevent the globalization of wine production from being complete (wine grapes grow best between 30 and 50 degrees of latitude in the Northern and Southern Hemispheres, ruling out much of the Southern Hemisphere). Globalization, however, is seldom truly global in practice for any product. Wine consumption is becoming more global, too, except in Muslim countries, where consumption of alcoholic beverages is prohibited or discouraged.

13. Gallo also sells brandy and fortified and sparkling wines, as do many other wine firms, but I won't include these products in the statistics I cite.

14. Rachman, "The Globe in a Glass."

15. Data cited are from Kym Anderson, "Wine's New World," *Foreign Policy* (May–June, 2003): 50–51.

16. Thanks to Kenneth Willman for pointing out the Two Buck Chuck phenomenon. For more information about Two Buck Chuck see www.traderjoes .com/new/chuckshaw.asp [accessed July 8, 2004].

17. Transportation costs matter and limit globalization. Brandy was invented when someone got the idea to distill wine to make it condense and reduce shipping costs. The idea was to add water to brandy to reconstitute wine after shipment.

18. See Tim Unwin, *Wine and Vine* (London: Routledge, 1991, 1996), 341.

19. The 2003 figure is 38.5 percent. See www.researchandmarkets.com/ reports/36340/ [accessed July 8, 2004].

20. See www.tesco.com [accessed March 31, 2004].

21. Data on supermarket sales found at enjoyment.independent.co.uk/ low_res/story.jsp?story = 469894&host = 5&dir = 223 [accessed July 8, 2004].

22. Lewis Perdue, *The Wrath of Grapes* (New York: Avon, 1999), 116–32.

23. Perdue, *The Wrath of Grapes*, 131.

24. There have been many wine market scandals over the years. Most involve fraud—the wine in the bottle isn't what the label says it is. Cheap wines are substituted for more expensive ones, young wines for old, or foreign wines for domestic. Such is the "mystery" of wine that these frauds often go undetected for some time. A more serious problem occurred in the 1980s when some Austrian producers added poisonous antifreeze to their wines as a cheap way to sweeten them, with truly deadly consequences.

25. Arthur Morris, "Globalization and Regional Differentiation: The Mendoza Wine Region," *Journal of Wine Research* 11:2 (2000): 145–53.

26. Morris, "Globalization and Regional Differentiation," 146.

27. Part of the price premium is due to simple demand and supply—you cannot just whip up another batch of that good 2001 vintage when your stocks run out—but this is only a partial explanation.

28. My source for most of this history is a beautiful and informative book by Michael Cooper, *Wine Atlas of New Zealand* (Auckland, NZ: Hodder Moa Beckett, 2002).

29. Gum diggers mined marshy areas for the amber-like gum of the kauri tree, which was for a time an important ingredient in shellac production.

30. A record 166,000 tonnes of wine grapes were harvested in New Zealand in 2004 compared with 89,100 tonnes in 2003 and 118,000 tonnes in 2002, the previous record year. Bad weather reduced the 2003 harvest.

31. Special thanks to Ken Willman for his comments on this chapter.

Chapter 7   Grassroots Globaloney

1. One of the things that I admire about Thomas Friedman's *The Lexus and Olive Tree* account of globalization is that he tries to tell both kinds of stories, giving the reader a choice, even though his bottom line is pro-globalization.

2. Karen Tranberg Hansen, "Transnational Biographies and Local Meanings: Used Clothing Practices in Lusaka," *Journal of Southern African Studies* 21:1 (March 1995): 131–46.

3. Now that agriculture and textiles are back on the negotiating table, you can expect trade agreements to be harder to reach.

4. I believe this figure includes shipping, which may be as much as a third of the cost.

5. Karen Tranberg Hansen, *Salaula: The World of Secondhand Clothing and Zambia* (Chicago: University of Chicago Press, 2000), 248. Hansen's excellent book is the source of much of what I know about the used clothing trade and the inspiration for this chapter.

6. Michael Durham, "Clothes Line," *The Guardian*, February 25, 2004, www.guardian.co.uk/g2/story/0,3604,1155254,00.html [accessed April 21, 2004].

7. You can learn about this family-owned company at www.savers.com/

8. George Packer, "How Susie Bayer's T-shirt Ended Up on Yusuf Mama's Back," *New York Times Magazine* (March 31, 2002), 54.

9. Karen Tranberg Hansen, *Salaula*, 229.

10. This same principle—small margins, huge volume—is what makes hedge funds profitable.

11. Scott Bailey's comments on an earlier draft "provoked" these remarks.

12. Thanks to Phil McMullin of Savers, who suggested this point.

13. Here is the website for the program: www.pbs.org/independentlens/tshirttravels/

14. Hansen, *Salaula*, 229.

15. Hansen, *Salaula*, 233.

16. Hansen, *Salaula*, 233.

17. Carlo Petrini, *Slow Food: The Case for Taste*, translated by William Mc-Cuaig (New York: Columbia University Press, 2001), ix.

18. Petrini, *Slow Food*, 26.

19. Petrini, *Slow Food*, 26.

20. Petrini, *Slow Food*, 32.

21. The details for this section are drawn from chapter one of Petrini, *Slow Food*.

22. ARCI today has over a million members in six hundred clubs in Italy. It remains a social club with political leanings and interests. It fights, as its webpage says, to eliminate social and political exclusions and to promote solidarity. It supports, among other things, activities for children and social and cultural tourism. See www.arci.it/present-ing.htm

23. There is no such thing as Italian cuisine, according to Mario Batali, only the regional cuisines of Italy.

24. Petrini, *Slow Food*, 5.

25. Petrini, *Slow Food*, 10.

26. The current version of the manifesto can be found on the SlowFood .com website: www.slowfood.com/eng/sf_cose/sf_cose_statuto.lasso [accessed April 20, 2004].

27. I find it interesting that "typical" in the United States generally means "unexceptional" whereas within the Slow Food movement it means "authentic."

28. Slow Food Planet currently exists as a frequently expanded web offering. See www.slowfood.com/eng/sf_sloweb/sf_arch_planet.lasso [accessed April 20, 2004].

29. www.slowfood.com/eng/sf_sloweb/sf_arch_planet.lasso?-database = sfesloweb&-layout = tutti&-response = sf_sloweb_dettaglio.lasso&-record ID = 35125&-search

30. See the complete description at www.slowfoodfoundation.com/eng/ presidi/lista.lasso [accessed April 20, 2004].

31. www.slowfoodfoundation.com/inc_sito/eng/bocconi_short.pdf [accessed April 20, 2004].

32. Paolo Di Croce, "Slow Food and Lula," *Slow: The International Herald of Taste* (July 2003): 4–5.

33. Di Croce, "Slow Food and Lula," 5.

34. The Republic of Tuva was an independent republic until it was absorbed by the Soviet Union in 1944. It is now a member state of the Russian Confederation.

35. Information about the 2003 winners is found at www.slowfood.com/ eng/sf_premio/sf_premio_vincitori.lasso

36. www.slowfood.com/img_sito/PREMIO/vincitori2003/pagine_en/ Brasile_03.html [accessed April 21, 2003].

37. Petrini, *Slow Food*, p. 63.

38. Slow Food Editore, *Italian Wines 1999* (New York: Gambero Rosso, 1999).

39. Slow Food Editore, *Osterie d'Italia 2002* (Bra, Italy: Slow Food Editore, 2001). Not available in English at this time.

40. www.slowfoodfoundation.com/eng/presidi/lista.lasso?lista = si& id_nazione = 1 07&id_tipologia = &id_regione = 5 [accessed April 21, 2004].

41. Patrick Martins, "Set That Apricot Free," *New York Times*, April 24, 2004, A-17.

42. The source of this insight is Alexander Stille, "Slow Food: An Italian Answer to Globalization," *Nation* 273 (August 20, 2001): 6. www.the nation.com/doc.mhtml%3Fi = 20010820&s = stille [accessed June 28, 2004].

Chapter 8 Globalization and the French Exception

1. Manfred B. Steger, *Globalism: The New Market Ideology* (Lanham, Md.: Rowman & Littlefield, 2002).

2. See Steger, *Globalism*, 43–80 for a discussion of the five central claims of globalism.

3. Balladur was prime minister of France from 1993 to 1995.

4. "Thatcherites in Brussels (Really)," *Economist* (March 15, 1997), 23.

5. Pierre Bourdieu, *Firing Back: Against the Tyranny of the Market 2*, translated by Loïc Wacquant (New York: The New Press, 2001). Viviane Forrester, *The Economic Horror* (Oxford: Blackwell, 1999).

6. He has written a book about this: José Bové and François Dufour (interviewed by Gilles Luneau), *The World Is Not for Sale: Farmers against Junk Food*, translated by Anna de Casparis (New York: Verso, 2001).

7. The lyrics have many references that suggest contemporary globalization besides those that are cited here. There is even one reference to a borderless world that eerily recalls the Henry A. Wallace versus Clare Boothe Luce debate that began this book. You should listen to the original cast recording.

8. Frantz Fanon, *A Dying Colonialism*, translated by Haakon Chevalier (New York: Grove Press, 1965), 35.

9. Edward M. Corbett, *The French Presence in Black Africa* (Washington, D.C.: Black Orpheus Press, 1972), 1.

10. Mannoni, O. *Prospero and Caliban: The Psychology of Colonization*, translated by Pamela Powesland (New York: Praeger, 1950).

11. Many former French African colonies used the French franc as domestic currency until the euro was introduced a few years ago, for example.

12. Hubert Védrine with Dominique Moïse, *France in an Age of Globalization*, translated by Philip H. Gordon (Washington, D.C.: Brookings Institution Press, 2001), 44.

13. Védrine, *France in an Age of Globalization*, 43–44.

14. All quotes in this paragraph as from Sheryle Bagwell, "A New World Sauvignon Blanc Built on French Soil," *Financial Times*, April 16, 2004, 10.

15. Védrine, *France in an Age of Globalization*, 3.

16. Bourdieu, *Firing Back*, 85–86.

17. Quoted in Jean-François Revel, *Anti-Americanism*, translated by Diarmid Cammell (San Francisco: Encounter Books, 2003), 44.

18. Revel, *Anti-Americanism*, 44.

19. G. Pascal Zachary has written about how people use globalization to construct distinct personal identities. See his *The Diversity Advantage: Multicultural Identity in the New World Economy* (Boulder, Colo.: Westview, 2003). Tyler Cowen discusses the result in his *Creative Destruction: How Globalization Is Changing the World's Cultures* (Princeton, N.J.: Princeton University Press, 2002). Cowen argues that the world seems more homogeneous to global travelers because each individual place is in fact more diverse and multicultural. In the final chapter, Cowen asks, "Should National Culture Matter?" You can see how that would infuriate a French imperialist, especially coming from an American.

20. I present this as the "conventional wisdom" even though I find the argument that America has always had a strong imperialist streak to be very persuasive. See, for example, Niall Ferguson, *Colossus: The Price of America's Empire* (New York: Penguin, 2004).

21. Revel, *Anti-Americanism*, 37.

22. Elaine Sciolino, "France Has a State Religion: Secularism." *New York Times*, February 8, 2004, WK4.

23. Fanon, *A Dying Colonialism*. See chapter 1, "Algeria Unveiled."

24. Meredith Anne Skura, "The Case of Colonialism in *The Tempest*," in *Caliban*, edited by Harold Bloom (New York: Chelsea House, 1992), 225.

25. Skura, "The Case of Colonialism," 225.

26. Skura, "The Case of Colonialism," 226.

27. Philip H. Gordon and Sophie Meunier, *The French Challenge: Adapting to Globalization* (Washington, D.C.: Brookings Institution Press, 2001).

28. Gordon and Meunier, *The French Challenge*, 8.

29. Gordon and Meunier, *The French Challenge*, 9.

30. Gordon and Meunier, *The French Challenge*, 9.

31. The link between cheese and public opinion comes from Charles De-Gaulle, who is said to have complained, "How can anyone govern a country with 246 cheeses?"

32. Todd Richissin, "The French Love Fine Food but also Have a Taste for Les Bigs Macs," *Seattle Times*, March 31, 2004, 1,

33. Richissin, *Seattle Times*, 1.

34. Revel, *Anti-Americanism*, 143.

35. Védrine, *France in an Age of Globalization*, 28.

36. Gordon and Meunier, *The French Challenge*, 18.

37. Gordon and Meunier, *The French Challenge*, 14.

38. Gordon and Meunier, *The French Challenge*, 21.

39. Carrefour translates as "crossroads" in English.

40. www.carrefour.com/english/homepage/index.jsp [accessed May 21, 2004].

41. www.walmartstores.com/wmstore/wmstores/Mainnews.jsp [accessed May 21, 2004]. The German and British operations are the result of the acquisition of local retail chains, not green field development of Wal-Mart stores.

42. See "Wal-Mart Aims to Set Up Shop across Europe" by Susanna Voyle and Daniel Dombey, *Financial Times*, May 25, 2004, 1. Wal-Mart's current position in Europe is due largely to its acquisition in 1999 of the British retailer Asada. According to this article Wal-Mart is considering several options for European expansion, including opening its own stores, opening Asada stores, and acquiring local retail chains.

43. Ann Zimmerman, "Ultimatum at France's Wal-Mart," *Wall Street Journal*, July 9, 2004, C1.

44. www.pret.com/philosophy/ [accessed May 24, 2004].

45. I'm not saying that these are the right factors to consider, only that they are popular indicators in the globalization literature.

46. See Dan Voelpel, "County Council Must Commit to Chambers Creek Golf Course," *News Tribune* (May 21, 2004) at www.tribnet.com/business/columnists/dan_voelpel/story/5095809p-5022922c.html [accessed May 26, 2004].

47. J. K. Rowling, *Harry Potter and the Sorcerer's Stone* (New York: Scholastic, 1997).

48. David Cannadine, "The Past and Present in the English Industrial Revolution, 1880–1980," *Past and Present* (May 1984): 131–72.

49. Cannadine, "Past and Present," 171.

50. John Maynard Keynes, *The General Theory of Employment, Interest, and Money* (New York: Harcourt Brace Jovanovich, 1964), 383.

BIBLIOGRAPHY

Alfino, Mark, John S. Caupto, and Robin Wynyard, eds. *McDonaldization Revisited: Critical Essays on Consumer Culture*. Westport, Conn.: Praeger, 1998.

Anderson, Kym. "Wine's New World." *Foreign Policy* (May–June, 2003): 46–54.

Angell, Norman. *The Great Illusion: A Study of the Relation of Military Power in Nations to Their Economic and Social Advantage*. London: Putnam, 1911.

Bagwell, Sheryle. "A New World Sauvignon Blanc Built on French Soil." *Financial Times*, April 16, 2004, 10.

Barber, Benjamin R. *Jihad vs. McWorld: Terrorism's Challenge to Democracy*. New York: Ballantine, 2001.

BBC News Online. "Profile: Jean-Marie Le Pen." news.bbc.co.uk/1/hi/world/europe/1943193.stm [accessed June 7, 2004].

Bell, Jack. "Soccer Report." *New York Times*, January 20, 2004, C16.

Bellos, Alex. *Futbol: Soccer, the Brazilian Way*. New York: Bloomsbury, 2002.

Bohmrich, Roger. "Terroir: Competing Perspectives on the Roles of Soil, Climate and People." *Journal of Wine Research* 7:1 (April 1996): 33–37.

Bourdieu, Pierre. *Firing Back: Against the Tyranny of the Market 2*. Translated by Loïc Wacquant. New York: The New Press, 2001.

Bové, José, and François Dufour (interviewed by Gilles Luneau). *The World Is Not for Sale: Farmers against Junk Food*. Translated by Anna de Casparis. New York: Verso, 2001.

Brown, Vivienne. *Adam Smith's Discourse*. London: Routledge, 1994.

Cannadine, David. "The Past and Present in the English Industrial Revolution, 1880–1980." *Past and Present* (May 1984): 131–72.

Congressional Record 89:1, 759–63.

Cooper, Michael. *Wine Atlas of New Zealand*. Auckland, NZ: Hodder Moa Beckett, 2002.

Corbett, Edward M. *The French Presence in Black Africa*. Washington, D.C.: Black Orpheus Press, 1972.

Cowen, Tyler. *Creative Destruction: How Globalization Is Changing the World's Cultures*. Princeton, N.J.: Princeton University Press, 2002.

Cuttler, David M., Edward L. Glaeser, and Jesse M. Shapiro. "Why Have Americans Become More Obese?" *NBER Working Paper* w9446. Cambridge, Mass.: National Bureau of Economic Research, January 2003.

Deloitte & Touche. *Deloitte & Touche Annual Review of Football Finance*. www.-footballfinance.co.uk/publications/arff2003release.pdf [accessed June 8, 2004].

Di Croce, Paolo. "Slow Food and Lula." *Slow: The International Herald of Taste* (July 2003): 4–5.

Dobson, Stephen, and John Goddard. *The Economics of Football*. Cambridge: Cambridge University Press, 2001.

Durham, Michael. "Clothes Line." *The Guardian*, February 25, 2004. www .guardian.co.uk/g2/story/0,3604,1155254,00.html [accessed April 21, 2004].

Fanon, Frantz. *A Dying Colonialism*. Translated by Haakon Chevalier. New York: Grove Press, 1965.

Ferguson, Niall. *Colossus: The Price of America's Empire*. New York: Penguin, 2004.

Foer, Franklin. *How Soccer Explains the World: An (Unlikely) Theory of Globalization*. New York: HarperCollins, 2004.

Forrester, Viviane. *The Economic Horror*. Oxford: Blackwell, 1999.

Frank, Robert H., and Philip J. Cook. *The Winner-Take-All Society*. New York: Free Press, 1995.

Frank, Thomas. *One Market under God: Extreme Capitalism, Market Populism, and the End of Economic Democracy*. New York: Doubleday, 2000.

Friedman, Thomas L. *The Lexus and the Olive Tree: Understanding Globalization*. New York: Anchor Books, 2000.

Galeano, Eduardo. *Football in Sun and Shadow*. Translated by Mark Fried. London: Fourth Estate, 1997.

Giulianotti, Richard. *Football: A Sociology of the Global Game*. Cambridge: Polity Press, 2000.

Gordon, Phillip H., and Sophie Meunier. *The French Challenge: Adapting to Globalization*. Washington, D.C.: Brookings Institution Press, 2001.

Greider, William. *One World, Ready or Not: The Manic Logic of Global Capitalism*. New York: Simon & Schuster, 1997.

———. *The Soul of Capitalism: Opening Paths to a Moral Economy*. New York: Simon & Schuster, 2003.

Haig, Matt. *Brand Failures*. London: Kogan Page, Ltd., 2003.

Hamilton, Gavin. "Adios Manchester?" *World Soccer* (June 2003), 6.

———. "United Ready to Splash Beckham Cash," *World Soccer* (August 2003), 10.

Hammond, Derek. "Class War!" *FourFourTwo* (January 2004), 83–86.

Hansen, Karen Tranberg. "Transnational Biographies and Local Meanings: Used Clothing Practices in Lusaka." *Journal of Southern African Studies* 21:1 (March 1995): 131–46.

———. *Salaula: The World of Secondhand Clothing and Zambia.* Chicago: University of Chicago Press, 2000.

Heijbroek, Arend. *Wine Is Business. Shifting Demand and Distribution: Major Drivers Reshaping the Wine Industry.* Rabobank International, January 2003.

Hessler, Peter. "Home and Away." *New Yorker* (December 1, 2003), 65–75.

James, Harold. *The End of Globalization: Lessons from the Great Depression.* Cambridge, Mass.: Harvard University Press, 2001.

Keynes, John Maynard. *The General Theory of Employment, Interest, and Money.* New York: Harcourt Brace Jovanovich, 1964.

Krugman, Paul. *The Great Unraveling: Losing Our Way in the New Century.* New York: Norton, 2003.

LaFeber, Walter. *Michael Jordan and the New Global Capitalism.* New York: Norton, 2002.

Lenin, V. I. *Imperialism: The Highest Stage of Capitalism.* New York: International Publishers, 1939.

List, Friedrich. *The National System of Political Economy.* Translated by Sampson S. Lloyd. London: Longmans, Green and Co., 1904.

Love, John F. *McDonald's: Behind the Arches.* New York: Bantam, 1995.

Lowe, Sid. "The Circus Starts Here." *World Soccer* (August 2003), 5–6.

McGinnis, Joe. *The Miracle of Castel di Sangro: A Tale of Passion and Folly in the Heart of Italy.* New York: Little, Brown, 1999.

"Management Brief: Johannesburgers and Fries." *Economist* (September 27, 1999), 75–76.

Mandelbaum, Michael. *The Ideas That Conquered the World: Peace, Democracy, and Free Markets in the Twenty-First Century.* New York: Public Affairs, 2002.

Mannoni, O. *Prospero and Caliban: The Psychology of Colonization.* Translated by Pamela Powesland. New York: Praeger, 1950.

Markovits, Andrei S., and Steven L. Hellerman. *Offside: Soccer & American Exceptionalism.* Princeton, N.J.: Princeton University Press, 2001.

Martins, Patrick. "Set That Apricot Free." *New York Times*, April 24, 2004, A-17.

Marx, Karl, and Friedrich Engels. *The Communist Manifesto: A Modern Edition.* London: Verso, 1998.

Miller, Karen Lowry. "Globaloney: The New Buzzword." *Newsweek Issues 2003* (Winter 2002/2003), 52–58.

Mintz, Sidney W. "Swallowing Modernity." In *Golden Arches East: McDonald's in East Asia*, edited by James L. Watson. Stanford, Calif.: Stanford University Press, 1997.

Mittelman, James H. *The Globalization Syndrome: Transformation and Resistance.* Princeton, N.J.: Princeton University Press, 2000.

Morris, Arthur. "Globalization and Regional Differentiation: The Mendoza Wine Region." *Journal of Wine Research* 11:2 (2000): 145–53.

Mueller, John. *Capitalism, Democracy and Ralph's Pretty Good Grocery.* Princeton, N.J.: Princeton University Press, 1999.

Murray, Bill. *Football: A History of the World Game.* Aldershot, UK: Scolar Press, 1994.

Ohamae, Kenichi. *The Borderless World: Power and Strategy in the Interlinked Economy.* New York: HarperBusiness, 1990.

Packer, George. "How Susie Bayer's T-shirt Ended Up on Yusuf Mama's Back." *New York Times Magazine* (March 31, 2002), 54.

Parker, Martin. "Nostalgia and Mass Culture: McDonaldization and Cultural Elitism." In *McDonaldization Revisited: Critical Essays on Consumer Culture,* edited by Mark Alfino, John S. Caupto, and Robin Wynyard. Westport, Conn.: Praeger, 1998, 1–18.

Parks, Tim. *A Season with Verona.* New York: Arcade, 2002.

Pemberton, Jo-Anne. *Global Metaphors: Modernity and the Quest for One World.* London: Pluto Press, 2001.

Perdue, Lewis. *The Wrath of Grapes.* New York: Avon, 1999.

Perot, H. Ross, with Pat Choate. *Save Your Job, Save Our Country: Why NAFTA Must Be Stopped—NOW!* New York: Hyperion, 1993.

Petrini, Carlo. *Slow Food: The Case for Taste.* Translated by William McCuaig. New York: Columbia University Press, 2001.

Polacchi, Stefano. "Ristoranti d'Italia Unitevi!" *Gambero Rosso* 135 (April 2003), 48–51.

Rachman, Gideon. "The Globe in a Glass." *Economist* survey (December 16, 1999).

———. "Passion, Pride and Profit." *Economist* special section (June 1, 2002).

Rai, Saritha. "Tastes of India in U.S. Wrappers." *New York Times,* April 29, 2003, W1, 7.

Revel, Jean-François. *Anti-Americanism.* Translated by Diarmid Cammell. San Francisco: Encounter Books, 2003,

Richissin, Todd. "The French Love Fine Food but also Have a Taste for Les Bigs Macs." *Seattle Times,* March 31, 2004, 1.

Ritzer, George. *The McDonaldization of Society.* Thousand Oaks, Calif.: Pine Forge Press, 1993, 2000.

———. *The McDonaldization Thesis: Explorations and Extensions.* Thousand Oaks, Calif.: Sage, 1998.

———. *The Globalization of Nothing.* Thousand Oaks, Calif.: Pine Forge Press, 2004.

Rohter, Larry. "Argentina in the Grip of Manu Mania." *New York Times,* June 4, 2003, C19.

Ross, Ian Simpson. *The Life of Adam Smith*. New York: Oxford University Press, 1995.

Rowling, J. K. *Harry Potter and the Sorcerer's Stone*. New York: Scholastic, 1997.

Schumpeter, Joseph A. *Capitalism, Socialism, and Democracy*. 2nd ed. New York: Harper and Brothers, 1942, 1947.

Sciolino, Elaine. "France Has a State Religion: Secularism." *New York Times*, February 8, 2004, WK4.

Severgnini, Beppe. *Ciao America! An Italian Discovers the U.S*. Translated by Giles Watson. New York: Broadway Books, 2002.

Shy, Oz. *The Economics of Network Industries*. Cambridge: Cambridge University Press, 2001.

Skura, Meredith Anne. "The Case of Colonialism in *The Tempest*." In *Caliban*, edited by Harold Bloom. New York: Chelsea House, 1992.

Slow Food Editore. *Italian Wines 1999*. New York: Gambero Rosso, 1999.

————. *Osterie d'Italia 2002*. Bra, Italy: Slow Food Editore, 2001.

Smith, Adam. *An Inquiry into the Nature and Causes of The Wealth of Nations*. New York: Modern Library, 1937.

Smith, Henry Nash. *Mark Twain's Fable of Progress: Political and Economic Ideas in A Connecticut Yankee*. New Brunswick, N.J.: Rutgers University Press, 1964.

Stead, W. T. *The Americanization of the World: The Trend of the Twentieth Century*. London: Horace Markley, 1901.

Steger, Manfred B. *Globalism: The New Market Ideology*. Lanham, Md.: Rowman & Littlefield, 2002.

Stevenson, Tom. *Wine Report 2004*. New York: DK Publishing, 2003.

Stille, Alexander. "Slow Food: An Italian Answer to Globalization." *Nation* 273 (August 20, 2001): 6. www.thenation.com/doc.mhtml%3Fi = 20010820& s = stille [accessed June 28, 2004].

Tustin, Michelle. "The Marketing Decade." *Wine Business Monthly*, April 2002 winebusiness.com/html/MonthlyArticle.cfm?AId = 53988&issue Id = 53965 [accessed June 27, 2004].

United Nations. *International Migration 2002*. www.un.org/esa/population/ publications/ittmig2002/2002ITTMIGTEXT22-11.pdf [accessed June 7, 2004].

Unwin, Tim. *Wine and Vine*. London: Routledge, 1991, 1996.

Védrine, Hubert, with Dominique Moïse. *France in an Age of Globalization*. Translated by Philip H. Gordon. Washington, D.C.: Brookings Institution Press, 2001.

Veseth, Michael. *Selling Globalization: The Myth of the Global Economy*. Boulder, Colo.: Rienner, 1998.

————, ed. *The New York Times Twentieth Century in Review: The Rise of the Global Economy*. Chicago: Fitzroy Dearborn, 2002.

Voelpel, Dan. "County Council Must Commit to Chambers Creek Golf

Course." *News Tribune*, May 21, 2004. www.tribnet.com/business/columnists/dan_voelpel/story/5095809p-5022922c.html [accessed May 26, 2004].

Voyle, Susanna, and Daniel Dombey. "Wal-Mart Aims to Set Up Shop across Europe." *Financial Times*, May 25, 2004, 1.

Wallace, Henry A. *The Century of the Common Man*. New York: Reynal & Hitchcock, 1943.

Wallerstein, Immanuel. *The Capitalist World Economy*. Cambridge: Cambridge University Press, 1979.

Watson, James L. "Transnationalism, Localization, and Fast Foods in East Asia." In *Golden Arches East: McDonald's in East Asia*, edited by James L. Watson. Stanford, Calif.: Stanford University Press, 1997.

———, ed. *Golden Arches East: McDonald's in East Asia*. Stanford, Calif.: Stanford University Press, 1997.

Weil, Eric. "Buenos Aires: Busyness as Usual." *World Soccer* (June 2003), 22.

———. "Carry On Selling." *World Soccer* (September 2003), 26.

Weiner, Jarrod. "Globalisation: The Political Function of Ambiguity." In *About Globalisation: Views on the Trajectory of Mondialisation*, edited by Bart Deschutter and Johan Pas, 19–49. Brussels: VUB Press, 2003.

White, David. "Choice between Demands of Club and Country Puts Africa's Soccer Stars in a Dilemma." *Financial Times*, January 24/25, 2004, 3.

Wilkie, Wendell L. *One World*. New York: Simon & Schuster, 1943.

Wilson, James E. *Terroir: The Role of Geography, Climate, and Culture in the Making of French Wines*. Berkeley: University of California Press, 1998.

Wolff, Alexander. *Big Game, Small World: A Basketball Adventure*. New York: Warner, 2002.

Wu, David Y. H., and Sidney C. H. Cheung, ed. *The Globalization of Chinese Food*. Honolulu: University of Hawaii Press, 2002.

Yergin, Daniel, and Joséph Stanislaw. *The Commanding Heights: The Battle for the Global Economy*. New York: Touchstone, 2002.

Zachary, G. Pascal. *The Diversity Advantage: Multicultural Identity in the New World Economy*. Boulder, Colo.: Westview, 2003.

Zimmerman, Ann. "Ultimatum at France's Wal-Mart." *Wall Street Journal*, July 9, 2004, C1.

INDEX

257

ABOUT THE AUTHOR

Michael Veseth is Professor of International Political Economy at the University of Puget Sound and director of the International Political Economy Program. He is the author of a number of college textbooks on economics and public finance and coauthor with David N. Balaam of *Introduction to International Political Economy* (Prentice Hall, third edition, 2005). Veseth's publications include *Mountains of Debt: Crisis and Change in Renaissance Florence, Victorian Britain and Postwar America* (1990), *Selling Globalization: The Myth of the Global Economy* (1998), and *The* New York Times' *Review of the 20th Century: The Rise of the Global Economy* (2002). Veseth has taught at the Bologna Center of the Johns Hopkins University School for Advanced International Studies and served as academic advisor to the interactive education website for the PBS/WGBH series *Commanding Heights: The Battle for the World Economy*. He lives in Tacoma, Washington, with his wife Sue Trbovich Veseth and their twenty-year-old cat, Yvonne.

GLOBALIZATION

Series Editors
Manfred B. Steger
*Illinois State University, University of Hawai'i, Manoa,
and Royal Melbourne Institute of Technology*
and
Terrell Carver
University of Bristol

"Globalization" has become *the* buzzword of our time. But what does it mean? Rather than forcing a complicated social phenomenon into a single analytical framework, this series seeks to present globalization as a multidimensional process constituted by complex, often contradictory interactions of global, regional, and local aspects of social life. Since conventional disciplinary borders and lines of demarcation are losing their old rationales in a globalizing world, authors in this series apply an interdisciplinary framework to the study of globalization. In short, the main purpose and objective of this series is to support subject-specific inquiries into the dynamics and effects of contemporary globalization and its varying impacts across, between, and within societies.

Globalization and Culture
Jan Nederveen Pieterse

Rethinking Globalism
Edited by Manfred B. Steger

Globalization and Terrorism
Jamal R. Nassar

Globalism, Second Edition
Manfred B. Steger

Globaloney
Michael Veseth

Forthcoming in the Series

Globalization and Warfare
Tarak Barkawi

Globalization and American Empire
Kiichi Fujiwara

Globalization and Law
Adam Gearey

Globalization and Feminist Activism
Mary Hawkesworth

Globalization and International Political Economy
Mark Rupert and M. Scott Solomon

Globalization and Labor
Dimitris Stevis and Terry Boswell

 Supported by the Globalization Research Center at the University of Hawai'i, Manoa